MW01253394

Competition, Gender and Management

Competition, Gender and Management

Beyond Winning and Losing

Jane Dennehy
Founder and Research Director, Gender Hub, UK

GUELPH HUMBER LIBRARY
205 Humber College Blvd
Toronto, ON   M9W 5L7

© Jane Dennehy 2012

All rights reserved. No reproduction, copy or transmission of this publication may be made without written permission.

No portion of this publication may be reproduced, copied or transmitted save with written permission or in accordance with the provisions of the Copyright, Designs and Patents Act 1988, or under the terms of any licence permitting limited copying issued by the Copyright Licensing Agency, Saffron House, 6–10 Kirby Street, London EC1N 8TS.

Any person who does any unauthorized act in relation to this publication may be liable to criminal prosecution and civil claims for damages.

The author has asserted her right to be identified as the author of this work in accordance with the Copyright, Designs and Patents Act 1988.

First published 2012 by
PALGRAVE MACMILLAN

Palgrave Macmillan in the UK is an imprint of Macmillan Publishers Limited, registered in England, company number 785998, of Houndmills, Basingstoke, Hampshire RG21 6XS.

Palgrave Macmillan in the US is a division of St Martin's Press LLC, 175 Fifth Avenue, New York, NY 10010.

Palgrave Macmillan is the global academic imprint of the above companies and has companies and representatives throughout the world.

Palgrave® and Macmillan® are registered trademarks in the United States, the United Kingdom, Europe and other countries.

ISBN: 978–0–230–38936–6

This book is printed on paper suitable for recycling and made from fully managed and sustained forest sources. Logging, pulping and manufacturing processes are expected to conform to the environmental regulations of the country of origin.

A catalogue record for this book is available from the British Library.

A catalog record for this book is available from the Library of Congress.

10 9 8 7 6 5 4 3 2 1
21 20 19 18 17 16 15 14 13 12

Printed and bound in the United States of America

For Amelia, Grace and Tim

Contents

Preface

This book was written to bring attention to competition as a concept which is largely invisible and yet active in our lives at work. Working towards new ways of thinking about gender remains central to my personal objective for writing, and I hope competition provides an interesting angle for people to engage with this vital component in our social worlds.

Acknowledgements

I would like to thank my partner and children for the endless support and cups of tea. I would also like to thank Diane for her patience through my Gender Institute journey.

To all the managers who have given their time and honesty – research is simply not possible without you, so thank you.

Thanks also to WomenWin, Second Base, the Guerreiras Project and Women in Film and Television (WFTV), four inspiring organisations who have shared their experiences and opinions with me during the writing of this book. In addition I would like to thank Debra Matsumoto and the other third parties who gave me permission to use their material.

Finally, thank you to Jackie, Sarah and Mia for your faith and my parents for encouraging me to always have an open mind.

1
Introduction

The subject of gender could be described as sitting in 'no man's land'. While such a suggestion affords gender an interdisciplinary approach, it also raises the well-founded idea that gender is simply about women. For some people the mere mention of gender sends them running for the hills, fearful that feminism is in hot pursuit. For others, working to increase the awareness and resolution of gender inequalities is often seemingly best achieved by limiting references to gender. The wide-spread energy afforded to keeping gender and feminism in a box continues to be both amazing and perplexing. In this book one of my central aims is to bring gender out of the shadows and into mainstream discussions in relation to management, competition and wider aspects of society.

The composition of our lives is often experienced as a series of frag-mented versions: the one we take to work, the one we have at home and a third suggesting a combination of both, often found in the relation-ships we have with wider communities, such as church, sport and our hobbies. Within the social world to which we belong the dynamic of competition varies along a spectrum of activities, some highly formal-ised such as sport, others less visible. How we experience and under-stand competition can be sophisticated and challenging, or it can rest on a stereotype which finds the concept negative and limiting. As with gender, competition is not widely discussed and often confined to innuendo and supposition rather than transparent and energetic discussion.

Management is increasingly being displaced by leadership discourses to the point where it is possible to suggest that managers, while perhaps less visible, continue to remain central to the success of large, medium and small organisations. What I contend is that management has

1

joined gender and competition to form a trio bound by a stifling societal internment. Whether individuals choose to be ignorant or blind (Wilson, 1996) to gender and competition in society, or take the view that such dynamics exist but are not important if it does not affect them, then the result is static and non-progressive workplaces.

Researching managers in the labour market as an integral aspect of the social world is a challenging activity. It may begin with a single question or hypothesis, later developing into a spectrum of issues demanding assessment and reassessment. What questions should be asked and of whom? What methods and methodologies should be employed and why? What role does the researcher play and what influence does this have on the inquiry and analysis process? Decisions taken during such an examination present both opportunities and diversions to the researcher. How problems, frustrations or revelations are dealt with can enrich the journey and the final publication of results and commentary.

Competition is a multifaceted dynamic that is ever present, yet it is often invisible and largely unarticulated amongst managers. For some it is only ever considered a negative, while for others it is merely a necessary part of operating in a market economy. For a few it is a motivating and meaningful contribution to their working lives and leisure activities. As an area of research which is generally neglected, the aim of this book is to add to the spectrum of definitions, experiences and perceptions that build a picture of competition as a dynamic concept. Defining competition is the first step to exploring gender and management in terms of access and participation rates for men and women which do not result in parity throughout the hierarchy. This book focuses on examining how competition in management is gendered

Gender and management standpoints

Management structures vary between organisations and industries, but gender research repeatedly finds collections of women managers' experiences, citing isolation, marginalisation and discrimination (Itzin, 1995; Collinson and Hearn 1996; Dopson and Neumann 1998). By contrast, research of men managers reveals shared experiences of mentoring, promotion, career development planning and progressive pay reviews (Massey, 1995; Fels, 2004; Arabsheibani, 2005). How careers develop can also offer insights into the structures which advantage some and disadvantage others. Such insights can also contribute to informing broader questions about how the practice of some organisational competitive systems can advantage one person over another (Schein, 2001; Ng et al., 2005; Nierderle and Vesterlunde 2007). Understanding the standpoints of individuals who apparently glide up the rungs of the management hierarchy offers the opportunity to explore how some organisational cultures are constructed and the mechanics which maintain them.

Acker (1990) identifies gender as an integral component of organisations operating in five ways. First, as a division that constructs boundaries at work both in terms of physical space and acceptable behaviours; second, in the use of symbols and images such as dress codes and language; third, in the interaction between men and women in the workplace and the devices used both subconsciously and consciously that reinforce gender roles. The fourth way gender operates in organisations is the manner in which the first three influence the individual in assimilating the messages into their own identity. Finally, how gender is performed at work carries over into the wider society by influencing the social fabric of individuals and all their relationships.

Acknowledging different standpoints also brings with it the awareness that research will never provide all the answers or the silver bullet to questions of inequality which lie within the intersection of competition, gender and management. Harding argues that 'the starting point of standpoint theory – and its claim that is most often misread – is that in societies stratified by race, ethnicity, class, gender, sexuality, or some other such politics shaping the very structure of a society, the activities of those at the top both organize and set limits on what persons who perform such activities can understand about themselves and the world around them' (Harding, 2004, p. 43). Unravelling how a manager's current and previous positions in an organisational hierarchy can be influenced by the relationships with superiors, peers and subordinates and how this intersects with their social, economic and political positions can converge to create a complicated picture. Drawing on the work of social theorists like Hakim and Beck (who I discuss in later chapters) is useful for teasing out how the multiple strands can be connected within a wider social context.

Preference Theory

Women's careers have historically been framed within a dominant male career model, which is inaccurate for explaining working patterns over the lifetime of a career. Hakim's Preference Theory (2000) makes an important contribution to rethinking women's multiple relationships with the labour market, particularly in the management sector. Four important tenets Hakim suggests have been pivotal in establishing women's place in the labour market. First, changes in Western society during the latter half of the twentieth century mean women now operate in a new scenario. These changes include the availability of more effective contraception, women entering the white-collar workforce in numbers, the growth of part- time work and equal opportunities policies. Second, there is conflict between a life dominated by paid employment and one centred on child rearing. Women as a group are heterogeneous in their work–lifestyle preferences as well as in how they deal with the issues that arise from them. Third, women will conflict with other women as preferences and interests diverge. Finally, the way women respond to social policy will vary according to their individual priorities, and because women have conflicting interests it 'makes it difficult for them to organize around any single set of common aims and women often find themselves in fundamental conflict over which policies genuinely benefit women' (Hakim, 2000, p. 283). These four tenets, Hakim suggests, are the foundation for predicting women's choices and preferences in combining work and family over their lifecycle using three classifications: work-centred, adaptives and home-centred.

Preference Theory predicts that women will continue to populate the lower tiers of management since only those women who are prepared to work in a similar way to men, and *compete with* them in the upper tiers of organisations where competition increases, will succeed. She argues with reference to Goldberg (1993) that psycho-physiological sex differences between men and women result in different behaviours. For example, testosterone levels produce behaviours in men that favour motivation, ambition and competitiveness. This essentialist argument presented by Goldberg (1993) and Hakim (2000) is important to include as it establishes the limitations of this position and the distractions which biology can present. Hakim also argues that men are a more homogeneous group than women, 'attuned to working in environments where it is necessary to be skilled in politics and diplomacy and to perpetuate the game so that there is more than one opportunity to succeed' (Hakim, 2000, p. 260). In explaining the work-centred classification it is important to note that it does not preclude women from motherhood and family life although this is not the priority. Family may be regarded in the same way as work-centred men regard them, as an 'expression of normality and a weekend hobby' (Hakim, 2000,

p. 280). For many women in this group work would be the priority, 'but it may equally well be political activity, religious activity, intellectual activity...all of which provide channels for competitive achievement and self-expression' (Hakim, 2000, p. 164).

The largest group, the adaptives, seek to combine a work–life balance with two foci – family (including motherhood) and employment. Hakim says this group of women opt out of choosing one path, changing priorities according to their changing circumstances. This may also be influenced by the industry or profession they choose. For example, teaching and health professions lend themselves to flexible working arrangements including shift work, locum work and school term-time work. Hakim's Preference Theory is clearly an important contribution to the genre of gender and work choice, as women's participation in the labour market is marked in modern economies by the existence and exercising of all three classifications by women (Hakim, 2000, p. 170). Within the classifications, it is important to take the generalisations made, see beyond them and unpack them to enable a more in-depth discussion of managers' working lives.

McRae's (2003) study collected empirical evidence to consider the claims of Preference Theory and found that choices and constraints fell into two areas: normative and structural. The normative issues relate to the person and their beliefs while the structural issues relate to day-to-day considerations. McRae also found that a major influence on women's choices about combining work and family is grounded in their beliefs about motherhood. She established that some women became family focused after having children, having, prior to this, planned to return to work. McRae argues that Hakim's classifications are not new but confirms from her own longitudinal study that employment is the priority for a small number of women. McRae contests that Hakim's premise in Preference Theory (that women have genuine choices in terms of employment) is flawed, as 'she appears to confuse voluntary action with genuine or unconstrained choice' (McRae, 2003, p. 333).

Constraint and choice are at opposite ends of a spectrum that has an important relationship with degrees of power, socially, economically and politically. The more choice one has in activating decisions related to these different aspects, the more likely it is they have some access to power. In contrast, the constraints which limit choice are likely to be responding to negligible degrees of power. Choice suggests an open competition where any number of individuals can achieve their objectives. Constraint conversely suggests that the only way an individual can win their selection is by changing the circumstances which negate access to choice. However, as Miner in Miner and Longino (1987) argue, choice and constraint are at the centre of what she describes as the 'ideology of competition', which does not take into account how power, control and access to resources are distributed and how this impacts on the choices available.

Working lives

For many people, the world of work is a central component of life, as remuneration allows them to meet the basic economic needs of shelter, food and clothing. How people will work in the future is a subject that invites a wide range of views that predict success for some and failure for others, often depending on how they approach the supply of and demand for skills in the market. Participation rates in the labour market for men and women are now largely equal, as singular notions of the male breadwinner and nuclear family have fractured to encompass a multitude of living conditions (Crompton, 1999). Increases in the rates of single households, a higher average childbearing age for women, more tertiary educated men and women and longer life expectancies have all contributed to changing notions of career. The emergence of portfolio careers, knowledge collateral and the growth of small businesses developing alongside linear careers in organisations that can be local, national or global, establishes a working environment that can demand much from workers.

Managers across all hierarchies therefore need to be flexible and adapt to constantly changing external and internal markets, ensuring that the resources they control deliver the expected results. Whether operating in a large business or a small enterprise, the demands for repeated optimum performance from managers can be relentless and can have a significant impact on how they manage and construct their career. Making decisions about which skills to develop in order to remain competitive within an organisation and in the wider labour market-place have increasingly become the responsibility of the individual (Beck, 1992). In such circumstances, the tools which may be advantageous in achieving career goals can include mentors, networks, progressive thinking superiors, good childcare facilities and an organisation which has a culture of inclusivity across functions and hierarchies. Remaining relevant in the labour market requires being vigilant about how the changing patterns of employment can positively translate into the everyday reality of managers' lives in terms of career development, cultivation of ambition and notions of success.

The perceptions and experiences of managers throughout their working history can provide useful insights into how individual managers reach and maintain their current position. Such information can highlight the positive and negative influences encountered providing examples of how attitudes and on-going stereotypes are experienced by some managers. How time and life stages can change outlooks can also contribute to identifying how different influences can distinguish the experiences of one manager from another, and examining the role of gender for managers is crucial to assessing how it can impact on other elements of work and career. Connell (2002) and Powell et al. (2002) discuss the ways in which men and women's behaviour and attitudes can be influenced by social and professional stereotypes assigned to their gender. For example, some women seek to control what they perceive as their gender weakness by embracing the attributes of their male colleagues. Such women are often cited as the group who act, dress and speak like men in order to lessen the visibility of their gender. Another side of this are the men who adhere to the accepted uniform assigned to their profession or trade (for example, the city banker). There was a great photo on Armistice Day 2011 (11.11.11) of the bankers in the Lloyds building, where four levels of escalators stopped to observe the minute's silence at 11am, filled with men and women in dark suits and white shirts.

At the centre of a manager's experiences are the relationships they have with the organisation as an entity and then with superiors, peers and subordinates. How cultures at work determine meanings and definitions of competition (if they do) is important for understanding the parameters managers use to define their experiences and perceptions within the context of what they do and how they do it. Relationships at work are also likely to change in response to internal and external factors like a promotion, departmental restructuring, merger or career break. What influence competition has in how relationships initiate and develop is likely to be more positive and constructive if the individuals in the relationship have similar approaches to a generalised version of competition. When competition is allowed to operate covertly by some individuals it is certainly going to affect how they are perceived by peers and superiors who are overt if limited in their competitive activity.

Contextualising competition

Competition, for me, is best described as a whirlpool of energy which quietly filters, often invisible, into many situations. When it is recognised it motivates a range of responses from excitement to anxiety. I first began thinking about competition when I was writing my dissertation for my masters on women and the glass ceiling. The term 'glass ceiling' was first coined by Hymowitz and Schellardt who used it in an article on 24 March 1986 in the *Wall Street Journal* on the corporate woman. The special report described a corporate world where access to the top for women was blocked by corporate tradition and prejudice. The term is often taken to mean the invisible barriers based on gender or race rather than on talent, education, ability and record of accomplishment to being promoted or employed at a higher level. 'Sticky floors' and 'glass walls' are terms that refer to vertical and horizontal segregation. Glass cliff is a relatively new addition to this group of terms, describing the situation where women who reach senior levels are given precarious roles in organisations, potentially becoming scapegoats for poor corporate performances (see Ryan and Haslam, 2005). It appeared that the whole debate on why women do not reach senior management positions was stuck. The barriers have been identified and researched repeatedly, the data is rich and the analysis informed and insightful. Yet somehow this has not made for transformative effects. While women managers, as Wajcman comments, have not been 'feminism's favourite daughters' (Wajcman, 1998, p. 32) because of their perceived privileged position with education and income, the focus on managers as a group has not accounted for the hierarchy of junior, middle and senior women managers who all are likely to have very different experiences. In the same way that second wave feminism was criticised for being dominated by white middle class women who have no sense of what it's like to be a poor, uneducated immigrant or live in the developing world, managers need to speak for their own history and experiences which establish women managers as a heterogeneous group.

What becomes apparent in reading the women in management research and now gender in management research work is how often 'manager' is a term used generically. This cannot accurately reflect the different positions which can construct a hierarchy. Consider Coca Cola, Nestle and HSBC, who have major sites of activity around the world. Within these organisations will be country and regional management systems which in turn feed into the global management team. The organisational chart of such a business will show multiple layers and strands of managers who will have different pay scales, responsibility levels, authority and ultimately power. Does a manager who runs a Nestle manufacturing plant somewhere in America have the same experiences as a manager who is responsible for the global marketing? For as long as we do not distinguish between different levels and sectors of management it is likely that the barriers to progress will be perceived with insufficient attention to detail. Detail is important. It is of little use to be talking about senior management pipelines to a group of managers who work in a medium sized enterprise of around five hundred employees when there are only three people on the senior management team and they are likely to remain there for the foreseeable future. My argument is that in order to effect change for women and men it is important that we spend more time breaking down contexts.

Detail and context means that reading an article which says that women managers cannot access top jobs and have a family unless they are exceptional should also point out that the number of senior roles are minimal pro rata to middle and junior management roles. Furthermore the global corporate world is going to have a different structure to a regional business. Women who aspire to be a senior manager need to place their ambition within the right context to build their road map accurately. Occupations and industries will also have an impact on how senior positions are counted. Does the senior management path have a discipline attached to it such as finance, operations or sales? This will have an impact on the education and jobs which are more likely to make the option viable. How is the senior manager role translated? Is it managing director, COO, CFO, director of sales and so on? Everywhere we look there is a plethora of job titles which makes standardising a plan difficult and, of course, job titles can change over time and be different depending on where an organisation is headquartered.

Mining existing research for data and analysis that adds more texture to the term 'manager' is not straightforward. There is not enough attention paid to job titles and job responsibilities and, in my own experience, I myself have been rewarded with title bumps as a way of trading perceived progression for limited pay increases. The title manager has been adopted by many people in many organisations that 50 years ago would have been called something different, like supervisor or team leader. In a similar way, 'executive' used to be the title of the senior team and yet has now been assumed by those at entry level. So what we now have is a mismatch of titles and jobs which can inflate perceptions and demotivate individuals. I have neither the inclination nor interest to resolve this puzzle and I suspect most people would agree. While I am interested in talking about people's experiences at work generally, I am especially interested in those experiences which have a management context. It is therefore important to define managers for the purpose of this book. A manager is defined as having responsibility for people and/or budget. This distinguishes senior and middle managers from project managers, managers without portfolio or junior managers who have limited responsibility and authority in respect of finance and direct reports. While I accept that this is still open to multiple interpretations, the other safeguard is to get an organisational chart which positions the management team so that people can be assigned accurately to more distinct groups. Also different organisations, depending on size and scale, will have career paths and models which outline potential routes for progress. This of course is blurred in small and medium sized businesses.

Recognising that management hierarchies are complex very quickly led me to the conclusion that identifying a dynamic such as competition would be useful for exploring what was happening to men and women at work. In my early research it became clear that competition was not a concept which had been given in-depth consideration in the workplace except in relation to competition in the marketplace relative to discipline of business. Yet I read stories where terms like 'level playing field' and the importance of knowing the rules were linked to discussions of careers, organisational politics and some work based relationships. The terms which remain part of the rhetoric of the workplace did not really make any specific links with competition and yet the reference points were sports related, suggesting that at least some connections were being made by some people at some time. As a trait, competition emerges as a strong component in the men as managers discourse. But the difficulty in unpacking competition as a trait is the lack of definitions to draw upon. This is an issue in management, gender and psychology where consensus on definitions remain allusive.

Thinking about competition as both a covert and overt dynamic sitting in different relationships at work made me evaluate my own experiences and opinions. If someone asked me if I was competitive I would have certainly answered 'yes'. For as long as I can remember I loved playing sports and I also loved winning so this made answering 'yes' to the question pretty straightforward, although when I started working I can honestly say that I gave competition about as much consideration as I did starting a pension. This is not to say I didn't recognise competition when I saw it, whether directly or indirectly, and I did find it interesting to see some people step away very quickly from such situations. But for most of us, what we learn from our own experiences usually comes retrospectively and this book is my conscious journey into exploring competition as a dynamic. I believe it offers new ways of thinking about how and why we work, how we construct success and ambition, and how the link between competition and confidence is useful.

The sense of anticipation I experienced when I appeared to have identified a gap in my field of specialism (gender and management) was exciting. However, as many will recognise, life is never that simple and my excitement was tempered by the lack of material available to work with. Stepping into the world of competition meant realising that the process was going to be slow and my own reference points found in sport were not going to be particularly helpful, at least not until they were reformulated alongside the accumulation of knowledge. In the process of learning about competition I have found there are a couple of dominant groups of thought. There are those people who do not think about competition at all and manage to walk through life without active engagement. Other people think about competition in a similar way to my original position with links to sport and the transference of winning and losing to other aspects of their life including work and leisure. There is also a group of people who take an oppositional view of competition; those who consciously opt out.

Competition is stuck in a stereotype which renders its value limited, and often portrays it as negative and the opposite of collaboration. Competition as a concept has, over time, been slaughtered by educationalists, media commentators, feminists, politicians, managers and many other sections of society. While there is widespread recognition that competition is an essential element in a free market economy, competition is often referred to as a necessary evil. To make claims that competition is evil is an undoubtedly strong response and made me curious about from where such claims could originate. It also doesn't take much research to uncover that competitiveness sits somewhat proudly among many management lists of necessary masculine traits associated with success. This is swiftly supported by arguments that competition can override most social behaviours to support a survival of the fittest argument. From this position it is quite easy to draw a picture that unless competition is controlled, as it is on the sports field, the outcome is often viewed as being only about winning, with winning perceived as being at the expense of others.

The fieldwork

Measuring equality in the labour market based on women's growing participation rates is misleading. Discourses of equality suggesting that access to education and jobs is adequate for achieving parity can distract from the on-going requirement to monitor and analyse the reality of women's working conditions and career trajectories as compared with men. Investigating the barriers for women managers at work and the impact on their careers was an important facet of my fieldwork. Exploring why men and women managers can experience work and career in different ways motivates questions as to where such differences are located, how they are maintained and why they may go unchallenged. The diversity within management in a context of industry, organisation, hierarchy and gender highlights the importance of continuing to explore the experiences of men and women managers.

This book is the result and extension of my PhD research which identifies competition as a lens through which to examine the ways in which managers understand their experiences and perceptions of work and gender. The main research question throughout the process of writing my thesis and then this book is how and in what ways is competition and competitive relations in management gendered? The competitive relations managers may experience across organisational environments and contexts are difficult to define. I use the five questions below as a framework for guiding the discussions in this book, particularly Chapters 4, 5, 6 and 7.

- How and in what ways do men and women in the workplace perceive and experience competition and competitive relations differently?
- How do competitive relations at work affect relationships between individuals of the same gender and those of different genders?
- What is the relationship between competition and success and/or failure in terms of career development/pathways/trajectories?
- Is engaging with competition and competitive relations at work mandatory and if it is, what effect does this have on workplace and career choices and the well-being of the worker?
- How do competitive relations at work impact on responsibilities and activities outside of work?

The fieldwork was undertaken in the UK and Australia between 2008 and 2011 with middle and senior managers from predominately media companies. The interviewees were sourced through word of mouth using contacts I had in media. I conducted in-depth interviews, some by phone and some face to face, of which all were recorded and transcribed. The number of participants for this project takes into account that qualitative research usually has smaller numbers than quantitative research projects and that the data collected using qualitative methods will produce intense and rich information. Because of the size of the sample (45), I did not aim to produce generalisations but to offer descriptions of human behaviour that influence a sector of the labour market – management. Given that grounded theory was the methodological approach for this study, after completing 45 interviews I considered that some points of theoretical saturation were reached, providing useful insights which overall met the research objectives. 'Like other forms of qualitative research, grounded theories can only portray moments in time. However, the grounded theory quest for the study of basic social processes fosters the identification of connections between these events. The social world is always in process and the lives of the research subjects shift and change as do their circumstances and they themselves change' (Charmaz, 2000, p. 522). Research is critical for society to extend our views and enables connections to be made at different points in time. What becomes apparent in the process of researching and writing is how much information we collect and analyse while waiting for a connection to happen. My key connection has been understanding how a media business offers a great example of success relying on the interdependence of different functions alongside transparent dimensions of competition.

Media and publishing

Within a publishing company there are four main sectors or 'work cultures' – editorial, marketing, advertising and production – and my participants are from all of the sectors. Before addressing the reasons for focusing on publishing it is important to define it, beginning with traditional publishing which is the production and dissemination of printed works such as books, magazines, journals and newspapers. With the advent of digital systems, publishing has expanded to include electronic versions of traditional products along with new products such as websites, blogs and social media. Publishing also belongs to the wider industry of media, which is defined as those organised means of dissemination of fact, opinion, entertainment and other information. Apart from publishing this includes television, radio, film, internet, DVDs and CDs. So with the many and diverse forms of media available, defining not just what media is but what it does is important.

As Engwall (1978) explains, a medium is what transforms experience into knowledge. Media, he says, provide signs which give meaning to the events of everyday life, and a medium is any instrument of communication that carries or mediates a message. He also highlights why the media industry is unique from other industries, stating three reasons. First, a media business operates a dual product, selling two different products to two different sets of buyers. For example, a newspaper will sell itself to readers/consumers and they also sell the relationship they have with those readers/consumers to a third party – the advertiser. The collateral of a media business is the advertiser and the audience who are intrinsically linked to the success of that organisation. The second reason media is unique is because it can access the mass market and this has traditionally come with a public service responsibility. It can play an important role by informing citizens about what they need to know in terms of their social and political life. Third, the role of media is a strong indicator of the democratic process operating in a country. The notion of 'free press' is generally understood to be a key element of a democracy.

My focus on media is grounded in my experience of working in newspaper and online publishing at a time when the industry was moving towards the digital platforms we now take for granted as mainstream. What I learned from my first job selling advertising in a daily newspaper in New Zealand is how seductive the energy is in a newspaper office. Being part of a daily competition within the business to deliver words and pictures and pages certainly made me appreciate temporal competition on an acute level. But what really strikes me about newspapers is the interdependent nature of the functions which compete for space and resources but would crumble without a co-operative approach. In writing this book I have been nostalgic for the regional press in the UK who have seen the highs of classified advertising making profits soar in excess of 30 per cent towards the end of the last century to the lows of the past decade when those profits have flowed online to non-newspaper sites. Journalism phone hacking scandals have plagued the profession, bringing elements into disrepute. However, the role of good journalism in society continues to be integral in exposing corruption and cover-ups and society owes some support to the people who bring us the news. How our future looks in terms of media is difficult to predict, particularly as newspaper publishing has been caught in a perfect storm of declining readership, declining advertising and declining relevance. What we will need is likely to be a mix of regional, national and global offerings which delivers news, features, information, advertising and comment in multi-media offerings.

Feminist influences

The engagement by feminists with epistemological debates critiquing positivism as androcentric and 'bad science' (Stanley and Wise, 1993; Harding, 1987) led to a view that removing bias (e.g. sexism and/or racism) from the research process combined with rigorous adherence to methodologies would result in value-free and objective outcomes. However, simply adding women into the social science equation did not change knowledge and did not challenge the relationship between epistemology and methodologies. Challenging the universal nature of women as a category, feminists argue that different women have different experiences based on not just their gender, but also race, class and sexual orientation (Mohanty, 1988; Hill-Collins, 1991; Stanley and Wise, 1993).

Hill-Collins states that 'epistemology is the study of the philosophical problems in concepts of knowledge and truth' (Hill-Collins, 1997, p. 198). Truth as an ideal for researchers can, I propose, serve more as a distraction than as a useful aim in explorations of the social world. What is believed as a truth or knowledge about one's life today may change tomorrow or into the future, resulting in 'knowledges', 'truths' and 'experiences' co-existing or being replaced over and over again to compose an individual's life story. Acknowledging that the social world is fluid locates not just this inquiry but my position as a researcher with the aim of adding knowledge to the body of work on gender, competition and management.

As someone who on first introduction sat in awe at the immense body of work feminist and gender theorists had amassed in 30 years, I admit to struggling with some of the complex ideas, but the intellectual challenge is rewarding and has certainly instilled a love of learning and debating. While I sit outside academia it does feel like the feminist voices are quieter and this is disappointing. I hope this book offers a window to those readers who had forgotten the socially focused intellectual passion of this work and an invitation to those who have not read feminist work in any depth. While it does seem that the feminist voices are getting quieter my hope is that gender voices are starting to be heard and unite in taking this body of work forward in new directions.

I accept that in any subject saturation points will be reached at different stages, but my cynical side thinks that the questions in the workplace have been silenced because too many cultural and societal changes are needed to move the barriers and this essentially requires some power rebalancing to occur. On the surface this may appear straightforward, but historically, power is never handed over without a struggle, and too often a war, whether physically or philosophically. While I am hopeful that such changes can happen I am not hopeful that they will occur without embedding new knowledge to allow the opportunity for some behaviours and attitudes to be challenged and modified. In seeking to find my own key to this on-going puzzle it became apparent that competition was not a concept that gender and feminist theorists had explored and yet it did appear to be active in the dominant masculinist organisational cultures operating in Western economies. My interest in competition grew, and this book examines the multi-dimensional dynamic which is ever present and yet too often invisible and unarticulated.

Working with the premise that truth is partial and located within an individual's world is an important influence on this how this research is framed. Standpoint theory argues that a position is achieved through understanding the location or locations from which a person's life is experienced. Standpoint theory rejects 'universal and essentialised woman' as a category, an important factor in pursuing discussions of gender. As Hartstock explains, 'A standpoint, however, carries with it the contention that there are some perspectives on society from which, however well-intentioned one may be, the real relations of humans with each other and with the natural world are not visible' (Hartstock, 1997, p. 153). Competition is largely invisible in gender and management, increasing the value of standpoint theory to draw out and discuss perceptions and experiences of managers.

My journey with reflexivity began with the feminist body of work which challenged the traditional orthodox role of the researcher as objective and value-free. My approach to this project was to be self-reflexive, acknowledging that in revealing my own values and attitudes I could be transparent about my role in the construction of knowledge generated from my project (Reinharz, 1992; Finch,1993; Oakley, A., 2000). In developing my position as the researcher I agree with Finlay (2002) who argues that as researchers, 'We recognize that research is co-constituted, a joint product of the participants, researcher and their relationship. We understand that meanings are negotiated within particular social contexts so that another researcher will unfold a different story. We no longer seek to eradicate the researcher's presence – instead subjectivity in research is transformed from a problem to an opportunity' (Finlay, 2002, p. 212). With my focus on gender and management it was useful to draw on the discussions of reflexivity by management researchers who in recent years, as Johnson and Duberley

(2003) suggest, are increasingly becoming engaged with the process of assessing the impact of their own attitudes and perspectives on how research projects are constructed. The use of reflexivity as a positioning practice which Alvesson et al. (2008) explore has particular resonance for me as I would position my subjectivity as a catalyst to explore new and different questions about managers and in so doing create an opportunity to contribute to the gender and management body of work.

Overview of book

Some people find the idea of being pitted against someone else in order to win as repellent. For others the opportunity to satisfy their desire for the adrenalin rush which comes from competing is attractive. This book is constructed over seven chapters which seek to increase the visibility of competition across a range of topics.

Chapter 2 will explore the most common frame of reference for competition – the sporting environment – where the scarcity and challenge models of competition dominate and rules govern the different disciplines. This chapter will argue that competition on the sports field does not easily translate into the work environment. However, for those men and women who played competitive sport as children and into adulthood the foundation for learning the rules of competition may offer distinct advantages at work in terms of communicating, building relationships, setting goals, winning, losing, collaborating and so forth. But research shows that boys are encouraged to play sport more actively than girls and for longer. Moreover, if girls do play sport, at what point do they need to be able to practise competition in the workplace in order keep building their knowledge base?

Chapter 3 defines the eight dimensions of the competition model: personal, interpersonal, external, internal, collective, positional, symbolic and temporal, drawing on a range of interdisciplinary sources. The dimensions are then discussed with reference to interdisciplinary perspectives to build a picture of how explicit competition actually is in the workplace.

Chapter 4 examines how relationships are a fundamental part of how we work, how we structure our work identity and how this manifests into the values and behaviours which direct our careers. Whether it is the psychological contract we as individuals have with the organisation or the networks we join to further our knowledge transfer, at every point we are meeting other people for whom we have to decide whether establishing a relationship is necessary, useful or simply enjoyable.

Chapter 5 explores the language of competition and opens a window on gender and competition as the story behind terms such as 'the rules of the game', 'healthy competition', 'necessary evil' and 'playing the game' is uncovered. The language of competition and particularly sport is often a subject accepted as being important to people, and in particular to men conversing at work. The images of competition in the media continue to be dominated by male sports. When women are engaged in competition at work the caricatures often default to images of masculinised women, reinforcing stereotypes that women who compete are de-feminised.

Chapter 6 explores different versions of confidence and success through the stories of men and women managers. The relationship between women's lack of confidence generally, as repeatedly cited in research, and their lack of confidence to compete at work will be examined. How one person feels or waits for feelings of confidence to occur in comparison to how another person displays confidence is perhaps learned in sporting environments and harnessed into the symbolic competition dimension. Standing on the starting line waiting to run a race it is expected that the competitors, no matter how well prepared, are likely to feel fear, anxiety, excitement and ambition which together can present as the confidence cocktail. So why is it that women cannot construct those legitimate feelings into a cocktail which allows them to exude confidence?

Chapter 7 discusses how time as a resource often presents a zero sum game and that in the workplace this is perceived as being in competition with the organisation. Time is explored with the managers who share their experiences of temporal competition as individuals, managers, parents, friends and extended family care givers. However, the pinnacle of the competition journey, I will argue, is that, if individuals fully understand and effectively manage other dimensions of competition, they re-negotiate their multifaceted relationships with time to secure a shift in how temporal competition is structured at work, home and at play.

In the final chapter, competition will be validated as multi-dimensional and actively influencing the lives of men and women managers at work. The conclusions will draw a picture which shows that competition is indeed gendered and that this has different impacts on the outcomes for men and women. However, the conclusions will also support the idea that sport is one key example of where the tools of competition can be learned and practised. Having reached this level of knowledge, managers will be equipped more generally to progress past the scarcity and challenge models and use what I call a competition cage which is nimble, adaptable and can be developed to embrace the ever changing situations and tensions experienced at work.

Conclusion

In her study of women, work and identity, McKenna (1997) met an editor who at 45 years of age had developed a solid career yet found that with increasing layers of hierarchy came less authority and more responsibility. For example, she was responsible for firing staff but could not solve simple problems without having to go through several rungs of approval. 'Corporate consolidation, more responsibility, lessened authority, all added up to more work with less quality in a dehumanized atmosphere' (McKenna, 1997, p. 37). This example illustrates how complex the business world is and how susceptible managers become to business decisions which may appear to be unpredictable or unforeseen. What becomes clear is how fast change can happen, and while pressure to perform is a constant, the managers who are connected with multiple components in their working life are likely to have more resources to draw upon in times of upheaval.

In response to the editor McKenna speaks to, I would suggest that the organisation's consolidation has probably been progressing over time and is responding to market conditions. The question therefore is, why is the business in decline and how could the role of editor contribute to rebalancing this situation? In this instance, external competition is probably the first entry point for engagement and without taking some ownership of responsibility for the overall performance of the company then progress is likely to be limited. I will argue in this book that competition is dynamic because it pushes the need for activity and connections with people and markets. My interpretation of this editor's remarks is that she is disengaged from the business and is focused on the difficulties in her role rather than how they are common to peers and superiors. Too often it is easier to steer away from the challenges which competition may bring, rather than confronting the active dimension of competition.

The connection of sport and competition certainly provides a foundation for thinking about and practising competing in a structured way. In my conversations about this subject I continue to be surprised by how many people state how they are not competitive. What is noticeable is not just the response itself but how fast it is delivered once the word 'competition' is aired. The sporting world is so much an international language of fun, fanaticism, passion, energy, failure, admiration and change, to name but a few facets. For those people who manage to bypass this huge monolith called sport and see limited or nil value in it, I would like to suggest that sport offers a window on how the social world co-operates, competes and depends on others. As a researcher I have witnessed how fluid and changeable the social world is, while simultaneously experiencing how static and rigid that same social world can be. The passion to explore a different way of examining gender inequality is inequality presents for me the opportunity to ask new questions which I hope will continue beyond the pages of this book. However, there is value in identifying seemingly well-established concepts such as competition and submitting them to a thorough exploration before utilising them as a lens to reinvigorate old debates and encourage new ones while seeking to find innovative ways of applying new knowledge to issues as yet unresolved.

2
Gender and Sport

> The most fruitful approach is not to ask why girls and boys are
> so different but rather to ask how and under what conditions
> boys and girls constitute themselves as separate, oppositional
> groups.
>
> Messner, 2007

The word 'competition' is derived from its Latin root 'competitus', which means to strive together, or to seek together. While competition exists at the core of sport, it is competition's interdependence with co-operation which underpins the success of sport witnessed in all corners of the world. Sport offers the opportunity to view kaleidoscopic images of competition on the field of play, which can be mobilised in other aspects of social life.

As a collective action, sport calls on the involvement of many different groups of people, including coaches, umpires, players and observers, to provide sustainable structures for playing. The flip side is the use of sport as means of calling on individuals to support a collective action which sees sporting programmes being used to address gender, health and education inequalities.

Broadly, there are two models of competition, scarcity and challenge, which are the mainstay of different team and individual sports disciplines. The models are supported and upheld by the rules which govern how each sport is played on local, regional and international stages. Entwined in these models is the access to moral aspects and interpretations of competition found most particularly in the discourse of fair play and sportsmanship.

Differences in access to sport for men and women are documented as early as the ancient Greek games where adult women were banned from attending the men's Olympics. Contravening the ban was met with the death penalty by being thrown off the nearby cliffs. Yet as Thomas F. Scanlon, Professor of Classics, University of California says, 'Maidens could attend the men's games, probably to familiarize them with the world of men.' Furthermore these maidens, legend says, had a sporting event for themselves, the *Heraia*, a footrace. What is interesting in this early tradition is the recognition by society that competition is best understood when observed and directly experienced. And tracing the provenance of competitiveness as a masculine trait, the relationship between sport and men is highlighted.

This chapter will argue that the sports field is where people begin the process of understanding competition through direct experience. When this direct experience extends into other contexts like work environments, the original reference of sport and competition remains dominant. So how does this impact negatively on women? The pivotal point rests in access to participation, where this first and critical stage of learning is experienced and practised. As competition moves off the sports field into society and the workplace the structures, such as rules and umpires, do not exist in the same way. Yet I will argue that possessing a foundation of knowledge about competition collected from the sporting arena provides some widespread points of reference. Elements such as communication, building relationships, setting goals, winning, losing, collaborating and. importantly, recognising the competitive approaches of other individuals in a hierarchy are recognisable. However, if access to sport participation and viewing is skewed in favour of boys and men, competition becomes part of the gendering process found in society and more specifically in management.

Scarcity and challenge models

Competition is often cast in the stereotype of winning and losing, driven by the association with sport. As a comfortable place to begin a discussion of competition, sport operates using the two distinct models of scarcity and challenge. The challenge model is the foundation of running races where it is possible for any number of the contenders to cross the line and win – or tie. The challenge model highlights that in sporting events where a minimum standard of performance is required to compete, on race day any number of differences can potentially advantage one person over another. For example, weather, training and preparation or even how one slept the night before the race may have an influence on the outcome. This aspect of the model makes for the suspense and excitement seen most effectively in the 100 metres final at an Olympics or world championships when we wait to see who is the fastest man and fastest woman in the world. For the viewers, the more well matched the competitors, the greater the challenge and the spectacle.

The scarcity model, or zero sum game, in sport is structured so there can be only one winner and the competition continues until this point is reached. So if at the end of the specified time allocation the position is a tie, many sports have rules to resolve the tie. For example in football there is extra time and if at the end of this period the game remains tied, a penalty shootout is held. In tennis, tie breaks are played at the end of a set for the first two or four sets and in the third or fifth and final set, two consecutive games must be won to declare a winner. For the viewer, this type of competition offers the opportunity to witness outstanding performances which often surpass the physical attributes of players and demonstrate the mental capacity required to break through the pain barrier and reach the finish line.

Found in both these sporting models are the stories of legends which bring to sport a dimension which transcends team alliances and becomes a shared experience. In sport a winner today may be a loser tomorrow, and this competitive scenario is the mainstay of particularly professional sport where the stakeholders are sponsors, television and radio broadcasters and, of course, fans. The partnership between sport and live television has certainly been a catalyst in bringing such shared experiences onto a global scale. The wonder of being in the moment when something phenomenal happens in sport is certainly difficult to replicate in other aspects of society and I am sure sports fans around the world have those moments etched into their memories.

What sport does is unite people and I believe it is the competitive element of sport which delivers the energy and momentum to excite players and participants whatever their age or level of experience. Yet this competitive component in sport is often assumed rather than contemplated and in this chapter I want to bring visibility to the dynamism of competition within the context of gender and sport.

History of sport

Sport in its widest context is interwoven into society and through the historical lens can provide markers which record responses to significant changes, economically, socially, technologically and politically. The transition in Britain from an agricultural based economy to the industrial age is possibly the most significant event which impacts on the world today. With the development of the steam engine and the spinning jenny came the growth of new ways of working and living. Factories, employment, structured working weeks and terraced housing in towns and cities meant that men and women lived in different ways, the household becoming the domain of women and the labour market the domain of men. So began the dawn of the breadwinner model.

Alongside these economic changes, which were direct responses to new technology, emerged the demand for activity and entertainment outside work, the catalyst for the transition from folk games to modern sport. Dunning and Sheard in their 1979 book *Barbarians, Gentlemen and Players* offer a comprehensive comparison of folk games and modern sport and for the purpose of this discussion I am going to draw on just two relevant elements. They describe folk games as diffuse, informally organised with simple and unwritten customary rules legitimated by tradition. In comparison, modern sports are specific, formally organised and differentiated at local, regional, national and international levels. The rules are formal, elaborate and worked out pragmatically by rational bureaucratic means.

It was the British public school system that was instrumental in bringing form and function to the modern sports. Horne et al. (1999) highlight that the game of 'association football in England can be divided into seven distinct phases; the folk game, the formalisation of the athleticist-amateurist codes in public schools; the spilt between association football and rugby football, and then later within rugby football itself – bound up with the emergence of the professional game, the insularity of the British game in the inter-war years of the twentieth century, the post-war years of austerity, the years of further commercialisation of the game in the 1960's and 1970's and 1980's and the more recent phase based upon the creation of a breakaway Premier league and sponsorship and media influences upon the game' (Horne, 1999, p. 36).

McIntosh (1979) suggests that competitive sport was developed in the public school system with an ethical rationale supporting the development of a moral compass for boys which they would carry with them into the world. Coming from the public school system, it was expected that the boys were destined to become the future business and political leaders setting the moral and ethical tone for wider society. The connection between sports, education and social values emanating from the public school system was crucial to the Victorians' rationale which was transferred into the colonies of the British Empire where sports such as cricket and rugby took hold. What is interesting is how many of those colonial countries have surpassed the United Kingdom in terms of leading the world in these sports. For example, cricket in India is as much a part of the culture as rugby is in New Zealand and the passion for these games is unquantifiable. The connection between sport and national pride is also something which is debated in the United Kingdom as the national football and rugby teams continue to disappoint. Perhaps professionalism has been critical in driving a wedge between the club and national teams which has diluted the commitment and pride required in serving two masters.

The language of sport and how it is enacted is wide and varied by discipline and the levels of interaction within that discipline. At the 2012 Olympics Games there 26 sports are presented breaking down into 39 different disciplines which offer an immense picture. Add to this all the levels from grass roots up and the 'sport' is best described as a generic term. Maguire (2011) makes the point that sport is bound in and around the social world and within that world are many areas which are contested such as politics and economics. He argues that sociologists must ask, 'What is Sport?' This will ensure that the connections with different aspects of the social world are identified and analysed. Maguire says, 'Attention must be given to the conventions that define sport worlds, but also the innovations and challenges that emerge out of these relations to other social worlds, such as the developments of "extreme" sports and the Gay Games' (Maguire, 2011, p. 860).

The ways in which people are active in sport are very different and can be useful for providing insights into the social world they occupy and the main influences on that world. A concise example of this was the Zola Budd story. As a young South African, because of apartheid her world best times in the 5000 metres were not recognised and so she became a British citizen in order to compete in the Los Angeles Olympics (1984) at 3000 metres. Sport is often a place where the politics of race, gender and power are witnessed, with racism in football currently a blight on sport in terms of players, managers and supporters.

In terms of sport and its relationship with education and with wider society, John Major, the prime minister of the United Kingdom from 1990 to 1997, is arguably the leader who most showed his passion for the value of sport. In a speech delivered on 14 July 1995 he shared his vision for a new direction and legacy:

'Sport, for most people in this country, is more than just a game; it is a way of life. And I think organised team sports is one of the gifts that this country has given to the world over the years...I believe sport is immensely important for children, it is an integral part of growing up. I think it is character building, but above all I think it is fun for children and they have a right to enjoy it.

I also don't accept the premise that competitive sport is bad for children. You only have to see youngsters together to realise that that frankly isn't true. Put any group of youngsters together in any environment and they are likely to compete. So I want to redevelop skills in competitive sport.

One of the sadnesses to me, and I think to many people in education as well, is the extent to which competitive sport has declined over the last 30 years and one aim...is to put competitive sports back where it belongs, right at the heart of weekly life in every school in the country.'

Major's speech highlights how the relationship between sport and society is one which changes, in response to the influences of educationalists, priorities for government money, and the value that citizens as individuals place on encouraging participation in and watching sport. History has been epitomised in great sporting moments like Jesse Owens winning four gold medals in the 1936 Berlin Olympics and President Nelson Mandela presenting the rugby world cup to the South African captain Francois Pienaar. The connection between the historical moments and the sentiment of Major's speech on competition shows how this dynamic is historically apparent in many aspects of society and yet does not receive the due respect and attention deserved, allowing the negative aspects to be mainstreamed.

Sense of fairness

One positively headlined aspect from competitive sport which is transplanted into many aspects of the social world is a sense of fairness or sportsmanship which can be embedded in an individual's moral compass. The *Evening Standard*, reporting on a cricket match in the summer of 2011 where the Indian captain retracted his call for a run out of an English batsman because of a misunderstanding, recounted a top ten of great examples of sportsmanship (Lucas, 2011).

For me, two of these examples stand out. First, 'West Ham striker Di Canio was commended by FIFA after passing up the opportunity to score a winner at Everton in December 2000 by catching the ball because goalkeeper Paul Gerrard was lying injured. It was a remarkable act of sportsmanship from a player who once pushed a referee over.'

This example is appealing because it could be interpreted that Di Canio learnt something about sportsmanship from his earlier unacceptable encounter with the referee.

The second example is that of the tennis player Andy Roddick who was leading by five sets to three in the second set of his quarter-final encounter with Fernando Verdasco in the Rome Masters of 2005, and with three match points, Roddick watched as his opponent spun a second serve close to the left tram-line. The line judge called the ball out, giving Roddick the victory. However, the American, seeing the ball mark in the clay, called the serve good, handing Verdasco a reprieve. The Spaniard took full advantage and held serve, before winning the set in a tie-break. Verdasco won the match and said, 'I have to thank him. He is a great sportsman.' This example illustrates how a sense of fairness can cost the player or team a win and can override the competitive element. Anyone who has watched Roddick play tennis will know he is an elite competitor.

Some critics argue that competition in sport accentuates egotism, cheating and selfishness. This is difficult to refute given the recent doping and match fixing scandals found in athletics and cricket, but sport is not the only place where we find ego, cheating and selfishness. The closure of the *News of the World* over the phone hacking scandal and of course the bankers' bonuses are two vivid illustrations. It is also easier to refute the claims that competition in sport sets individuals against one another in some gladiatorial type forum which results in either winning or losing. What this argument misses is all the processes which lead to a final outcome which is repeated again and again. The examples above highlight how out of competition comes winning, losing and a whole bundle of other experiences, including respect of rules and for the enforcers of those rules, respect for other players, the probability of human error and the positive pressure to play with integrity.

To ensure a competition can take place, it is vital that there is co-operation from those taking part and those officiating. The interdependent relationship between competition and co-operation is fundamental to the success of sport and sporting contests. The term 'a level playing field', something many people refer to in the workplace, arguably represents the voluntary nature of accepting a competitive sporting challenge where interdependence with co-operation is accepted as essential. But outside of the sporting context the playing field can never be equal or the outcome of a parallel interdependent relation, as the social world is complex, without referees and agreed rules of engagement. As such this term is loaded with expectations which are repeatedly unable to be met because the essence of a sense of fairness found in sport simply does not translate outside these parameters. Furthermore, if we try to translate this essence of fairness onto a global stage what becomes apparent is how cultural aspects of society are an additional layer which can increase the likelihood of misunderstanding and disappointment.

Participation and access

Making the distinction between the basic benefits of participation in sport – health, self-respect, co-operation with team, learning to be a good loser and winner, improving skills, learning to accept criticism, and fun – and the more scarce benefits of fame and fortune is important in exploring the multiple levels of sport, as English (1978) argues. Fame and fortune are direct products of the growth of professional sports over the past forty years or so and in today's media frenzy can present a utopian picture of how accessible fame and fortune can be. Football is highlighted as the crème de la crème of professional sport because of the sizeable weekly payments made to world class players. However, what we do not see in the sports pages of newspapers and websites are all the professional players in football or many other sports who live a life of uncertainty, waiting to break into the big leagues and believing that their time will come or accepting the life of a journeyman professional. Golf probably provides the best example of a two tier professional model where the majority of professionals are employed by clubs (quoted as 95% by GolfPro.com) to coach, play and act as a beacon for delivering the skills of the sport to club members. This is distinct from the professionals who play on the circuit travelling the world vying for the chance to qualify to play in the grand slams where those scarce benefits of fame and fortune wait for the few.

However, for those men and women who played competitive sport as children and into adulthood, the foundation for learning the same rules of competition may offer distinct advantages at work in terms of communicating, building relationships, setting goals, winning, losing, collaborating and so forth. But two issues arise: first, data, trends and research show that boys are encouraged to play sport more actively than girls and for longer. Second, at work practising competition is often deemed to be part of the culture of the domain of men so if girls do play sport, at what point does their base knowledge and experience of competition pass its 'use by date'?

For most people, early childhood is when we learn to play games as way of mastering the physical skills of walking, running and jumping. As we grow and enter education systems, the games we play gain structure and rules, beginning our transition into the world of sport. However, the sporting journeys for girls and boys become distinct from an early age and from this time the relationship with sport develops as a participant and/or viewer in a gendered way. While there is a broad body of research on why girls and boys have such different experiences, the bigger picture shows how the entrenched traditional social roles society determines for men and women, boys and girls, prevail. The depth of this prevailing pattern is different across economic, geographic, education level, religious and ethnic components.

Sport England released their Active People Survey figures in December 2011 for the fifth consecutive year and found that 6.927 million adults aged 16 and over participated in sport three times a week for 30 minutes, with 14.759 million adults participating in sport at least once a week during the period October 2010 to October 2011. The Women's Sport and Fitness Foundation, who are funded by Sport England, broke down the data from the 2009–2010 Active People Survey and found that 2.76 million women take part in regular sport every week, which they claim is a non-significant increase since 2008/09. What they also found was that women are more likely to participate in individual sports such as swimming, going to the gym and athletics. Only 8.3 per cent of women take part in organised sporting competitions, 2.5 times less than men. While competition is most likely to be associated with youth sport, the different rates of participation are significant from an early age. Sport Scotland have been collecting data about sports participation in children aged 8 to 15 years since 1998. They found that the most popular activities are football, swimming, cycling, dance and running, with football being the most popular activity by more than 50 per cent. There was also a noticeable drop in participation in sports for girls from 95 per cent in 1998–2000 to 89 per cent in 2006–08. Swimming is the most popular sport for girls with 44 per cent participating. What was also noted was the sharper decrease in girls' participation rate between the ages of 12 and 15, where the drop of rate fell from 96 per cent to 88 per cent over the same time period.

It is claimed that 4 per cent of the world's population are involved in the game of football, accounting for approximately 265 million players. FIFA have done two surveys of their sport, one in 2000 and the second in 2006, and while in 2006 26 million women were counted as playing the game, this equates to only 10 per cent of the total number of players. The biggest growth in women's football has been recorded in the CONCACAF (Federation of North, Central American and Caribbean Association Football), which registers 23 per cent of all women players. The top three countries with registered players are Germany, USA and Brazil for men and USA, Germany and Canada for women. With both men and women the difference between the first and second country is approximately double.

Participation in sport and especially team sport is dominated by boys and men. This is replicated in the television viewing figures which build the foundation for my argument that girls and women are being disadvantaged by not engaging in competition at this sporting level. With sport as a mainstream part of masculine cultures it becomes clear to see why competition has been constructed as a masculine trait and couched alongside terms such as 'aggression', 'ambition' and 'leadership'. The key element of competitive sport is not the taking part but the repetition of different cycles of experience. This includes winning, losing, changes in teams, changes in coaching, players retiring or moving from junior to senior levels, moving away from playing one particular sport to play other sports, and building friendships and networks. What competitive sport fundamentally teaches is that there is always another game, another contest, another tournament; winning and losing is only part of the overall process.

Sport and media

As a product of the social world sport presents a good opportunity to examine the gendering process. At the time girls move from playing games to engaging in competitive sport they can become more attuned to the role of media in reflecting and reinforcing social roles of men and women. Messner is a sociologist who has written widely on gender, media and sport and he comments on how sport remains one of the final sites of male domination and privilege. While women are participating in sport in their millions, they are largely locked out of media in ways that are meaningful and reflect their athleticism and power. Messner comments that 'televised sport has continued to juxtapose images of powerful male bodies against sexualised images of women's bodies in ways that affirm conventional notions of male superiority and female frailty' (Messner, 2007, p. 165). The media is as much entwined in the social world as sport, and their interdependent relationship is one which requires exploration to understand how to shift the emphasis to be more reflective of diverse societies.

Removing gender from sport, particularly when you are a woman, is difficult. The gravitational pull in sporting entertainment is dominated by men's professional sports where often highly masculinised images and high contact sports dominate. Why as sports fans do we consider men's sport worthy of pay-to-view while women's sport is what we watch when there is nothing else on, with the exception of the Olympics, tennis grand slams and some sporting world championships? The Women's Sport and Fitness Foundation (WSFF) released a report looking at media and sport (2010) and found from data collected in 2009 that men as a group are the largest audience for sport, with tennis and particularly Wimbledon being the exception for women. This may be due to the fact that it is shown on BBC free-to-air television and dominates the scheduling for two weeks in the summer. For male viewers football was by and large the most viewed sport on free-to-air television. To add more contrast to this picture, 79 per cent of the viewing audience for the Women's Cricket World Cup final and 76 per cent for the Women's Rugby World Cup was male.

Learning about competition generally is experienced first-hand through sports and games at school. There is no doubt that some children have memories of competition and sport which are filled with dreaded moments of waiting for everyone else's name to be called before being picked last. This is undoubtedly cruel and with some minor adjustments could be removed from the process. By letting the two people picked last, pick first next time, the power of this experience could be shifted and become more inclusive. Sad as it is for those who are stuck with such experiences, the actual feeling of playing till the final minute in the hope you may win can be an adrenalin rush which is difficult to match. Furthermore, beyond the elation or devastation of winning and losing sportspeople and sports fans will admit that some wins are sweeter than others.

Watching sport while growing up in New Zealand, there are a couple of moments which are etched in my memory. The first is New Zealand winning the gold medal in the men's rowing eight in the 1972 Munich Olympics and seeing these men stand on the podium proudly saluting the national anthem. The visual memory of this picture is viewed in black and white because colour television did not reach New Zealand until 1974, in time for the Christchurch Commonwealth Games. Fortunately the rowers were wearing black kits, which further defined the moment. What I didn't know until researching this book was that the International Olympic Committee President, Avery Brundage, was so elated by this victory of amateurs over professionals that he presented the medals himself, and 'God Defend New Zealand' was played at an Olympic medal ceremony for the first time. This picture, etched in my memory for many years, now has another layer of knowledge which for me personally renews it and adds to its sweetness.

One of the other key moments in New Zealand sporting history is the tour of the South African (Springboks) rugby team in 1981, the first tour since 1965. For both nations rugby is part of the national identity, the difference being that in New Zealand there were no racial restrictions on who could play. This tour can only be described as a pivotal moment in New Zealand's political, social and racial history. In 1977 New Zealand, along with other commonwealth countries, agreed through the Gleneagles Agreement to discourage competition with South Africa. However, Prime Minister Robert Muldoon declared that politics had no place in sport which the rugby union (NZRFU) took as an opportunity to organise a tour. As the tour moved closer to starting, New Zealander Pakehas (whites) came under increasing scrutiny about their own race relations as more Maoris (indigenous people) entered the debates. The tour went ahead but violence plagued every game and two games were cancelled because of the clashes between pro and anti-tour groups. When the news of the anti-apartheid action reached Mandela in Robben Island, it is said that he commented that it is as 'if the sun had come out' (Atkinson, 2011b). Two lessons I recall coming out of this event are first, sport and politics can never be separate because both are integral to society and, second, sport is an emotive way to challenge traditional thinking. As a postscript in 1984, the government was ousted by a landslide Labour victory and shortly after nuclear-free legislation was introduced and homosexual law reform was taken forward.

In each of these moments it is the magic of live television which invites the viewer to connect with experiences beyond what often seems possible. The role of television has been critical to the development of professional sport and the wider sporting industry. According to a report, 'The Sports Market: Major Trends and Challenges in an Industry Full of Passion', from global management consultants A.T. Kearney (2011), the global sports industry is worth between 350 and 450 billion euros and is growing faster than the GDP rates around the world, and there are predictions for further significant growth. The report illustrates how sports create value through the events, media and marketing rights, creating what is described as a virtuous chain. One of the early exponents of this was Kerry Packer who in 1977 established World Series Cricket having been denied the television rights to the game by the Australian Cricket Board. Packer's initiative was scorned at first. 'Because of the players' coloured flannels, it was dismissively known by the old school as pyjama cricket, but it helped to bring the game up to date and established Packer as a world influence in sport' (Zinn, 2005). The introduction of colour to television and cricket has over time added a new dimension to the game away from the five day test match. In recent years the one day game has also undergone some challenges, with the introduction of the high speed Twenty20 cricket competitions in response to the demands of TV.

The global sports industry provides some useful context for thinking about the relationship between women and sport. The 2011 Forbes list of the top ten female and male earners in sport is worthy of further comment. The women's list is dominated by tennis players (seven out of ten) with number one on the list, Maria Sharapova, earning twice what the number two, Caroline Wozniacki, earns. However, the spilt between sponsorship and winnings from tournaments is skewed towards sponsorship. The top ten men athletes earn a combined figure of four and half times what the women top ten did, which is also probably representative of TV coverage. Sponsorship opportunities have been instrumental in changing the face of professional sport and not least women's sport. While women's tennis is held up as a leading light in achieving equal pay in the grand slams following a campaign led by some very strong women such as Billie Jean King and Martina Navratilova, sponsorship in tennis and other women's sports reflects demands which are grounded in sexualising women athletes.

'Sexploitation' is a term used by the Australian Sports Commission (2011) to describe the 'forms of marketing, promotion or attempts to gain media coverage which focus attention on the sexual attributes of female athletes, especially the visibility of their bodies'. The tension which unfolds with sexploitation is a dilemma. To secure sponsorship to fund their further development female athletes (individuals and teams) open themselves to being portrayed and judged in terms of body type rather than athletic prowess. While some male athletes would claim similar dilemmas, it is their athletic prowess which is used as the foundation for delivering the sponsor's message which could be humorous, clever or approachable. An example of using humour is the famous shaving trio featuring Roger Federer, Thierry Henry and Tiger Woods, icons in their respective sports, who were successfully used to advertise razors at men. I doubt we would see Serena Williams, Paula Radcliffe and Marion Jones advertising tampons!

In a research project currently being undertaken in Brazil, Caitlin Fisher, a former professional footballer turned researcher, is exploring how the professional women's game has developed in recent years within the context of 'futebol' the national game and 'futebol' the women's game. She shares in our conversations how during her time in Brazil she has seen a clear shift in how successful women's football teams are treated by the community and their sponsors. The demands placed on the women players to deliver on and off the pitch a 'highly feminised' image have become much more prevalent. This highly feminised image is seen in players having long hair and wearing make-up when they play. Her research is building a picture which suggests that while football offers some choices for women, especially in the professional arena, narrow gendered social norms are the constraints. In her own words she espouses her frustration of gender and sport as merely one element of the wider world: 'Listening to women both inside and outside of football I can see distinct parallels to imprisoning and oppressive experiences of gender. What upsets me, but also motivates me in working towards change, is how strongly these narratives resonate with women who otherwise do not seem to be able to hear each other.' The point illustrates how fragmented the world has become for women and how the navigation is often isolated and unconnected with the experiences of other women.

Increasingly women can see a complex spectrum of choices and approaches to creating a life of their own. How education, work, career interests, family and lifestyles are planned varies according to opportunities presented and the fundamental issue of being economically active and independent. In such a divided range of commitments, women can often find themselves operating in a life bubble which can make them vulnerable to tensions and dilemmas. This may be the sexploitation scenario described above but equally may be in respect of time and of society's predetermined pressure to push women towards domestic and caring responsibilities.

The relationship between media and leisure time resonates in many households with viewing and participating in sport. Bittman and Wajcman (2000) argue that leisure time has become more fragmented with unpaid work being a dominant feature. They argue that although men have more pure leisure time than women, the difference between parents and non-parents is as marked as that of gender. For women and men with children, leisure time can be a combination of domestic and care work and entertainment which would include sport. What the universality of sport offers many men, whether from playing, viewing or a combination of both, is an arena for connecting on number of levels. While there are obviously a wide range of preferences within this arena, sport does provide men with an understandable structure which offers a comfortable counterbalance to the nuanced versions of their individual lives.

How we as viewers, listeners and readers experience sport in terms of gender is predictable, with men's sports dominating coverage. A number of studies have been undertaken to measure the actual coverage. In 1991 the third IAAF World Championships were held in Tokyo and in 1992 we were treated to the Olympics in Barcelona. For both these events the BBC coverage of athletics was collected by Alexander (1994) who decided to choose these two platforms because of the comparative participation rates between men and women in the majority of events, that is sprints, middle distance, long distance and field events. In both these championships men competed in more events (25) than women (19) because of the ban on pole vaulting, triple jump, 50k walk, steeplechase and shot putt. (The 50k walk remains a race which women cannot compete in at the 2012 London Olympics.) The findings showed that men's live events in the World Championships amassed 57 hours, while women's events accounted only for 41 hours. In the Olympic Games, the ratio was 84 to 55 hours (men to women). While there is a the need to acknowledge that at any such sporting event, winners from the broadcasting nation will collect additional coverage, at the 1992 Olympics the BBC gave Linford Christie 38 minutes after he won the men's 100 metres. Sally Gunnell, the 400 hurdles gold medallist, received less than five minutes. The viewing hours beyond the national team are the most interesting. Alexander found the women's coverage was dominated by British women competitors whereas the men's coverage had a global perspective in addition to following the national representatives. This clearly positions men's athletics as a viewer preference after nationalism is satisfied.

Duncan and Hasbrook (1988) in their research of televised women's sport found what they describe as four aspects of ambivalence. First is qualitative limitation, which is simply about token coverage of women's sport; second is narrative and imagery, which is where the camera is on the women but the commentary is on the male athletes. They found this particularly when they were watching the New York marathon. Macro and micro ambivalence are the other two elements, with macro accounting for the overall positioning of women's sport combined with broadcasting which can see battles between commentators around sexist comments. Micro ambivalence centres on individuals making comments either off or on air with little or no regard for what they are saying. A recent example from the UK is the sacking of a high profile pundit from Sky Sports for making sexist comments about a female referee (BBC, 2011). For as long as the media are at the centre of the sporting world it is important to challenge those outlets that reinforce stereotypes about men and women.

In 2001 in a journal article George, Hartley and Paris analysed the representation of female athletes in textual and visual media. They tested the hypothesis that female athletes are unfairly reported in the British press, using the *Sun*, *Mirror*, *Mail*, *Independent*, *Daily Telegraph* and *Guardian*. Unfair was defined as use of sexist language, negative coverage, emphasis of femininity and physical characteristics, less coverage and trivialisation of achievements. The newspapers were viewed over nine days of the 1995 World Championships. Most telling in the results is the total picture area which had 33,000 column centimetres of which 21 per cent was devoted to female athletes and 79 per cent to male athletes. As for the editorial coverage, of the 18,300 column centimetres, male athletes filled 72 per cent and female athletes 28 per cent. The conclusion supports Hargreaves' point that 'sport constitutes the most male-dominated area of the media' (Hargreaves, 1986, p. 151) and perhaps reinforces the idea that women's sport is less competitive and interesting than men's sport.

In January 2012 I decided to take three titles from the British newspaper market and replicate aspects of George et al.'s study to establish whether outside of a major championship the profile of women's sport had gained mainstream coverage ten years later. The *Daily Mail*, the *Sun* and the *Daily Telegraph* were collected from Friday 6 January to Thursday 12 January. In terms of high profile events the FA Cup (football) competition was taking place but to all intents and purposes it was a relatively normal week in terms of sports events.

Over the week the *Daily Mail* ascribed 108 pages to sport, of which 103.55 pages were editorial and 4.45 advertising. Photographs accounted for the equivalent of 22.5 pages. Football was the number one sport with 70 pages. The rest of the pages were spilt in the following way: rugby 7.5, cricket 3.9, racing 8, boxing 2.75, tennis 1.7, Olympics 1.5 and golf 0.5. Sports results accounted for 2.9 and snippets were 4.7 pages. Snippets are defined as stories which are no more than four lines of one column and are often used described as 'News in Brief'. In the sports coverage of that week women's sport was assigned to only a handful of snippets where the coverage included a tennis story, a horse racing trainer and Olympic gymnastics. Just 1.8 per cent of the total editorial content was devoted to women's sport.

Though the *Daily Telegraph* is a broadsheet, the design template was scaled to tabloid size to enable direct comparisons to be made. Its sport allocation was 152, pages with an editorial spilt of 141.75 to 10.25 advertising. Photographs accounted for 49.35 pages. Football again was dominant, amassing 72.85 pages of news and features. Rugby was number two in the sports rankings with 24.7, cricket 9.7, Olympics 9.6, racing 9.3, boxing 7.4, tennis 2.1 and golf 0.4 pages. Results accounted for 3.55 pages and snippets 2.15 pages, of which 50 per cent of the stories were Olympic based, with one about a women boxer who is a medal hope. Again, as seen with the *Daily Mail*, women's sport was covered in the snippets section but during this week the newspaper published a 16-page Olympic supplement which featured Victoria Pendleton, a cyclist, across two full pages with a mix of big glamour and smaller action pictures. The other woman featured was Fran Halsall, a swimmer, whose photos were mostly action. Aside from this supplement, regular women's sports coverage amounted to just 1.4 per cent, less than the *Daily Mail*.

The *Sun* devoted 95 pages to sport with an editorial split of 87.8 to 7.2 pages of advertising. Of that space 23.25 pages were photographs. Football was the winner on coverage with 55 pages, followed by racing with 21.3, Olympics 3.8, rugby 2.2, snippets 1.9, boxing 1.25, cricket 0.75 and tennis 0.6 pages. In the snippets the women's sport covered was diving, cycling and a boxing medal hope for the Olympics. In the Olympics coverage was a double page spread on Rebecca Adlington, the swimmer, where the main shot was her fully made up in a swim-suit. What was striking about the shot was the sexualised manner in which her body was thrust into the centrefold. However, this feature brought the percentage of editorial coverage in the *Sun* to 2.6 per cent, the highest of the three titles. Without it, the *Sun* would have recorded the lowest coverage.

Over the three newspapers the total percentage of sport attributed to women was just 1.8 per cent or 16 of 333 editorial pages. This figure excludes the *Daily Telegraph* supplement, where the ratio was 60:40 men to women athletes. In similar data collections undertaken since the 1980s the average is reported to peak at about 10 per cent, although many of the data collections take place during a period of a major event. This was an average week of sport and represents what readers see on a daily basis; without a seismic shift in editorial approaches it is difficult to see how these ratios will do any more than stagnate.

Without the London 2012 Olympics gaining momentum in the British media the smattering of women's sport reported would be non-existent. Since 1996 when George et al. took the temperature of women's sport in newspapers not much has changed and men's sport still dominates the media profile. Sport editors will obviously argue that they are giving readers what they want. (This is difficult to dispute unless readers are given other editorial offers and accept or reject them.) The other argument is that if a person follows a specific sport or team which is not mainstream it is likely to have some online news platform which can be accessed. Football remains the most popular sport and reported as such. As a sport the English Premier League has a global following and has invested in players, managers and infrastructure, presenting itself as a brand leader where some of the clubs, such as Manchester United, are top global consumer brands.

To challenge the interdependent relationship between football, merchandising, attendance and media coverage would require a remarkable shift in our cultural preferences. So the battle for women's sports coverage sits within the minority sports package where news usually comes from a world stage. In this space the opportunity does exist to raise the profile of different sports and the men and women who play them. However, to achieve this, the role of sponsors needs to be refocused to encourage women's sponsorship beyond tennis where it remains quite distinct from other sports. Women's tennis has been fortunate in having insightful and passionate players who over time have challenged the Women's Tennis Association (WTA) to present the women's game as a sport in its own right. They have also put pressure on the sponsors to demand profile and coverage, especially at the grand slam events. As a result, I would think most people would be able to name some women tennis players (or at least recognise their names) and certainly more so than in other sports.

Sport as a right

Bringing sport to the developing world as a mechanic to empower girls and women has become popular with governments, international aid agencies and non-governmental organisations (NGO). In this context there is a sense of the circular as history serves us with the stories of colonisation which brought religion, education, health and sport to far flung corners of the world. The connection between sport and social change is certainly seductive, and I think it is important to view the sport in development model as in many ways still under construction.

The United Nations has led the way on taking a rights based view of rest and leisure for individuals within the social and cultural life of the community. The International Charter of Physical Education and Sport states: 'One of the essential conditions for the effective exercise of human rights is that everyone should be free to develop and preserve his or her physical, intellectual, and moral powers, and that access to physical education and sport should consequently be assured and guaranteed for all human beings' (UNESCO, 1978). This charter was then extended into the Convention on the Rights of the Child where it states that the 'development of the child's personality, talents and mental and physical abilities to their fullest potential' should be one of the aims of education (UN, 1989).

In 2000, a pledge was made by 189 nations to free people from extreme poverty and multiple deprivations by 2015. The pledge was developed into the eight Millennium Development Goals (MDGs). In September 2010, the world recommitted itself to accelerate progress towards these goals. In 2005 the UN Year of Sport and Physical Education was launched to focus the MDG's on sport. This included targeting the sports industry to create employment opportunities to promote sport in education and use this as a platform to develop children's confidence.

In 2007 the UN Division for the Advancement of Women, Department of Economic and Social Affairs published a report, 'Women, Gender Equality and Sport', which presented a range of projects working to bring sport into a place where it served the interests of men and women. The projects cover issues like media stereotyping and coverage of women in sport, leadership, coaching, health and education programmes around the world, professionalism in sport and representation in national sporting bodies. This report identified the sheer number of people, projects and organisations which are amassing information and data which is likely to be rich and useful. However, there is not enough evaluation of the projects to assess their strengths and weaknesses and there is also an opportunity to collect qualitative and quantitative data to build a layered picture of what works and what does not. which remains a work in progress.

Sport in development

Sport has been described as the 'new engine of development' (Levermore, 2008), and the examples of sport being harnessed by corporates, public/ private partnerships and NGOs as a way of addressing social and health inequalities in the developing world are widespread and numerous. Whatever the rationale – building on the rights approach supported by the UN, the work being undertaken in the HIV/AIDS epidemic, political corruption, diluted citizenship, illiteracy or poverty – using sport in development is changing the lives of some people. However, suggesting that sport is the silver bullet to all the ills of world is not without concerned critics, and Spaaij (2009a) argues that while there may be useful outcomes there can also be a reproduction and reinforcement of inequalities. The way sport is used in programmes needs to be sensitive to the environment because sport carries cultural and symbolic meanings in a local and global context which does not always translate across such great divides. Kunz (2008), in assessing the Bam post-earthquake project in Iran, made strong reference to the workers and coaches modifying the positioning of competition in the sports programme by focusing on tolerance to achieve more positive effects for the participants. As with sport in the developed world, the processes of a social kickabout with some friends in the park and a more structured team based league where scores are recorded and rankings compiled are very different. One of the other aspects of sport which becomes more acute in the world of global sport is the distinction between amateur and professional sport. These operate to provide different forms of entertainment, but for professional sport, capitalism is the ultimate driver and there are many who do not make the grade. Managing expectations in sport is a difficult balance and requires the wisdom of forethought rather than hindsight when establishing and encouraging a programme. Spaaij comments that 'Certain sports seem better suited than others to address or change gender relations and to empower young women, facilitating a radical rethinking of things we tend to take for granted. The key, then, is to avoid naive and unrealistic generalizations about the transformative capacity of sport' (Spaaij, 2008, p. 1266). Sports which are non-contact and do not require specialist physical skills are likely to be the most gender inclusive, such as throwing, catching, running and kicking based sports which do not rely on hand–eye co-ordination where a bat or racquet is involved.

In 2010 Professor Fred Coalter with John Taylor of the University of Stirling published a report commissioned by Comic Relief and UK Sport to test the hypothesis that 'sport contributes to the personal development and well-being of disadvantaged children and young people'. The aim was also to build a resource of good practice and to enable the development of monitoring and evaluation assessments. What Coalter found from the data collected from six sport-for-development programmes in different countries was that the deficit model needed to be re-evaluated. The deficit model in most sport-for-development programmes is based on an assumption that young people from disadvantaged communities are themselves deficient in one or more aspects of their development. The rationale that deprived communities produce deficient individuals is a dangerous and generalised approach which was discounted in the majority of self-evaluation measures of self-esteem and self-efficacy. In the sports programmes Coalter found that setting objectives, collecting data and having the expertise to analyse that data was generally lacking, which made it difficult to assess good practices. This was further complicated by issues such as staff moving on fairly regularly and the fundamental problem of trying to establish whether sport on its own made an impact or worked with other mechanics to support progress in terms of health, education and citizenship. So what of gender attitudes, the mission of many of these programmes? Coalter found mixed outcomes with what he says were few clear and consistent differences between participants and non-participants on women's roles in society. The social institutions which influence and direct beliefs about gender roles are entrenched and it will take more than sport programmes to shift them.

The Nike Foundation is probably the most visible global corporation vehicle for supporting the empowerment of young girls and women through their movement, the Girl Effect. Founded in 2008, in collaboration with the Novo Foundation, the Girl Effect is a movement which seeks to bring attention and action to some serious inequalities. Their website states that they exist as a direct response to a number of key facts. First, more than 70 per cent of the world's 130 million out-of-school youth are girls. Second, between 25 per cent and 50 per cent of girls living in developing countries will give birth before the age of 18 and third, 75 per cent of young women (15–24years of age) in Africa are HIV positive. Describing the programme as a rallying point, the Girl Effect build awareness of education, health and economics as the key to unlocking girls from a life where they are not visible and live in poverty. The programme offers multi-media platforms, research and tools and the reach achieved in such a short space of time is impressive.

But before and after the foundation of the Girl Effect, different organisations and governments have been addressing the blatant inequalities facing girls and women in societies within the developing world. Health and sport continue to be useful allies in shifting the visibility of girls and women in the social world. Go Sisters is a programme in Zambia which provides adolescent girls with sport, leadership and health training to facilitate the spread of information through peer leaders. Between 2002 and 2006 Go Sisters trained over 5000 girls as peer leaders, reaching approximately 56,000 girls with the programme. Moving the Goalposts in the Kilifi District of Kenya uses football as an outreach tool to tackle health, education and employment issues for girls. The football games and tournaments provide a safe place for girls to build and experience positive social relationships and access accurate health information. U Go Girl in South Africa is delivered by Sports Coaches Outreach and encourages female participation in traditionally male dominated sports. The Ishraq programme in Egypt is centred on rural communities where sport it not considered appropriate for girls. After reaching ten years of age, girls are not allowed to play games and become less visible as members of the community year on year. The programme uses traditional games to increase self-confidence, and build citizenship and leadership.

The sport in development programmes are often found to be tackling one central issue such as gender based violence or sexual health. What is important, however, is understanding that for people who live with the tragedy of poverty, their lives of inequality are not about one issue but an intersectionality of issues which makes for minimal progress. Intersectionality is defined as an integrated approach that addresses forms of multiple discrimination on the basis of racism, racial discrimination, xenophobia and related intolerance as they intersect with gender, age, sexual orientation, disability, migrancy, socio-economic conditions or status. Intersectional discrimination is a form of racism and racial discrimination which is not the sum of race plus another form of discrimination to be dealt with separately but is a distinct and particular experience of discrimination unified in one person or group (United Nations, 2001). For those programmes that can make connections between issues utilising the same resources but differently the opportunity for success is likely to not only increase but be more sustainable.

WomenWin are a rights based NGO founded in 2007 which supports programmes that deliver sport and physical activity as a means of addressing intersectionality for girls and women in the developing world. The organisation is focused in three areas: gender based violence, sexual rights and economic empowerment. The objective is to empower girls at a grass roots level to facilitate choices beyond what are currently available to them. So how does this work? WomenWin work with partners supporting them with tools, evaluation and impact assessments to ensure the programmes are of a high quality and deliver on the objectives. They also advise on how to bring an issue such as HIV/AIDS to sit alongside the need for girls to go to school and learn life and employability skills.

Starting with the premise that girls in the developing world are likely to be discriminated against in multiple ways creates a framework which allows sport to be utilised as a catalyst for change. Maria Bobenrieth is the executive director of WomenWin and oversees the global operations, programmes, partnerships and strategic development. In a recent conversation Maria and I discussed the issue of programme monitoring and evaluation, an in which the sport in development group was criticised. While Maria recognises the problem, she says the longitudinal data is not available and it will take time to collect. But, as she comments, this criticism needs to be framed in terms of short, medium and long term objectives for data. Furthermore, we discussed the opportunity for using a range of methodologies which evolve with the participants so that the questions are relevant to them and their lives, increasing the opportunity for collecting rich useful data. This certainly adds weight to the anecdotal evidence which many programmes collect and use to bring awareness to their specific issue.

What I found interesting about WomenWin is their holistic approach which advocates recognising sport as a tool which can teach life skills but also recognises that sport can be a catalyst for encouraging girls to take charge of their lives which can lead them to thinking about employment. Taking charge, as Maria explains, can be about getting up earlier to get chores done so that a girl can come to a sports practice. Each little step is a step forward to broader empowerment, and to be economically empowered it is important for girls to stay in or get back into school to learn to read and count so that they create some choices, be it getting a job, starting a business or running a home and a household budget.

WomenWin is a young organisation and is working towards investing in 25 partners in low income countries to produce best in class examples of rights based programmes for girls and women. What strikes me about the sport in development context is the passion and energy which emanates from people like Maria Bobenrieth, who agrees with my perception that the South have hope and no resources, and the North have resources and no hope. The imbalance of the world and drive to make a difference is what I now recognise as the seduction of sport and development. While there is plenty of work to be done in the monitoring and evaluation, bringing abuse of children by adults out into the open, and in bringing sustainable models which address intersectionality, I support and admire the people working in this area.

The idea that sport can be used to make social impacts, resolve conflicts and enable equality is idealistic but seductive. At football world cups or other world championships we are usually captured for a period of time in the human stories of hard work and dedication over-coming all other obstacles, in order to take part. Eric the Eel at the Sydney Olympics is one story which illustrates this point. One year before the 2000 games, Eric Moussambani did not know how to swim and had never left his Equatorial Guinea home. As with other countries run by despots, this oil rich country does not support its citizens who live in poverty on less than one dollar a day. When Eric lined up in the heats of the 100m freestyle his two competitors were disqualified for false starts and he was left to conquer the pool on his own in front of millions of people. His entry into the Olympics was through the wild card system which does not require performing qualifying times. The aim is to encourage people from developing countries to compete in the games either for the first time or in a sport which is not widely practised in their country.

Of course this story makes for great sporting moments and in September 2000, the *Guardian* reported that Moussambani in one of his hundred interviews after his race said, 'I would like somebody to sponsor me and pay for a coach. It is all very well doing these inter-views and having all this publicity but it will not be worth anything if nobody is willing to help me.' He went on to say that he hoped the world would not forget him once the Games were over. But what happened when everyone went home and what happened to Eric the Eel? Gary Glendenning, deputy sports editor of the *Guardian*, found that Eric went about training for the Athens Olympics and trained hard. He was offered a scholarship to a Wisconsin university but it was with-drawn when paperwork was not submitted by local bureaucrats. By the time Athens came around in 2004 Eric was a poor engineering student living in Valencia with his sponsorship money from Speedo finished. While he wanted to go to the Olympics this was not possible because his passport photo was mysteriously mislaid.

Sport in development is an area which is attracting high profile managers from different industries, as seen at WomenWin, who work directly for the organisations or lend their support through sitting on advisory boards or raising money. The attraction of different versions of sporting platforms provides a useful foundation for thinking about where and how competition fits.

Sport and competition: an exemplar for managers

Some of the managers in this study when discussing competition and competitive relations at work used the language of sport and sporting analogies. There is also evidence to suggest that the unspoken rules which managers refer to in this and other studies (White, 2000; Rindfleish, 2002) are an important aspect of the relationship between competition and sport which extends into the work environment. The main difference is that while sport offers widespread access to competition, competition found on the sports field has agreed and enforceable rules which do not, as discussed earlier, translate into the workplace. However, this does not mean that the sporting arena is not a useful place to learn about elements and dimensions of competition, as one of the managers I interviewed discusses:

> David: Sport is a very pure form of competition in a very defined set of rules. In other environments competition is less well defined.
>
> Int: Do you think playing sport is a good place to learn about competition?
>
> David: I think people who have been involved in team activities definitely have a huge advantage in competition at work.
>
> Int: Is it just in sport?
>
> David: It doesn't have to be sports, it can be part of a musical band or a scout troop but you have to learn about interdependence, learn about teams and you can't learn about this from books. I think you have to experience it, you need to learn both individual and team issues. Sport does teach this and it is an advantage but it is not the only place.
>
> Int: What sort of advantage do you mean?
>
> David: One thing you have to learn is both winning and losing. You don't win all the time and it's all right to lose, it's not the end of the world, it just happens. Where you learn about competition isn't important, it is the fact that you do learn it.

The sporting model offers some learning opportunities, already widely used by men, for women to compete on more equal terms in management hierarchies. That men and women perceive and experience competition in different ways suggests that the starting point for understanding and practising competition is not the same for each gender.

Richman and Shaffer (2000) argue that participation in sports is neither encouraged nor reinforced for women as it is for men. This suggests that the gateway to understanding competition is accessible to, but just not widely advertised to women. Kelinske et al. found in their study that there were no socialisation differences between men and women. They suggest that 'women who play sports seem to have the same advantage as men in terms of fostering competitive behaviour, learning to be a team player, perseverance and networking' (Kelinske, 2001, p. 82). The advantage referred to in Kelinske's study is important to this study as it reinforces the value of learning about competition in the sporting context which was found in the accounts of some managers in my research. Suggesting that women and sport exist in a sporadic vacuum which randomly brings it into the lives of some women and not others continues to highlight how gendered processes can result in constraints which can continue unchallenged.

DeBoer (2004) argues that at its basic level, competitive behaviour is about a struggle to achieve. Furthermore, she argues that when gender enters the equation the process of competing for men and women is different. She gives the example of a person who coached men and women cross country runners. The coach found that when a male had a breakthrough in his time his male teammates had a surge in training, finding motivation in the possibilities. Counter to that, when a female runner excelled her teammates teased her by saying she wanted to be a star. The men's response was to aim for better performances, for women it was about the team rebalancing its chemistry, with the best performer being encouraging and running only just ahead of the group.

DeBoer is an athlete-turned-coach who uses her experience to unravel the different attitudes and resulting behaviours to understanding gender and competition. Sport is an arena where competition is relatively pure, the rules are defined, there is an umpire to enforce the rules and the aim of the game is to win. She argues that the nature of the contest is where the difference between men and women becomes apparent. 'Males define contests as self-contained events during which normal rules of decorum be momentarily suspended. Females define contests as just another activity and expect all the usual rules of decorum' (DeBoer, 2004, p. 55). DeBoer argues for the importance of broadening the concept of competition from being one dimensional to multidimensional and for moving discussions beyond the sporting situation to understand how competition, gender and management intersect.

So how does gender fit into the mix of competition and management? It appears as if competition and competitiveness 'lurks' in the background of discussions of management and gender often only recognising it exists. As Harold Leavitt observes, 'Twenty years of Jean Lipman-Blumen's research on achieving styles with more than 20,000 male and female managers around the world comes up with one consistent difference between the sexes. Men everywhere score higher on competitiveness than women. But women managers score higher on competitiveness than non-managerial women. Managers, that is to say, are competitors, and competitors' egos "want report cards" (Leavitt, 2005, p. 3). Jean Lipman-Blumen is a professor of organisational behaviour at Claremont Graduate University. She co-wrote 'Hot Groups' with Harold Leavitt, Professor Emeritus, Stanford Graduate School of Business. She was nominated for the Pulitzer Prize for her 1996 book *The Connective Edge: Leading an Interdependent World.*

Like other management commentators, Leavitt only goes this far with this acknowledgement of competition and gender rather than developing the discussion further. However, emerging from economic perspectives are discussions of gender and competition in relation to the labour market. Booth (2009) uses data from students using psychologically based variables to assess the relationship between gender and risk assessment to explain the impact of competition on the supply side of the labour market. Similarly, Kleinjans (2009) argues that gender differences in an individual's taste or distaste for competition can contribute to explaining occupational choices. Both these studies argue that more research should be conducted in the area of gender, competition and the labour market. But the lessons drawn from gender, sport and competition translate fairly effectively into gender and management debates, as commentators such as DeBoer (2004) highlight.

Conclusion

The broad range of activity we refer to as sport is a part of many people's lives around the world, whether as a participant, a viewer or a supporter. How sport is portrayed in the media governs the different positioning of one sport from another and has created a lucrative rights market supporting sponsorship platforms and the brands which some sportspeople and clubs have become. As professional sport has grown, a hierarchy has emerged where the elite sportspeople occupy the top levels of performance and pay and dominate the media. On the other rungs of the hierarchy are sportspeople who are paid to play in what might be best described as minority sports and as such do not attract the same levels of attention as the elite.

Sport offers people from a young age the opportunity to play within a structured framework and begin the process of learning about competition within a scarcity and challenge model. Through play individuals also begin the process of learning how to watch and understand other sports which they may not play. This may be as a result of parental preference in supporting a team and sport or as time goes on through individual choice. Alongside this are the aspirational global events which deliver to an audience feats of human brilliance combined with acts of courage, determination and pride. The pleasure of watching sport has become an activity which live television has capitalised on and as the technology has developed has become accessible to people around the world.

Sport has also become a mechanic used to bring attention to the rights of the developing world. Capturing the energy of sport as an activity enables health messages and education to be addressed as the first part of an empowerment programme especially for girls. While in the developing world there is evidence of girls being receptive to the messages of empowerment, these are lessons which could be implemented in the UK and Europe to deliver the same empowerment messages to girls. As a language which is international, sport offers a way of understanding the cultural complexities of societies by observing how communities engage with sport locally, regionally, nationally and internationally. It is difficult to find another example of an activity which has such a mix of competition, money, success, ambition, media, fanaticism and dedication working in multiple interdependent relationships.

3
The Competition Cage

> Management makes organizations possible; good manage-
> ment makes them work well and management's real genius is
> turning complexity and specialization into performance.
>
> Magretta, 2002

Introduction

The interest afforded competition once we move it out of the sporting
arena is scant, and what interests me is how many of us subsume
competition into our lives without question. The trouble with such a
passive transaction from sport to society is that competition is likely
to be stuck in one's own experiences, which can feed the stereotypes
that seek to reconcile those processes and outcomes. For some these
experiences are from childhood where the world was rationalised in
terms of black and white. The central stereotype I want to dissect is that
competition is simply about winning and losing and, as a result, a raft
of opposing emotions for example fear and aggression, disappointment
and elation, anxiety and excitement. Getting stuck in this emotionally driven quagmire of winning and losing can stifle broader experiences of competition which provide some individuals with challenges,
satisfaction, motivation and pleasure.

So for the child who stood wishing they would not be the last one
chosen for the team the experience of competition is couched in
anxiety. However, that same child may be the top maths student and
sit proudly when the weekly test results are handed back. Similarly
the child who is the best athlete and is usually the first picked for any
physical game may shrink in fear as the test results are shared. For both
these children, competition is likely to be couched in different terms

and experiences. The physically able child is likely to find sports and competing a useful platform for learning and being accepted, whereas the maths student is likely to gravitate to the stereotype that competition is about winning and losing.

While I fully accept that throughout our schooling we as children can have defining experiences I would argue that these experiences may be less defining if they were explained more accurately. If the two children in the example found they have the same response of anxiety to similar situations where they were going be highlighted for their weaknesses perhaps they may redefine their relationship and even be supportive of overcoming such anxiety. In this chapter I will explore how the concept of competition has been examined in different disciplines and share my approach to exploring this dynamic to challenge the stereotype that competition is simply about winning and losing.

I will introduce my eight dimensions of competition: personal, interpersonal, external, internal, collective, positional, symbolic and temporal, and develop the model to construct a 'competition cage'. The competition cage will be used to illustrate how competition can be inclusive, exclusionary, gendered, power-laden, protective, restrictive and transparent, resulting in a range of processes and outcomes which advantage some and not others. The competition cage will contribute to understanding how valuable it is for individuals to seek out different dimensions of competition to enable informed decisions to be taken as to how to engage and manage this dynamic at work.

Extracting dimensions of competition

In order to explore the dynamism of competition I developed an eight dimensional model. While Ackoff (1979) argues that 'All models are a simplification of reality,' with which I agree, models can provide a useful platform for exploratory thinking. My competition model was designed with two intentions, first, to map a collection of experiences from managers and, second, to provide a structure for conducting an examination from a range of work on defining and researching competition as a social influence.

In deciding on the eight dimensions I am not suggesting that this is an exhaustive list but, more importantly, a manageable one to enable data analysis. Because this work is based on a qualitative approach to data collection the aim was to identify themes and trends rather than advocating generalisations. Capturing the dynamism of competition is at the core of the data collection, analysis and discussion. The model has been instructive in directing the interaction of the different dimensions to cope with the complexities which emerged.

While society accepts the presence of competition as a concept, it is treated with complacency. Competition is consistently influencing different relationships and situations, and whether individuals accept or reject its importance as a dynamic remains active for as long as one person is engaged. I argue that the reason individuals reject competition is because they have not had access to a framework for thinking about the concept outside the boundaries of winning and losing. Furthermore I would argue that those people who consider themselves competitive are often only thinking in terms of the competitions they can visualise. Whatever the perspective, it is difficult to fully engage with concepts unless there is definition which enables the same starting point for discussion, debate and development. Through the process of designing a model the objective has been to create a point of origin which draws on the multidisciplinary work that already exists. Also important in the thinking was to present a framework which could be applied to specific industries or broader categories. While I use the lens of competition to explore inequalities in management hierarchies, this lens could be used conceivably in any context where there are questions about the construction of situations and relationships.

The eight dimensional model

Figure 3.1 is an illustration of the model followed by definitions of each dimension and a key question which drives discussions in the following chapters.

External competition

Focus on the relationship between an individual manager and the organisation in the context of being a front person representing the interests of the organisation in the local, regional, national and global marketplaces.

- Is engaging in external competition considered mandatory for managers?

Many managers view external competition as an integral part of their contract with an organisation implied in their position of performing in a marketplace.

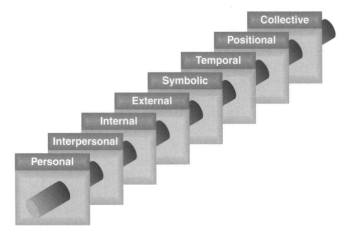

Figure 3.1   Eight dimensional competition model

Personal competition

Focus on the relationship an individual has with the skills used within their current job and on-going career development.

• How do managers organise their career goals and skills development?

Managers use different reference points to construct their goals from work and non-work perspectives. Individual performance as a measure for self-development is common among people who use benchmarks to assess their strengths and weaknesses. In a work context this can be in terms of knowledge and practices; outside of work it can be across sports and fitness or hobbies. Personal competition sets people on a road of self-challenge which is linked to motivation, achievement and a sense of satisfaction.

Interpersonal competition

Focus on how available resources are utilised by individuals to further their progression in an activity, task or project as an individual and/or part of a team.

• How do managers experience and perceive this dimension and how does this affect wider perceptions of competition?

Going head to head with another person outside of a sporting challenge attracts negativity from people and is where the stereotype of competition is most prominently located. The anxiety associated at times with the mere thought of interpersonal competition can only be described as extreme.

Internal competition

Focus on how departments and divisions access power, authority and resources to achieve specific strategic and tactical goals.

- How does this dimension affect how managers build relationships with peers and superiors?

The necessity of managers to think strategically about internal competition is important to keeping this dimension on track to be focused on resources. Misunderstanding internal competition for interpersonal competition is the second part of locating the stereotype of winning and losing.

Symbolic competition

The activity of individual managers imposing their own attitudes and values on situations.

- What role does competition have in developing and practising management and leadership styles?

The development of a style which fits with an authentic manager is an area where there are many personal struggles. An influence in those struggles is an often unspoken conflict with competition which is interpreted as being about ambition, aggression and the male traits which have been assigned to management.

Positional competition

The experiences of different internal and external work based relationships which occur as an individual climbs the management hierarchy.

- How important are different relationships in achieving career progression in management?

The role of relationships in careers is increasingly important in work environments which are fast paced and changing as the economics of national and global markets converge. The value of gaining knowledge requires building layers of relationships both within and outside an organisation.

Collective competition

How group resources can be used to gain knowledge and advantage in terms of achieving goals and aspirations in order to progress as an individual and/or as a group.

- Do some collectives have greater power and authority both informally and formally?

Groups of people have by the nature of numbers usually held some power in some context. However, when it comes to work based networks the essence of power is usually linked to positions related to hierarchy and in the world of management the groups who have been operating the longest hold the greatest amount of power. This is retained because access is limited.

Temporal competition

The ways and means time as a fixed resource and a commodity, directly or indirectly, becomes a competitor with an individual in all aspects of their life.

- Do static temporal structures prevent new ways of working and thinking about work?

How we work and why we work have not changed – purpose and money. Yet time remains stuck in the traditions of career models where other demands on time were related to leisure. As society has fragmented the roles of care and work for men and women, time has remained stuck in an era of past times when traditional social roles were easily defined.

Perspectives on competition

In 1999 *Time Magazine* published a series on the century's greatest scientists and thinkers. Named on the list was anthropologist Margaret Mead (1901–78) who was referred to as a cultural icon. Her quote 'Never doubt that a small group of thoughtful, committed citizens can change the world' is perhaps better known to some people than the woman herself. But Mead holds a pivotal position in terms of building a body of work which explored the central premise that cultural environments shape human behaviour. In the first stage of her career Mead spent years living in and observing primitive societies in the South Pacific, including being cut off on an island during World War II. She published widely on her fieldwork and began the journey of moving towards emerging the discipline of public anthropology. This discipline had a broad activist framework which moved anthropology into the wider social mainstream, making its methods and insights accessible for application to different aspects of society. Mead's biographer, Nancy K. Luthehaus (2002), describes her as a compelling and provocative social commentator who was able to draw on her work on non-Western societies to offer interesting insights on American culture. What is interesting about this picture is how it highlights the intersection of Mead transitioning from her work on primitive societies to American society when America itself was re-positioning itself in the world as global leader with a formidable military.

But what I want to explore is Mead's 1937 book *Cooperation and Competition Among Primitive Peoples*. Mead was commissioned by a committee of psychologists to look at 12 different cultures to assess what influences and impacts competitive and co-operative habits have on the cultural personality. A number of interesting insights are drawn, first, that competition does not necessarily lead to conflict and that co-operation does not necessarily lead to solidarity. What was found in co-operative societies was that competition can be introduced to act as a mechanism which can increase productivity. For example, the Maoris of New Zealand were eager to outdo one another in bird snaring and were honoured for the largest catch. But what is important to note is that the birds was shared equally among the families in the tribe so the competition was about the challenge and the glory, not the catch.

Another insight is that no society is exclusively competitive or exclusively co-operative, with the two concepts having a symbiotic relationship but recognising that social systems can be described in a multitude of ways, with competition and co-operation not being the most significant. But in defining the concepts Mead makes a distinction between competition and rivalry, co-operation and helpfulness. Competition is defined as a behaviour which is goal oriented, where the other competitors for the goal are secondary, in contrast to rivalry, where the behaviour is oriented toward another human being and the goal is secondary. In co-operation the goal is shared and it is the relationship to the goal which holds the co-operating individuals together. Conversely, helpfulness is not about the goal but the shared relationship with the individual who has the goal.

Since Mead's work, research on competition and co-operation has remained dominated by the schools of psychology. Morton Deutsch, Professor Emeritus at Columbia University, is a social psychologist and scholar of conflict resolution. In 1986 he founded the International Centre for Co-operation and Conflict Resolution (ICCCR). This Centre is culturally sensitive and aims, as it states on its website, 'to develop knowledge and to practice and promote constructive conflict resolution, effective cooperation and social justice'. Deutsch's interest lies in theorising conflict negotiation, using competition as the counterbalance to co-operation, suggesting that positive outcomes are unlikely if the approach is not co-operative. In conflict situations, particularly those highly charged around religion, politics and/or land, history documents how difficult or even impossible resolution is. Even when interested parties meet on some co-operative agenda which can be leveraged for progress, co-operation is unlikely to exist without some dimension of competition. Of course, conflict resolution on the scale that involves governments and groups of citizens, as seen in the ICCCR, extends far beyond those that are likely to be found in any organisation. However, I would reiterate Mead's point that co-operation cannot exist in a society without competition so it is a question of balance rather than an either/or dilemma.

A further challenge to Mead's proposition comes from Alfie Kohn (1992) who in 1986 wrote *No Contest: The Case Against Competition* which presents the idea that competition is undesirable and destructive in education, at work and at play. Competition faces accusations from Kohn which include contributing to anxiety, low self-esteem, lack of motivation and an increase in aggressive behaviours and destructive relationships. He professes that by dismantling competition in society and replacing it with co-operation. society will be more productive, moving from valuing winning to valuing excellence. Kohn's work focuses on education and parenting, where he has been critical of school systems from homework to rewards based systems. While Kohn has picked up a following, including the media, for being provocative I like the description Dan Wallingham, a professor of psychology, offers about Kohn's work. He says, 'I think of Kohn as a honeyguide of education. The honeyguide is a bird that leads humans to bee colonies. Once the human has found the honey the bird feeds on the wax and larvae left behind.' The attraction to Kohn is often found in the education sector which is seemingly always looking for a silver bullet to rectify all that is wrong with schools. While Kohn calls attention to competition as a dynamic which for me 'is the honey', his placement of competition as the binary opposite of co-operation has limitations.

Stanne et al. (1999), leading educational psychologists and researchers, published a literature review of over 185 studies conducted in the twentieth century which examined competition. They found it had been defined as a situational variable, a cognitive variable, a trait, a motive, a behaviour and an attitude. Tjosvold et al. (2003) progressed their research on competition maintaining that focusing on experimental studies in laboratory type settings, often conducted with undergraduate students or school classes, does not allow competition to be researched in a multi-dimensional way. They conclude that extending our knowledge of competition requires a greater focus on the importance of relationships and different behaviours in a variety of competitive situations. In order to achieve such knowledge I would argue that definitions are essential to lay down the framework for analysis and integration of competition across multiple dimensions.

While competition has a long history of research by psychologists, social scientists have been slower to excavate mines of interest. Social theorist Beck, in his risk society, reflexive modernisation and individualisation theses, explores the breakdown of industrial society and the emergence of a new modernity which challenges how we think about gender, family, occupation, science and technology. Beck argues that work has increased its dominant influence on individuals and he points out that, 'Wage labour and an occupation have become an axis of living in the industrial age' (Beck, 1992, p. 139). He presents the labour market as having three key interrelated dimensions: education, mobility and competition. Applying Beck's ideas suggests an individual entering the labour market will experience mobility in multiple forms as they transition from education to employment, career development, geographical location and social positioning. In modern society, Beck says, more people want to lead a life of their own, which is illustrated in many Western cultures by the dominant 'nuclear' family unit, often disconnected from tribe, class and origin. In the labour market deregulation, contract work and weakening unions are keys elements in enforcing a culture of individual workers having to adapt to the destandardisation of working hours and conditions. This is further enforced by the breakdown of the 'job for life' concept as well as the fact that the clear line between work and non-work has blurred and become more fluid and pluralised.

Individuals engaged in the labour market may be required to take any number of decisions during their career directly in relation to work and more widely in relation to life. Different dimensions of competition may be invoked at each decision making juncture as it becomes apparent that other people have the same objective. As a career progresses, it becomes increasingly likely that one individual will be pitted against similar individuals in terms of education, societal status and aspirations in the desire to achieve their career objectives. Beck asserts that, 'Where such a shared background still exists, community is dissolved in the acid bath of competition' (Beck, 1992, p. 94). In this context, competition could have a range of outcomes including isolation, suspicion of others, a sense of failure or success and the breakdown of existing relationships. While acknowledging the existence of competition, Beck does not explore this phenomenon for its effects on individuals or their biographies.

Beck addresses gender specifically in his work with Beck-Gernsheim, building upon the argument that in the labour market and the individualisation process, women often want a life of their own but remain financially dependent on men and the state, especially while raising children. Women dominate the part time work sphere and continue to suffer inequalities in pay and promotion. Furthermore, women also face the risk of divorce, widowhood, redundancy and insufficient education. Confronted with such risks some overcome them, adapting successfully to changed circumstances, while others may struggle, eventually becoming another statistic facing poverty. Beck describes the feminisation of poverty as the 'other side of the coin of when thinking about the desire for more people to have a life of one's own' (Beck and Beck-Gernsheim, 2002, p. 67). He also admits that with such scenarios evident across Western societies it is unclear how women, especially young women, will cope with the disappointment of their decisively expressed goals. That Beck is anticipating disappointment certainly adds realism to the progress which is often perceived to have been made in society for women. In historical terms, change in the past 50 years is arguably fast paced with women in the Western world having access to education, travel and work as well as choices about marriage, children and family. The world does allow women to construct a life of their own, but only if they make all the choices which do not require any degree of dependency either financially or socially. Whether society will be able to accommodate and support all the versions of people's lives is hard to imagine, because as a society we still rely on the knowledge and skills of others to survive and flourish. At a base level this is found in taxation which supports our societal infrastructure. So having aspirations of choice without compromise calls into question whether the possibility of having a life of one's own is truly a reality.

Gender and management

As a cornerstone of this discussion I want to define gender as a social construction which can produce, maintain and use a range of discourses, operating in isolation or in combination across different relationships, locations and cultures. I agree with Butler and her assertion that no one account of gender is sufficient, because if gender is singular in form and function, it limits how it can be understood within different environments and cultures. Butler has been critical of defining gender in a regulated way and her view is that gender, as she states it, is 'not exactly what one *is* nor is it precisely what one *has*. Gender is the mechanism by which notions of masculine and feminine are produced and naturalized, but gender might very well be the apparatus by which such terms are deconstructed and denaturalized' (Butler, 2004, p. 42). In other words, as Le Feuvre (1999) argues, gender is not so much about biological differences but more about social processes and how the relationships which take place in society can incorporate and encourage hierarchies which can favour one individual over another. Connell (2002), like Butler, argues that gender relations and their arrangements are always changing in response to new societal circumstances. Drawing on the work of Butler (2004), Connell (2002) and Le Feuvre (1999), Martin's picture of gender suggests a concept which is multi-functional and can include a range of 'meanings, expectations, actions/behaviours, resources, identities and discourses that are fluid and shifting yet robust and persistent' (Martin, 2003, p. 344).

Braidotti and Connell argue that to view gender as merely having a biological relationship with individuals underplays the importance of recognising social and/or culture practices and that gender cannot 'simply express bodily difference' (Connell, 2002, p. 11). Bruni argues that gender is a 'social practice, not a biological attribute, and that it must be looked for in everyday interactions, read in relation to broader symbolic-cultural domains and considered as the outcome of mediation and representation in these various domains' (Bruni et al., 2004, pp. 410–11). For Braidotti (2002) gender as a concept should be researched on three levels: personal identity, as a principle of social organisation and as the basis for normative values. The language and social texts which influence the development of normative values are an area of concern for me here. Making the distinction between gender being a social construction and not a biological one provides the basis for dismissing essentialist arguments in terms of attributing competition to any biological foundation. What interests me is the exploration of practices, both formal and informal, of individual managers to discover how and in what ways competition is gendered. To use the term 'gender' as merely a replacement for sex is to undervalue the construction of the concept and to assign it potentially stereotypical attributes.

The reason I chose Margretta's quote at the beginning of this chapter is because it captures my interest in management as a broad and complex discipline. Managers are the people within the infrastructure of organisations who are often invisible and yet deliver products and services which enable society to function. The wide ranging skills and knowledge that are found in a manager become immense when one manager joins with another to build layers of efficient and effective activity. However, as with any discipline there are variations of expertise ,and weaknesses are not always readily identifiable until it is too late, often casting management as the culprit for a failure. The burden of management is unquestionably huge and for this reason I appreciate the simplicity of Margretta as I am sure this explanation is the result of much thought and experience. There is value in the definition of 'manager' from the Australian Institute of Management (AIM) (2010): a manager is 'a person who plans, leads, organises, delegates, controls, evaluates and budgets in order to achieve an outcome' Because of the broad base of management it is important to highlight that management has a hierarchy which I suggest has senior management as controlling which objectives are set, while middle and junior management are assigned the day to day responsibility of achieving the desired objectives.

Management across the world looks very different in the early years of the twenty-first century from just 20 years ago when globalisation, technological development and increasingly sophisticated consumers were beginning to claim the attention of management consultants and practitioners, as both key indicators and drivers of future market economies. In the increasingly fast changing world of work, managers are key to ensuring that staff continue to adapt to new environments and develop business by embracing change, whether internally or externally motivated. Management as a sector supports an estimated £4 billion industry which includes studying the discipline and associated publishing, educating, consulting and commentary activities (Whipp et al., 2002). As a strand of management I am interested in the concept and practices of power which, like competition, are dynamic, fluid, unstable and bound in values, attitudes and behaviours for individuals and organisations. I recognise that it is difficult to isolate power from competition and I am drawn to the work of Foucault, a French philosopher who has been instrumental in discussions of power.

For Foucault power is not limited, nor is it zero sum, which suggests it cannot be competed for or with, yet Foucault argues that discourses are where power and knowledge combine. He suggests that this intersection of knowledge and power is where we must focus in order to establish through the promotion and maintenance of discourses whose agenda is being served and why. Discourses are defined as a series of statements held by a community. He states, 'we must conceive discourse as a series of discontinuous segments whose tactical function is neither uniform nor stable. To be more precise, we must not imagine a world of discourse divided between accepted discourse and the dominated one; but as a multiplicity of discursive elements that can come into play in various strategies' (Foucault, 1979, p. 100). The importance of discourses to examining competition underpins the rationale of the eight dimensional model, for as long as competition is left to those who want to engage with it, the power of the discourse remains unchallenged. Avoiding competition in the workplace makes it easier for those who do not avoid it to gain advantages which become accepted as just the way things are. The words which reinforce the stereotypes of competition and management being the domain of men makes it quite clear whose interests are being protected and where Foucault would locate the power. But if power is everywhere then how can it be organised, measured or competed for ,which underpins why power is a dilemma for on-going discussions. I agree with Grimshaw (1993) who says that without being able to distinguish between effective and ineffective forms of resistance, how can power, which Foucault argues is always shifting and is unstable, generate resistance, sustained or otherwise? Furthermore, Ransom (1993) argues that discourses are not only structured ways of knowing but have strands of power within them which can influence and direct institutions and their practices. These issues highlight how power and competition are likely to have a complex relationship, although for this discussion my focus remains on competition. However, it is important to keep in mind that power remains potent in the discussions which follow. What is interesting to me is how much time and energy we spend on the subject of power and yet the outcome of resisting change remains steadfast. It is difficult to think of examples of power being relinquished voluntarily except in democratic elections and yet even here we have legal petitions to challenge the count.

Personal and interpersonal competition

Conceptualising personal development competition using the theory of hyper-competition, Ryckman and Borne (1997) define it as an indiscriminate need for individuals to compete and win (avoiding losing) at any cost. However, in a competition it is important that the individual maintains feelings of self-worth. Personal competition is defined by Ryckman and Borne as an attitude, with a primary focus not on winning, but on the experience, with the process enabling an opportunity for self-discovery and learning. Within the process success and winning are important but tempered by what goals can be achieved. They argue that personal development competition and hyper-competition are related in the endorsement of individualistic values such as working hard to achieve personal and material success. However, the major distinction is in the individual's relationship with people. Hyper-competitors view social power and the domination of others as important whereas personal development competitors find the welfare of others and treating them as equals essential.

Houston et al. (2002), in their study of personal development competition, identify two key factors: self-aggrandisement (validating one's own superiority) and interpersonal success. Furthermore, the benefits of competition were deemed important but not at the denigration of others. Interpersonal competition is prevalent at certain career and life points, influenced by the theory of social comparison as found in Stapel and Koonmen's (2005) study. Social comparison, where we evaluate and verify mental, physical and social attributes in relation to others, is one way of learning about ourselves. Stapel and Koonmen argue that the impact of upward and downward social comparisons on self-evaluation can have positive and negative effects for individuals. For example, an individual's success in achieving a goal may be an inspiration to some yet a source of self-doubt to others. Social comparison is shown therefore to be a highly subjective concept motivated by individual perceptions of others who may or may not be valid as a comparable.

For Stanne et al. (1999) competition is well placed in the context of social interdependence theory where how goals are structured determines how individuals interact with others and with a situation. For example, goals may be arranged so people need to work co-operatively, against each other or alone. They identify three types of competition:

- Zero sum competition when one winner takes all and everyone else fails.
- Unclear competition where procedures are vague and .badly communicated. The rewards are subjectively based on perceived contributions.
- Appropriate competition when ultimately winning is not important with all participants having a reasonable chance of success. The rules are clear and participants can monitor each other and engage in social comparison.

Exploring internal competition

Exploring the role of competition in organisations, Handy (1993) begins with the premise that organisations are communities of people, not machines. Like most communities, individuals bring with them behaviours which are diverse and potentially can compete and/or conflict with other behaviours. Handy makes a clear distinction between competition and conflict, arguing that 'competition is useful and beneficial, conflict damaging and harmful' (Handy, 1993. p. 292). For managers, he argues, the challenge is to stop competition becoming conflict.

Conflict for managers can be perceived as negative. Yet conflict and the management of it can reflect a pluralistic organisation where there is any number of stakeholders with varying covert and overt agendas. Arguing that managers are often constrained by conflict, Eisenhardt et al. (1997) suggest that it is a necessary, natural and essential part of decision making and brainstorming. In their study Eisenhardt et al. observed 12 companies to ascertain what role conflict has in organisational politics, management and strategic decision making. The main findings were as follows:

- four organisations had little or no disagreement over major issues
- four had high levels of conflict appearing difficult to resolve
- four employed a range of tactics to effectively manage interpersonal conflict by making clear distinctions between issues and personalities.

In the study six tactics were identified as being necessary to work effectively with conflict:

- more rather than less information
- developing alternatives
- shared commonly agreed goals
- injection of humour
- balancing the power structure
- no consensus by force.

The introduction of two or more of the tactics was a crucial part of the process as this was found to prevent conflict from becoming personal and destructive. As Eisenhardt et al. conclude, if conflict cannot contribute positive and effective influences to working relationships and task completion, it is likely the conflict is being mismanaged.

'Without conflict, groups lose their effectiveness. Managers often become withdrawn and only superficially harmonious. Indeed, we found the alternative to conflict is usually not agreement but apathy and disengagement' (Eisenhardt et al., 1997, p, 85). A manager's role often demands a mix of skills which develops through experience and increasing one's understanding of how their position relates to other positions in the organisation.

For Kanter (1989) internal competition was driven by one or more of the following six circumstances:

- mergers and acquisitions putting external competitors in the same organisation
- pressure for limited resources
- performance comparisons within an organisation as a means of motivation
- flatter management structures which lessen promotional opportunities
- decentralisation and the establishment of divisions or business units that are autonomous and can place other units or divisions in competition
- the natural competition which occurs when groups are defined in terms of other groups and comparisons are made and rated in terms of performance and productivity.

What is found in the research and commentary of Handy and Kanter is that internal competition can stimulate and motivate groups within an organisation by encouraging them to set common goals, potentially finding that the combined team effort is greater than the sum of the individual contributions. The shared sense of purpose and achievement can be positive in terms of building loyalty and support that allows for the possibility of greater innovation and creativity. Internal competition can distinguish the excellent from the good and the good from the poor which can be applied to products, services and people and enable organisations to be more effectively externally. How competitions are constructed and implemented internally can reflect how an organisation operates as a whole and as the conglomeration of departments. These competitive processes can provide insights into the practices of managers across the hierarchy in terms of how they understand not just the concept of competition, but also its multiple and interacting dimensions.

Handy (1993) compares the differences between open and closed (or zero sum) competition. Open competition, in a similar way to the challenge model, is not a matter of 'first past the post' as there can be as many winners as desired providing that each meets the agreed measures for success. Handy is clear that successful open competition depends on how all the competitors engage in the practice, suggesting that three conditions have to be met:

1. It has to be perceived as genuinely open i.e. everyone can ultimately win.
2. The rules and procedure for arbitration must be seen to be fair and adequate. No one is likely to be collaborative if the umpire is biased or the rules unknown.
3. The major determinants of success in the competition must be under the control of the competitors. They must have only themselves to blame if they fail. (Handy, 1993, p. 295)

Tjosvold et al. (2003), in seeking to combine competition and management, make an important contribution to this investigation. Their research clarifies not only the nature and role of constructive competition but the need to further explore this knowledge gap. Tjosvold et al. hypothesise that constructive competition occurs when competition at work is a positive enjoyable experience. This, they propose, results in increased efforts to achieve goals and more positive personal relationships, and maintains psychological health and wellbeing. They use five variables against which to measure the existence of constructive competition: the role of fairness, the low importance of winning, the equal probability of winning, the role of task type and the effect of prior relationships.

At a management workshop in China, 68 managers were invited to participate in the study along with a subordinate employee from their organisation. The average age of the 61 men and 30 women participating was 31 to 34 years. Of those, 64 were managers and 28 were subordinates. (One person did not specify gender and the gender ratio of managers was not given). The main procedure used in the study is called the critical incident technique, designed to ask participants to write a full report of a competitive incident before answering questions based on a predefined scale. This procedure was originally developed by Flanagan (1954) to study complex interpersonal phenomena. Each participant is asked to describe a specific situation in which they competed with a fellow employee as honestly and accurately as possible.

They were asked to describe what led to the situation, who they were working with and what happened. They were then asked to rate on a scale factors that affected the competition and its outcome ranging from personal benefits to enjoyment, strength of relationships and commitment to the organisation.

The findings support constructive competition as existing in work environments. Numerous incidents reported enjoyment, learning, strong positive relationships and increased confidence as outcomes. Other variables show contradictions to the proposed hypotheses. The importance of winning was found to increase the constructiveness of a competition. Where there was an advantage this overshadowed the importance of having an equal probability of winning. Contrasting with past psychology studies, where simple motor tasks have been employed to research competition, this study found that using intellectual problem solving was reportedly a positive contribution to greater self-efficacy and task effectiveness. However, fairness, as predicted, is important to facilitating task effectiveness. Tjosvold et al. (2003) conclude that the role of long term relationships among employees who operate in contexts beyond a singular competitive situation could influence constructive competition. For example, organisations that need to be profitable may actually provide an overall co-operative goal from which task oriented competitions can take place in a constructive way. The role of positive and strong relationships at work contributing productively to constructive competition is a significant finding in this study.

Symbolic and positional competition

Contextualising a style within the management arena provides a baseline from which to discuss why managers in the same organisation do not necessarily operate in the same way. Belbin and Meredith (2000) define the core work of a manager as assigning tasks, responsibilities and contracts to others and highlights how crucial internal relationships are in performing these functions. Mintzberg (1973) identifies a manager's working environment as having several key characteristics including long hours, enjoying action, doing work in short bursts with frequent interruptions and spending most of their time with other people both internally and externally. How an individual processes these conditions alongside the knowledge and experience they have already amassed can be best defined as a management style (Kakabadse et al., 2004). This style includes the values and morals that they hold as individuals and how they interpret and deliver this in relation and response to the needs of the business, their position and their staff.

Management styles are often side-lined by discussions of leadership styles which appear to attract more attention. Some argue that this has encouraged a situation where no one wants to be a good manager; they all just want to be leaders (Gosling and Mintzberg, 2003). Yet without managers, would there be leaders? And does a leader need to know how to manage? Clarifying answers to such questions when not addressed in literature encourages a situation where the titles of leadership and management become interchangeable. The position this study takes is one that accepts this crossover in the literature, recognising that definitions of 'manager' and 'leader' operate along a spectrum that makes distinctions in terms of degrees of responsibility and authority. For example, the title of manager has become all-encompassing and does not necessarily mean heading a team and controlling a budget; in a similar way 'leader' does not necessarily mean top of an organisation, but may mean the head of a team. How this terminology is portrayed questions whether job titles have become too generalised and removed from a role and its responsibilities. Mintzberg (2004) describes the heroic and the engaging manager, Kanter (1989) portrays the cowboy manager, Rosener (1990) describes interactive leadership as a style women have developed and Wajcman (1998) explores whether there are masculine and feminine styles of management. How these different styles link to the role of competition presents a tangible means of engaging with managers to investigate not only how they perceive and experience categories of competition but how this translates into the ways they practise it in their working lives and their organisations.

How managers are perceived in their organisational role can be influenced by a range of variables. This includes the relationships they initiate and conduct with subordinates, peers and superiors. Relationships formed at work can change over time and in response to both internal and external variables such as mergers, acquisitions, promotions, redundancies, maternity leave, sickness and care responsibilities. How a manager develops the skills required to deal effectively with the spectrum of scenarios that may emerge can be strongly influenced by the experiences and observations they engage with. Drawing on a range of management and organisation literature, I define four factors contributing to the development of a manager: first, the current organisational culture, combined with experiences of cultures from previous organisations; second, the interaction with role models and mentors who can guide a junior individual manager through the complexities of understanding the organisation, its politics and the manager's role in it; third, the ability for an individual to understand and embrace the range of skills required to be a manager; and finally an individual's ambition to join a management structure and climb the hierarchy to reach their desired position.

For many managers, positional competition can become a major junction for the interaction of different dimensions of competition which can result in a variety of negative and positive results. For example, badly managed interpersonal and internal competition can be found in the experiences of many managers at some point in their careers. Such experiences can be instrumental in defining what sort of manager they aim to be, which is often found in the stories of contrast, for example where a manager has behaved badly to such an extent that a standard is set to never be like this manager.

Management identities

Social identities for managers can encompass a multiple and complex set of meanings which stem from the roles and situations which reflect an individual's reality. Competition as a masculine stereotype in management has maintained some on-going status within organisations, particularly with those managers who operate a heroic type management style as described by Mintzberg (1973) and Sinclair (1998). Adhering to such gender based stereotyping has being repeatedly studied by Schein (1975), Schein and Muller (1992), and Schein et al. (1996), who concludes that 'think manager – think male' remains a dominant discourse in organisations, particularly at the middle and upper echelons of management hierarchies. Being part of the norm provides the opportunity to develop an identity which is accepted and judged in a completely different way to those individuals who sit outside the norm. Think about the white educated man who is described as eccentric, one of the lads or leadership material, and it is easy to paint a picture of acceptability. Yet if one sits outside, the description might go something more like ordinary, tries too hard to be like us and hard-nosed. How to decipher the interpretations of one's behaviour becomes more complicated when the norm is not you. For women, who despite progress continue to be seen in opposition in management, being authentic can be risky and isolating.

Competition portrayed in managers as a masculine trait can, as with similar traits, present a confusing and challenging picture for women managers who may find themselves comfortable embracing such traits. The collision of masculine and feminine traits being translated as requiring male and female ownership respectively makes it harder for women to personalise masculine traits without being stereotyped. The outcome of aligning with one or other set of traits can be a double negative for women: too masculine an iron maiden and honorary man, or too feminine and a pet or seductress, as epitomised by Kanter (1977) and McDowell (1997) as capturing the difficulty women face in engaging with competition at work. Butler (1999) argues that discourses can be important to maintaining the framework of scripts and behaviours which regulate and reproduce the dominant cultures found in organisations and their management hierarchies. Proposing that competition is a negative trait in women can limit their engagement as they anticipate that full participation may result in negative outcomes.

Alongside these stereotypes are those which focus on women in management as pioneers. Often charged with being role models and mentors, senior women managers particularly can suffer if they do not meet the expectations of younger or junior women managers. Queen bee syndrome, a term used by Staines et al. (1973) and Abramson (1975), continues to pervade language used to criticise women managers who do not subscribe to the solidarity of the sisterhood. 'Queen bee syndrome' refers to women who are actively opposed to changes in traditional gender roles and can deny any systemic discrimination against women. An attitude that 'if I can do it all without help or a movement, then so can everyone else' is a major characteristic. The use of the term 'queen bee' can be found in media to describe, challenge or refute the allegation, underlining its impact as important enough to explain but without acknowledging that no such term exists for men in management. Expecting that women who have overcome barriers and reached positions of power and authority to act as initiators of change highlights the complex nature of the gendered environments they can experience. Mavin (2006) argues that the women in management literature has diverted attention away from negative discourses such as the queen bee syndrome by opting out of exploring its existence and influence. She says a dilemma exists: if ignored, queen bee discourses can continue to feed stereotypes of women, keeping them in second place in management, and if investigated, there is a danger that a 'blame or fix the women' perspective develops.

In her study of senior women managers in Australia, Rindfleish (2000) found a mixed range of attitudes to whether women face barriers at work. Some (the smallest group) denied the existence of them outright. Others conceded that they exist but believe that each individual controls their destiny. The group labelled 'reluctant feminists' suggest that despite barriers being in place, they were unable to specifically identify them and consequently unable to enlist actions to counteract their impact. Definite feminists (the largest group) had personal experiences of discrimination and structural barriers to their career progression and generally believed that legislation is important in addressing equality. However, organisational cultures need to embrace change, including redefining terms such as 'merit' to base it on skill and talent rather than the right man for the job. The notion of a female misogyny (Mavin, 2006, 2008) suggests the dynamics of women's relationships at work are not fully understood and potentially can encourage suspicions which destabilise relationships and collectives while also manifesting in interpersonal competitive behaviours.

How women, as individual managers, deal with the tension of diverse attitudes and behaviours found in both stereotypes and gender based expectations which may follow them through the organisational hierarchy, is fraught with complexities. How a manager constructs their management style over time is influenced and guided by their past experiences of working relationships, hierarchies and organisations. The command and control style found in the think manager, think male stereotype continues to be the basis of management styles for some men and women managers.

Coward's (1992) study explores the satisfactions, fears and anxieties which determine women's choices in Britain. Her work contributes to my study as competition is an issue which is raised and discussed. She examines in 150 interviews the subjective side of obstacles women face at work, at home and as wives and mothers. Competition is explored in relation to work, with negative themes dominating the experiences of the women interviewed. For some women this includes confrontations of competition at work and making decisions not to engage in any way and actively withdraw. Coward found that this is increasingly likely when the competition was about recognition and was individual versus individual. For other women, recognising they were competitive but were unable to translate that into a work environment resulted in feelings of envy towards those women who could. Women who left jobs to have a family also experienced feelings of envy when they compared themselves to their peers who were succeeding in careers.

Coward argues that women find it difficult to define their attitude to competition because of the bundle of complications influencing both the process and the outcome. In order for women to engage with competition more openly and effectively they need to rationalise that 'what they feel most strongly is not the thrill of the chase, but the destructive spoiling impulses that characterize envy' (Coward, 1992, p. 43). Identifying a relationship between perceptions of competition at work and in other areas of life is important to understanding how emotions may result in practices of competition which reinforce the scarcity model because there is no other model to use. A typical comment from men and women has been that women take competitions too personally which, if founded on envy, as Coward argues, will generate personally felt responses. Envy is not competition and this position needs to be accepted before the value of the competition model can be useful. Taking competition too personally suggests a lack of variety in competitive experiences leaving a limited or singular frame of reference, and this links to sport and competition as a platform for learning.

Typographies for competitors

To further explore how competition is actively found in different situations and executed in different ways I used the competition model and the competition cage to build three profiles of managers. The aim is to exemplify how the complexities of different interacting dimensions of competition can embody a manager's identity and influence the development of their working and management style. The intention is to reiterate how understanding the dynamism of competition and competitive relations at work can be important to creating a concept which is more transparent to more managers.

The three profiles I created are called *players*, *careerists* and *the frustrated*. It is important to note that these typographies are by no means considered a definitive list. However, they are intended as a means of showing how competition can, with greater recognition and understanding, be used as a lens to discuss gender and management, which is the focus of this book, but can be equally applied to other elements.

Players

Players accept and welcome the scenario that in the market and in the organisation a serious game is on. They have a tool box of strategies and tactics easily adaptable in most situations. They have usually had a series of mentors and belong to a number of networks which meet their social (including sports), business and strategic career needs. Although they claim they have no career plan, they do have a plan to accumulate opportunities from which they can make decisions based on the financial and professional challenges presented. External competition is where they find the game most interesting, accepting that internal competition for resources is largely fixed with finite resources available. They are driven by a personal desire to improve their own performance but equally find social comparison with peers and superiors motivating. As they reach the later stages of their career they may reduce the degree to which they compete, finding younger players attractive to watch and maybe mentor. In their private lives, if they are married their wives/husbands are unlikely to be in paid employment if there are children. The career model for a player is the dominant one in a household and meets the traditional breadwinner model.

Careerists

Careerists are usually managers who have amassed a wide range of skills to meet the needs of their position. They enjoy the challenge of climbing a hierarchy, embracing the challenges which come with each new position. Although they do not enjoy zero sum interpersonal competition in terms of promotions, they accept the situation, often avoiding the terminology of competition to describe such processes. The focus on collective competition becomes an important facet of their career as they build and manage effective teams to perform, in their terms, co-operatively for the good of the organisation. They use personal competition as a means of motivating their own performance and use terms like 'healthy competition' as a way of accepting that competition exists but does not have to be conflicting or negative. Discussing competition per se is difficult and while articulate on many other issues, they can stumble on this subject, showing how difficult they find the concept, locating it most comfortably within the categories of external and personal competition. They will often be found mentoring subordinates and will be good networkers with peers and colleagues across their industry. They can often be found to have long tenures with organisations but are not naive and are constantly prepared to be the next cut back. In their private lives if they are men, they are likely to be married with a part time working wife if there are children, and if they are women and married they are as likely as not to have children.

The frustrated

The frustrated can appear confused on whether they themselves are competitive or not, seeking comfort in an approach that is non-committal. As they progress in their careers it becomes difficult for them to accept that competition and competitive relations is something people do but never talk about. Climbing the hierarchy, it becomes apparent to this group that competition is all around and they largely describe it as being OK as long as it is healthy. This does not enable them to engage with the dynamism of the concept at any level and their inability to find platforms from which to explore and practise competition leaves them vulnerable to those managers who are simply better at understanding the workings of this dynamic. Internal and interpersonal competition is potentially where the frustrated find the most conflict and the most competition, and for middle managers this can present a scenario which confines and limits them as managers.

Frustrated managers do not usually leave middle management regardless of whether they want to, and they often embody a sense of bitterness which can be directed towards a range of issues which have been a source of frustration in their position. They may have had mentors who have been ineffectual in enlightening these managers to the wider contexts of organisational cultures which can exist, including being able to identify the roles and agendas of peers and superiors. For women who are in this group, gender is often a barrier which becomes embedded in their work identity as a woman manager. They can experience marginalisation and informal gendered practices but are often left without a frame of reference or a support system to help them identify and process such gendered situations. For men in this group they are likely to be inflexible to the changing conditions of careers, wanting to continue the simple concept of a job for life.

While it is probable that there will be managers who fit into only one category, it is equally probable that other managers will move between at least two categories, either concurrently or sequentially. The process of building a model, and then developing that model into other representations is useful and necessary to fully explore the dynamism of competition. Whether one sees the value or connection with one or many of the dimensions of competition it is hoped that Mead's sense that co-operation cannot exist without competition holds strong as a base from which to unpack the stereotypes and take a fresh and more structured view which moves beyond the stereotype of competition as just a zero sum game.

Table 3.1   Typographies

Players	Careerists	The frustrated
Strong networkers	Like to mentor and network	Likely to have had mentors
Always looking for opportunities to build career	Motivated to build career based on skills and knowledge	Want to have a career but find it difficult to accept some of the realities of management which may challenge their code of ethics
Like to operate directly in external market	Strong ties and loyalty to organisation; identify with being team member and/or team leader	Want to be a team member but often marginalised because of attitude, gender and perceived lack of engagement in competitive relations
Meet traditional breadwinner model of one income household. Children likely if man and less likely with women	Meet mixed income household model of one main and one part time worker. Children likely if man and unlikely if woman	Meet transitional income household model of one main worker who if man is likely to want a job for life type career. If woman then likely to be before children, part time and then resumed when children independent
Focus on all dimensions of competition	Focus on external, positional and symbolic competition	Focus on external and personal competition

The competition cage

So what is the value of the competition model and the perspectives which explore different processes and outcomes of competition? To begin I want to reiterate the idea that competition is largely invisible once it walks off the sports field. Such invisibility has a number of consequences; first and most importantly the concept remains hidden in the complacency of a lack of definition, challenge and debate. Off the back of this outcome is the building and maintaining of a stereotype which puts competition in the box which is simply about winning and losing. Without actively recognising the multi-dimensional nature of competition individuals can be excluded from accessing the resources, including power, which are often associated with competition. To this end I want to paint a picture which builds upon the competition model

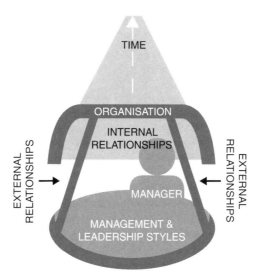

Figure 3.2   A competition cage

to create what I will call a competition cage, shown in Figure 3.2. This cage is a visual representation to illustrate how by thinking strategically and experientially about different dimensions of competition, individuals can amass knowledge which can have an impact on their relationships with subordinates, peers and superiors and more broadly with organisations.

As Ackoff (1979) says, models are a simplification of reality and with this in mind I wanted to take the competition model through to the next stage. Having spent some time trying to find a visual representation I could usefully adapt I was channel surfing one evening when an off-road car rally captured my attention. I was drawn to the roll cage sitting inside the structure of the rally car. Whether you want to call it a light bulb moment or any other kind of moment, I was struck by the cage because of its dual function – protecting the driver and navigator while concurrently enabling clear visibility. Such visibility works from the inside out – that is, one's own engagement with competition can be separated from the actions, attitudes and behaviours of others as they engage with competition. Being able to choose whether to compete or not in any given competitive situation is likely to present a strategic advantage for some managers who are able to identify the actions and motivations of those individuals involved. Similarly, the knowledge to modify the competition can be important in protecting one's position, whether as part of a role or a team. Like the roll cage, the competition cage can grow to become more sophisticated depending on the user and the levels of knowledge and experience they accumulate over time. For example, Mercedes in the late eighties developed a roll cage that locks into place using sensors when a roll-over threat is detected.

The idea that competition is dynamic is central to my exploration of this concept, both as an abstract and an experience. So to identify the cage, a structure which can encompass these ideas is certainly valuable. I have focused on defining competition as a multi-functioning dynamic which influences managers and the way they work. Using the experiences and individual accounts shared over the course of the fieldwork, it has become evident that dimensions of the competition model can operate singly or in tandem. One of the key findings is that for all the managers interviewed, external and temporal competition have some significant impact on their experiences, both personally and professionally. While the other dimensions did not have the same overwhelming degree of impact, the stories of perceptions and experiences crossed a wide range of themes. These will be discussed in later chapters. However, in seeking to find frameworks to accommodate and make sense of stories and emerging themes I concluded that when a concept is maligned as a stereotype, in this case as simply being about winning and losing, the stereotype is often personified in clear cut positive and negative ways.

Conclusion

Gender inequality continues to exist in the labour market and this book aims to explore why women are not equally represented in management hierarchies relative to their labour participation rates. Exploring how as a concept and a practice competition can operate in organisations and in the individual careers of men and women managers is the main focus of the discussion. To provide a framework for defining competition I drew on the work of Bradley (1999) and her model of gendered power, establishing a series of eight dimensions which are investigated to examine how and in what ways competition is gendered. Within organisations and management hierarchies, competition, some managers claim, remains distant from their experiences at work and is not widely discussed. For others, external competition located within the marketplace is strongly identified with, whereas other managers cite personal competition and its role in their own self-development as the base for their experience. Suggesting that competition is a single concept or has a single location for practice has limitations and weakens the position of those individuals who try to engage with the dynamic in this mode. The competition model is designed to explore the concept as operating across multiple dimensions. What is central to the examination is the requirement to bring competition out of the shadows and into a workplace where it can become transparent and visibly identifiable in the actions and behaviours of subordinates, peers and superiors. In this way competition can break away from its stereotype of winning or losing and be utilised within a competition cage to provoke change and transformation of structures which support inequalities.

4
Work-Based Relationships

Competition has always been a dirty word for me. As long ago as I can remember, I have never felt comfortable competing with others...Why was it necessary to be pitted against others in order to discover one's potential? I like to think I am no longer as naive as I was at school and after being in the workforce I've come to view competition less simplistically.

Matsumoto, 1987

How individuals conduct relationships across all aspects of their life and work can be a window on how they perceive and experience interdependence as an element of those relationships. Yet many of us do not clarify how we value different interactions with people as individuals or as representatives of organisations until challenged by a barrier or breakdown. This is exacerbated in societies which increasingly promote the individual as the norm, leading to the conclusion that interdependence is an oxymoron. However, every day in some way most of us will unconsciously experience some degree of reliance on someone else to do their job. Such functional relationships are a useful place to begin thinking about interdependence: the train driver who took you safely to work, the barista who made your coffee this morning and the bank administrator who processed your salary so there was money to pay for your train ticket and coffee.

Taking these individually experienced interactions onto a larger scale is the realisation of how many societies across multiple geographies have interdependent relationships with those individuals who service and maintain our communication, transport and technology infrastructures. Without too much thought, it is interesting how quickly we start to recognise the sheer scale of people on whom we blindly depend.

My immediate thoughts go to air traffic controllers and waste management providers who keep our quality of life stabilised. While I do not have much patience for queuing, the philosophy of stopping to take the time to realise how many services we rely on is perhaps only reinforced once we comply with the system of waiting to be served.

Unlocking interdependence

When I began thinking about the spectrum of power or powerlessness experienced in different relationships I struggled with trying to pin down where that power is located and whether the sites of power change in different situations. While I accept the notion of interdependence in terms of people delivering services, the psychological contract in other relationships is more difficult to rationalise because of the fluid and unpredictable nature of individuals. The bottleneck, I suspect, comes from my first response which is to think of interdependence in terms of equal input for equal output which, in many functional relationships, has a financial element. But in many relationships this is simply not possible. To push past this ingrained position I welcomed reading Mary Bateson's (1989) *Composing a Life* where she shares her interpretation of a sermon by a Tibetan Buddhist, Nechung Rinpoche.

This sermon was delivered at the Lindisfarne Association founded in 1972 by academic William Irwin Thompson. The association comprised a group of intellectuals from science, art and philosophy who were interested in exploring alternatives for humanities to develop in scientific and technically dominated societies and this included drawing on Buddhist teachings. The essence of Rinpoche's sermon was that throughout eternity reincarnation has opened a route for us to find the core of compassion as we conclude that all living beings have at some point being someone's child – this highlights life and compassion as an asymmetrical connection we all share. Yet in the Western world such a concept is difficult on a number of levels. First, connections with our mothers and reincarnation are not as inherently strong as in other cultures. Furthermore, symmetry is more dominant as we are more inclined to measure society in terms of equal and unequal, fair and unfair, just and unjust, leaving little space for the ebb and flow of life. Bateson says, 'Nothing in our tradition gives interdependence a value comparable to symmetry. It is difference that makes interdependence possible but we have difficulty valuing it because of the speed with which we turn it into inequality' (Bateson, 1989, p. 104).

To consider the asymmetrical nature of relationships at work there is value in using repertoires as a means of capturing the patterns and nuances of managers' experiences. By accepting that relationships at work change and evolve in terms of importance, value, enjoyment and support, I will argue that interdependence is a useful way for thinking about how gender and competition operate within those relationships. There is much work on the gendered nature of organisations, and the challenge of asymmetrical thinking is to move away from looking for differences based on biological essentialism. While there is an array of gender based structural barriers such as pay gaps and parenting penalties, I want to maintain the focus of my discussion on gender and competition in management. As Potter and Wetherell (1987) explain, individuals face an ever changing kaleidoscope of situations in life and need to draw on different repertoires to construct and understand their social realities.

Using this position I want to explore the different relationships managers directly and indirectly experience and what influence the multiple dimensions of competition have on how interdependence is perceived. The competition cage, as outlined in the previous chapter, is a useful reference to illustrate how competition can be found in the realities of individual managers and, with the knowledge to recognise the dimensions, how future thinking may be modified for a more productive outcome. In the managers' stories I identified three repertoires: management based relationships, career journeys and managing a relationship with the organisation.

How competition impacts on different relationships at work can be influenced by the structures, attitudes and behaviours which dictate the importance or value of each relationship. They can also be influenced by how different individuals position the role of interdependence in developing and maintaining a range of relationships. For example, a manager climbing up the rungs of a hierarchy has a number of challenges to confront in terms of ensuring that their need for knowledge, networks, sponsors and profile is balanced with the need to offer similar opportunities to subordinates and peers. A constant reality for managers is strategically and tactically keeping track of how the politics, power and competition in work environments respond to different scenarios. How a manager develops their approach to these fast moving elements can be critical to navigating a path which balances performance and creativity.

How and to what degree managers up and down management hierarchies decide to spend their time and energy in developing relationships can offer insights into where points of power exist. The role of networks, repeatedly cited as a key component of career success, continues to be an issue of access for many women in management. Networks are sites where developing relationships can be important in soliciting invaluable support, advice and profile. However, the gendered nature of both formal and informal networks is often premised on distinguishing women as different from men, isolating them from the knowledge and connections made via such relationships.

Networking for knowledge

Networks fall into two categories, formal and informal. Formal networks functioning within an organisation enable prescribed relationships to be formed to achieve a desired outcome. An example may be a committee, team or group that is set a task loosely connected to their positional roles. Such a network is likely to include representatives from a range of hierarchical levels and often has a deadline which is marked at the end of the assignment or task. These groups may be learning platforms, providing opportunities to build a profile with colleagues, and can assist in developing relationships across an organisation. This may be most useful for more junior managers who are seeking to identify and develop their management plan and want to broaden their experiences.

Informal networks cross the boundaries of work and social bases and the old boy network continues to be widely recognised as a network which houses powerful and influential men. This long established approach of exclusivity has certainly served some groups with positive outcomes (Schwartz, 1992; Coe, 1992). In J. Oakley's work on why women CEOs are scarce, she cites a number of explanations including behaviours such as double binds (a behavioural norm creating a situation where a person cannot win no matter what they do) and leadership styles, but also in the top three are old boy networks. She argues that, 'Throughout history, double binds have been used by those with power to oppress those without power' (Oakley, 2000, p. 324). Women since the beginning of the twentieth century identified the old boy network as an establishment (Edwards et al., 1996; Davidson and Burke, 2000) which could not be challenged directly on the basis of gender. Yet emulating the peer to peer relationships seen in the established old boy networks was found to be very useful with groups of women.

Women's networks

In the UK, Beatrice Holmes Gordon is held up as the founder of the organisation Business and Professional Women (BPW) in 1938 – yet this piece of information alone does not serve the history of women's work oriented networks. Born in 1884, Beatrice started her career as a typist and ended up working in a financial issuing house for a man named Thorolds. With the outbreak of the war in 1914 Beatrice was charged with running the business when the whole management team enlisted. While the business remained intact throughout the war, on his return Thorolds wanted to give jobs to returning soldiers and so constructively pushed Beatrice out. Not one to take no for an answer, she formed a partnership with Thorolds' company secretary, and together they raised enough money from the city to open a stockbroking business in 1921. It is this mantle of being the first woman stockbroker in Great Britain which Holmes Gordon is most often associated with, but her experiences beyond this are worthy of documenting in order to provide context to the value of women's networks.

The 1920s were a socially challenging time for young women in Great Britain as they found themselves immersed in phenomena which served as a catalyst for changing the way women thought about themselves and put a spotlight on how society thought about them. In the 1920 census it emerged that the number of unmarried women had reached two million – an unexpected trend. Yet with the loss of a generation of young men who had fought and died in the Great War (some 750,000), it was in retrospect not difficult to predict. Lord Northcliffe, owner of the *Daily Mail*, is reported to have said in conversation with a reporter who was looking for a story, 'Tell your chief to find out what's to be done with the two million superfluous women we now have in England' (*Indiana Gazette*, 1921). So what happened to these women? Some went into further education and joined professions, some built businesses and many simply worked to sustain themselves. Often overlooked in feminist history and overshadowed by the second wave of feminism in the 1970s and 1980s, this generation of women took the journey into business and the professions and recognised that there was value in connecting with other women who shared similar work environments.

In 1923, with only minimal numbers of women in business and professional careers, Holmes Gordon experienced isolation in her business and wanted to connect with similarly placed women. After several trips to America she discovered a women's network, the

Soroptimists, who, it transpired, had a Greater London branch, to which she was invited. What I found refreshing in reading about this network was Holmes Gordon's comment on her first impressions: 'I was impressed to note how many women directors of business houses there were. Names I had known and had taken for granted were men's names, were now revealed to be women's. I noticed with admiration that many of these women had large staffs and handled their staffs admirably. If I had ever had a tendency after my successful years in the City to regard myself as something unique, joining the Soroptimists stopped it.' What this captures is the motivation for women to join networks to find companionship with peers in the work environment which in essence remains the premise for women today. Connecting in a safe and secure environment has over the decades proven to provide many women with the opportunity to share ideas, frustrations, wisdom and mutual support in a quasi-social environment.

One aspect of Soroptimists meetings was the requirement for each member to share the story of their career, establishing the value of knowledge transfer. This act of sharing is found in a mentoring programme created by Women in Film and Television (WFTV) in response to a report in December 2009 by Skillset, the sector skills council for the creative industry. The report found women's representation in creative media, a £50 billion per year industry, to be only 42 per cent compared to 46 per cent in other sectors and, critically, this number is dropping. Also found in decline were numbers of older women across the sector. Nicola Lees, who directs the WFTV mentoring programme for mid-career women, now into its second year, told me what a valuable exercise it is for the mentees to describe their roles and responsibilities. The six-month programme comprises of six hours of face to face mentoring with a matched mentor alongside meeting as a group every fortnight. During the group sessions each person is required to give a presentation about an area of their expertise which gives the rest of the group vital insights into other parts of the creative industry. As a result of this knowledge transfer a number of the women from the first intake have combined their skills to develop new projects together. Nicola says that this trend towards collaboration is expanding into the new group. For example, a producer from the first mentee intake hired a director of photography from the second group after Nicola made an introduction. Why mentoring is important for women is found in the repeated findings that women do not feel confident. This was also found to be the case among the women applying for the WFTV mentoring programme. A lack of confidence, for example, prevented the women asking for promotions, pay rises and career development projects. Careful matching with a mentor can ensure confidence is instilled in the mentee; furthermore, the women reported that even the simple act of being accepted onto the scheme was hugely validating and instantly increased their self-belief. Although the process of being mentored was seen as valuable, at the end of the inaugural scheme the mentees predicted that the strong, supportive network they had formed with their fellow mentees would also have a positive and long-lasting effect on their careers.

Halford and Leonard (2001) argue that networks offering support to deal with the stresses and strains of being a woman or member of a minority group cannot offer the same degree of career development as an old style network. This raises the issue of whether industry networks are more outward facing than organisational or occupational networks. Waldstorm and Madsen (2007) suggest that a generational effect is apparent in the formation of networks, with the development of young women's networks responding to the number of women in the labour market and in management. However, the value of these networks in terms of actual career development or business growth is difficult to determine. They suggest that such networks do not have members with enough power or influence to change situations to positively impact on a person's progression at work.

The number of women's networks has grown at a remarkable pace over the past 15 years and the use of online platforms has certainly contributed to this rise. In 2004 the independent think-tank Demos produced *Girlfriends in High Places* (McCarthy 2004), a research and discussion report on the growing phenomenon of women's networks. The report points to the dynamism of the many women's networks built on an identifiable need which is harnessed and shaped by a group of women. The report recommends that large organisations continue to start or support women's networks which are aligned internally and use them as means to gather rich insights into how the culture is experienced. While many large organisations already do this, they may be missing an opportunity to fully integrate the network into informing the strategic direction of the business. Another aspect of women's networks which I find personally disappointing is the lobbying void on wider social, political and economic issues. Whatever the central aim and location of a women's network, it is difficult not to question the thinking as inward facing.

Connections and associations

Explaining the importance of analysing networks, Ibarra (1993) makes the distinction between instrumental and expressive ties. An instrumental tie stems from a work role and can include information, expertise, advice, political access and material resources, all of which can assist personal and career development. Although a mentoring or coaching relationship falls into this category, it is only one element of a range of relationships which offer a wide scope of support and resources. An expressive tie primarily provides friendship and social support and is not as bound to work roles. Holmes Gordon argues, 'Our faith is that business and professional women have something new to contribute. The trained woman as a class is just 30 years old. She comes as an outsider...She represents a new source of power, an unexplored field of thought. She brings what the world has been waiting for; an entirely new perspective on old problems' (Hall, 1963, p. 15). Yet one perspective unresolved in the world of networks is the role and placement of friendships which fall between work/network/social relationships.

In their exploration of friendships at work, Markiewicz suggests that interpersonal work relationships are important and whether instrumental or expressive, they present men and women with experiences that can positively or negatively impact on their employment, career decisions and development. Friendships are defined as a 'voluntary, reciprocal, equal relationship which is seen as unique and special and which enhances the sense of self' (Markiewicz et al., 1999, p. 161). The study researched how same gender and mixed gender friendships operate among managers, solicitors and technology workers and what impact this has on levels of job satisfaction. The results found that salary tends to be higher as the proportion of men increases in the workflow and friendship networks and that homophily characterises these relationships. Homophily refers to the degree to which pairs of individuals who interact are similar in identity or organisational group affiliations. Interpersonal similarity increases ease of communication, improves predictability of behaviour and fosters relationships of trust and reciprocity (Ibarra, 1993, p. 61). Also concluded was that close relationships with men indicate a better outcome for women in terms of career success than similar relationships with women.

These findings continue to observe women being disadvantaged at work because of their gender based exclusion from or partial membership of networks complicated by time, family responsibilities or a preference for networking by necessity. So do women need to be more strategic in identifying their relationships at work? Do women need to better understand the role of interpersonal competition in different relationships to ensure they have a repertoire of responses? In many conversations I have had with managers in my research one remark repeatedly made is how women take competitive working situations too personally no matter what the outcome. Perhaps this is an example of why there is value in thinking about distinguishing work friends from colleagues and associates. In an increasingly competitive labour market where women too often remain at the lower end of management hierarchies, it is important to question how initiating, developing and managing relationships more effectively could increase the opportunities for advancement. Markiewicz suggests that, 'Greater competition may lead workers to place more emphasis on making strategic choices about relationships, ones which would make females' lower status even more salient and thus these friendships less desirable' (Markiewicz et al., 1999, p. 176).

How important, therefore, is networking to advancing women's careers in management? Ibarra and Hunter (2007) identify and define three types of networking they argue are necessary for managers to be successful: first, operational, which is primarily about building relationships that enable jobs to be completed; second, personal, which involves widening one's circle of contacts based on common interests; and finally, strategic networking. This is perhaps the most difficult to manage as it involves predicting future issues and identifying stakeholders who may be important in such scenarios. Ibarra and Hunter suggests that networking is not an easy skill to master and can often be a reason for a manager's slow progress up the hierarchy. Her solution is to seek a role model who is successful at developing networks and learning the skills and practices from them.

Networking puzzles

Grace, a middle manager interviewed for this book, discusses her experiences of the advantages and disadvantages of not networking. She accepts she may have had better opportunities to progress if she had committed to networking at events and activities outside of prescribed working hours. However, she believes that in presenting herself as a neutral character allowed her access to more groups internally because her alliances were difficult to define. How Grace rationalises her experience of networking appears to suggest that her priorities outside of work were balanced with those at work, accepting that with every decision comes a compromise. This approach requires a degree of confidence, enabling a person to remain in control of their life by managing the various components efficiently and effectively.

> Grace: I think I may have paid a price for not networking outside of work, but on the other hand I never saw work as any more than a part of my life. In some ways this made me more approachable because I was not aligned with any one group.

Another interviewee, Pat, is also pragmatic about her role in networks at work and the purpose they may serve. She sees them as a means of gaining information to build power bases that suit her individual working agenda and its objectives. It is apparent in Pat's organisation how the value of information is paramount to being able to achieve certain goals and being in the information loop makes relationships and accessing internal networks important. Like Grace, Pat sees networks in the plural, recognising the value in being accepted in multiple internal and external environments. This approach is a strategy used by a number of the managers I interviewed and supports the notion that internally sourced information is crucial to being able to perform their jobs and to building a career.

> Pat: One thing I see here often is that information is power. In this sector it is one of the most vital things, sharing information but often the opposite happens. The common thought is I have power simply because I have information. It is important then to build liaisons or networks so that I become part of the power chain.

Networks which operate outside of the formal parameters of an organisation are most frequently cited by women managers as discriminating based on gender (Itzin, 1995). As a structure this type of network can be active in reproducing stereotypes which disadvantage some women and men (Coe, 1992). The value of networks is not usually underestimated by those that belong to them, nor by those who do not, as being involved in a network can be useful to career progression. In terms of collective competition, networks provide an opportunity to communicate with peers and senior figures often outside, but associated with, an organisational structure or industry. This can increase personal confidence and collective notions of solidarity based on belonging to a particular gender, industry, profession or social position. Such collective notions can be instrumental in engaging in collective competition where supporting one person over another in their career is based on membership rather than meritocratic mechanics.

A male interviewee, Mark, presents a picture where networking and information is necessary for business development and admits a male dominated approach by his all-male team as the normal practice. Based around sport and events which usually take place outside of working hours, this form of networking, he says, appeals particularly to the younger men. Although Mark says that such types of networking are not essential to being successful, it remains a consideration for him when interviewing for positions. He suspects this is also the case for his competitors. Networking in this situation is viewed as an informal requirement and clearly makes it difficult for women to compete equally for positions. The relationship between age and this type of networking may, as Mark suggests, reach a point where it is no longer of interest or necessary. Whether it is replaced by a more sedentary approach as individuals get older is not clear.

> Mark: The only broader observation I'd make is that it is a pretty blokey space and that can be a tough element to break through. It's not old boy stuff, it's more sport stuff. This is a very relationship driven business and there's a real flow of information and we need to have an edge... so it's for the young who are in their late 20s through to late 30s.
>
> They go to the rugby, go to the cricket, go to the pub, it's that kind of world. It's not an essential element, I mean even within our 'shop' there are those who love it and are happy to be in that kind of flow. There are others who are equally successful without feeling the need to be as mixed up in this.
>
> But it's an element and I can't help but think that as you go through the process of interviewing people to come in and I'm sure some of our competitors have looked around and thought how well is this networking thing going to work?

The role of networks can be different depending on the objectives they are seeking to serve. If the aim is to gain information on an internal basis then relationships and networks across an organisation could be an advantage. If the information required is in the wider marketplace then relationships built with outside networks could be a priority and seeking to find platforms to access these would no doubt include sporting events where corporate hospitality can be a useful and popular means of introduction. Networking outside of office hours can be a barrier for some groups who have responsibilities that do not enable a freely available commitment of time.

Life expectancy of role models

Gibson defines a role model as 'a cognitive construction based on attributes of people in social roles an individual perceives to be similar to him or herself to some extent and desires to increase perceived similarity by emulating those attributes' (Gibson, 2004, p. 136). He argues that in organisations women have fewer role models in terms of gender and therefore face a difficult challenge of interpreting male role model behaviour and assessing it in terms of acceptable behaviour for them.

Role models may be important, however, at different life stages. For example, at a young age it may be aspirations which need visual realities followed later with comparative realities found in commonly used comments like: 'if he/she can do it then why can't I?' (Rindfleish, 2000). Singh et al. (2005) suggest that role models are important for young women managers who are constructing their working identities and Ibarra (1999) found in her study that young professionals who use multiple role models are more successful in their early careers. Singh et al. found that the women managers interviewed used a range of role models from family members to high profile public figures. Such global or distant role models were cited as being useful in terms of addressing the often cited lack of confidence in the managers' careers, identifying with figures who are perceived as being successful, in control and having power.

Flattery or self-serving

Being a role model is often assumed, rather than agreed to. The mixed messages and blurry line between role model and celebrity have increased in recent years. The cultural role models society throws at young people can create unrealistic expectations rather than demonstrations of attitudes and behaviours which could be positively emulated. While role models dominate cultural landscapes, especially in the sport, entertainment and media arenas, role models in the work environment are not such an easy sell to young people.

There are certainly some gender based issues which emerge. Women managers can be held up as role models without their knowledge or agreement. In this process an unfettered package of unrealistic behaviours and attitudes can be assigned, setting up the individual role model to fail in the extreme or at a minimum disappoint. Another of my interviewees, Amy, has experienced a series of conversations with her CEO who has sought to harness her gender and position as a device to entice her away from her current role – which she loves – to a global role – which she is not interested in. She has been explicit in her disinterest and was becoming increasingly frustrated. Amy now feels a little bitter over this episode where she feels her feminist beliefs were used as a tactic to manipulate an organisational challenge.

Amy: Our global CEO was again trying to convince me to move to anywhere in the US or London, he used my gender as a tool by telling me that oh I know you're a really strong feminist and if you move you would be a tremendous role model for other women in our organisation who would see you in this terribly important global role.

The importance of role models for young women, as Singh et al. (2005) suggest, provides a source of ideas for building a work identity. Apart from Amy, the managers I spoke to did not mention role models in terms of having had one or indeed being one, although they themselves may not know they have been assigned this position.

My argument is that cultural role models have a shelf life and are often set up by external forces such as the media. Organisational based role models are often established by either senior managers who want to hold up a picture of what a successful woman looks like, or by junior staff members who are simply looking up the ladder. Men in management do not experience such blatant gendered flag-flying in respect of their position as their women counterparts. I would further argue that organisations can overuse the role model tactic and as a result dilute the original intent. For example, at a recent meeting around the subject of women's representation within a leading national sporting body I was asked about the value of role models for women. Sitting around the table were the Chairman and CEO and my question to them was this: 'When did you personally stop looking for role models as reference points?' While there were some audible intakes of breath it was quickly recognised that role models are important, but to engage with women it must be acknowledged that they are not a homogeneous group and different tactics are required. Role models are useful for young people and then it becomes important to be sensitive about using role models without being patronising. To view role models as only one aspect necessary to convey a message is a positive move towards building a dialogue which has multiple aspects of communication about an organisational picture which shows men and women across the hierarchy in fairly equal numbers. In this process, as individuals become more engaged in building their work identity, it is likely they need to engage more directly with their managers, not with role models.

Mentored to death

In a similar way to role models, mentoring has become, I would suggest, an overused practice for solving all the ills of gendered management systems. Women are increasingly standing up and vocalising that, at certain points, mentoring is not the answer. While this response is valid and links into discussions of sponsors, mentors can be useful on multiple levels. I have come across only one manager in my research who spoke of having a traditional mentor. Mark developed a mentoring relationship in his teenage years with his godfather after his father passed away, which provided him with long term wisdom and guidance. This lengthy relationship is not the norm, with short term and functional mentoring being more popular. Pat is someone for whom mentoring has been instrumental in her career development. She uses mentors to strengthen her weaknesses either in a lack of information or in a skill based capacity.

> Pat: In fact it's kind of interesting that you're bringing this up because I've been thinking recently that I sort of need a new mentor for myself. But at this stage I need to answer a few questions on the parameters: should the mentor be someone at work or outside of work, as I need some help about what to do next in my job and to work out some options.

Matt has a different view and says he has never had mentors but has experienced valuable relationships with some individuals at work who have been useful in supporting him to develop skills and experiences. This view would be regarded by other managers as describing a mentor, which illustrates how broad the mentoring spectrum is becoming and how it is also becoming an aspect of management styles, as Angela describes:

> Angela: My last boss is my mentor. He gave me responsibility and authority for a group of 35 people so I could further strengthen my management skills. He has confidence in my abilities and

let me get on and do the job while always being there to offer support and guidance. The key lesson has been when and how to 'play' the politics with the organisation. To pick the arguments you're going to have and when to get on with things as arguing and challenging won't make a difference.

Matt raises the explosion of business/executive coaches which he thinks are filling a gap that people need to continue to their career journey. I would certainly agree with Matt that there has been an increase in the number of coaches and that the trend continues to grow.

> Matt: For me the mentor is the wise person whereas the coach helps you learn through self-discovery.

A number of the managers had executive coaches assigned either by their organisation or through some personal development platform. The experiences of coaches did come across as quite vague and they appeared to be useful in setting objectives to develop particular skill deficits. I have had one session with a coach to see for myself what the parameters were and, while my response is ambivalent, I can see how the support could certainly be useful in some precarious management positions.

Mentoring in management

The mentoring experiences of the managers I interviewed were largely positive and did not suggest strong gender influences in the relationships. The relationships are best described as informal, with no one having been part of an organised formal scheme. A number of managers refer to having male superiors who acted as mentors and the experiences described are positive, contributing confidence and knowledge to their portfolio of skills. The relationship that develops with a line manager can be the first insight a new entrant gets into how an organisation works. Developing this relationship is the opportunity to assess what type of management style is practised, what can be learned and from whom. Encouraging a productive and positive relationship with a line manager is an important stage in being included as a member of the team (Ely, 1994). One female manager remembers with a measure of fondness her (male) manager, upon becoming a junior manager herself. The relationship was based on mutual respect and a belief in Martha's skills. He did not see gender as a reason not to have a woman manager, even when they were operating in a male dominated area of the business. Experiencing this degree of confidence from a superior is positive and has allowed her to appreciate the opportunity she was offered.

> Martha: I moved into my first management job in a sector that was male dominated and I was pretty young at the time so it was even more of – oh my gosh what is this chick doing on this side of the company? My manager at the time was such a great guy that he allowed me the opportunity and it was a really good thing to do.

Another shares her fortune in having two superiors who offered to teach and guide her through the transition into management and beyond. Becoming a good manager is for many managers a process of trial and error which is made easier with good support, particularly at the early stages of a management career.

> Clem: I had two bosses, a man and a woman who were very supportive and I felt they took it upon themselves to be my mentors and to share information and experiences to the best of their knowledge with me. They helped me develop my managerial skills as it was my first manager's job.

Managers who experienced line managers with a mentoring element to their management style found this largely positive for their development as managers. Having a line manager who opens the door to an organisation's unwritten rules can certainly be advantageous, especially when it is combined with challenging projects and experiences. Getting a good manager at the right time can be critical as a success factor for some men and women's careers and certainly ignites the argument that leadership should not overtake or dismantle management discourses. Whitely and Dougherty (1992) argue that as careers become more fluid, short term mentoring is becoming increasingly developed as a management tool, and mentoring did emerge as a performance measure in terms of a good manager and a bad manager. While many managers recognise that having talent and ambition is not enough to progress, good managers see their role as helping subordinates realise this and helping them to build their skill base to prepare for future roles. What junior staff require to have the best chance at success is strong and knowledgeable managers who can teach them how to develop and apply their skills within a range of business scenarios. The downside of having a bad manager may mean it takes longer to find a mentor and network where such support and direction may be available. While some interviewees prioritised mentoring as part of their management style and see it as an asymmetrical relationship, boundaries are sometimes overstepped, leading to degrees of resentment.

One interviewee stated that she actively tries to present herself in a mentoring role to staff but explains how over time this is diminished by people who exploit the time and effort offered. She is increasingly weary of offering too much mentoring energy to individuals.

> Elaine: I have always tried to offer advice in a mentoring way and I have seen some staff progress and move onto bigger and better jobs and it makes it worthwhile when they ring out of the blue to say how well they are doing. This I have to say is the exception; most people take from you and bugger off with the energy you have given them. It makes me choosy now about who I offer help to over and above what is required by my job. Let me also say there is no difference on this between men and women, it's a human deficiency.

Whichever side of a mentoring relationship an individual occupies (mentor/mentee), the degree of attention given to considering competition appears negligible. The legacy of not engaging with competition on a multi-dimensional basis is a situation where knowledge and experience of competition is limited. This may contribute hugely to why this dynamic remains largely invisible in management. While mentoring is loaded for some managers with the pay-it-forward philosophy, it is equally loaded with changing their own bad experiences by doing things differently. Both approaches arguably lead to concluding that people management is a multi-skilled operation which has a wide ranging spectrum of effects on individuals. What should be a concern for managers is how effective informal mentoring is and whether, outside of direct people management, formal mentoring is a better option. While I think we would all like to have a mentor, the definition of 'the mentor' is arbitrary and has got lost in the crowds of mentors and mentees apparently available in all sectors of society.

Multiple work identities

A manager's professional identity is influenced by their position and the values of the organisational culture within a sector and/or occupation. Different industries will attract certain types of people and we are all quick to distinguish between, for example, the creatives, techies and bankers who assemble a group identity which lays the foundation for individual identities. The function and visibility of external competition in an industry will also be influential in the process. Management identities in newspaper publishing are interesting because it is an industry where the distinctions between departments, primarily advertising and editorial, are so clearly defined. The interdependence of the relationships which exist in a newspaper office is often tense but creates what can best be described as a buzz. This buzz has declined in the last couple of decades as we have witnessed the decline of newspaper publishing. Yet one only has to get on a London underground train in the mornings and evenings to see how daily newspapers remain an integral part of our daily lives. Content is the lifeblood of all media, and the responsibility for the collection, assembly and dissemination of such material is the editor's. The imagery of 'hold the front page' perhaps best epitomises the importance of unique content and being first. Ultimately, getting an exclusive is a zero sum competition where only one publication is the winner. Competition is therefore entwined with the content but again, it is a limited version of the scarcity model.

Advertising is about yield (the revenue related to volume), with the business objective being simply about meeting the agreed ratio of advertising to editorial content to meet financial necessities. This is even more important when the newspaper is free, negating cover price income. The competitive environments therefore which underpin the management functions of advertising and editorial in commercial media are good examples of how positional and external dimensions of competition operate simultaneously and in an interdependent way.

John explains how advertising and editorial work together out of necessity rather than a desire to compete internally.

> John: I sit in marketing, probably the meat in the sandwich between editorial and advertising, who in my experience merely tolerate each other. Working with both functions I can see why they struggle to compete for anything other than money to spend because they ultimately need each other to do well and that just doesn't sit well. So it's mostly a standoff.

Peter is an editor and is very precise about saying that he is competitive at work. He views competition as an essential element of his position and his role is a good example of how different dimensions of competition impact and collide in the media. Juggling a combination of external, internal, positional and of course temporal dimensions of competition are for a daily news product in play on a constant basis. Peter is clear in articulating the necessity to engage with competition and competitive relations at work, stating that being first is of ultimate importance to the success of his newspaper and his position as editor. How the market measures success and failure in terms of a media manager's role is perhaps more acute than other industries. Ultimately it is the readers and viewers who make the decision about what to read, listen to or watch.

> Peter: My job is to have the story first for my newspaper. There is no second place. Yes I am competitive, no question. My success and the success of my team and the publication rely on me being competitive. It's what and who I am.

Peter's position as an editor is a good example of why it is important for managers to understand other positional functions within an organisation. In so doing managers can observe competition and competitive relations specific to a position and role and lessen unnecessary tensions by being able to distinguish one competitive practice from another. Extending this point illustrates the diversity of relationships individuals have with their organisation, peers and subordinates and, in Peter's case, newspaper readers.

The career journey

Beck and Beck-Gersheim (2002) argues that work is increasingly dominant in Western societies and that the responsibility for planning and development of one's career journey rests with the individual. For many managers this requires navigating work environments while keeping abreast of the labour market in terms of the requirements for education, mobility and competition. Success, he claims, is influenced by the ability of individuals to understand the importance of leveraging each element on its own or in combination with the other elements. The managers I interviewed claimed that personal competition is a dimension they easily identified with on some level, whether as a device for benchmarking their performance or to measure skill development. Many managers recognised the value of personal competition within their own education and career history so far.

However, interpersonal competition did not have such positive responses with some managers. When I interviewed Ella she has recently found herself in the centre of a competitive relationship with her subordinate as a result of a situation initiated by her superiors. The 'big boys', as Ella refers to them, began having direct conversations with her subordinate, bypassing Ella and in her view undermining her position. She describes how she witnessed the subordinate being treated like a senior manager. What is interesting in this situation is how Ella does not project herself into the situation as the senior manager she is, suggesting that she does not perceive that she too is part of the 'big boys' club. Second, while Ella experienced the negative outputs of a competitive relationship, this did appear to be one-sided, with the subordinate quite likely unaware of exactly what was going on, although likely to recognise something was up. So the question is how often do we find ourselves in competitive relationships involuntarily and/or unknowingly and does this account for some of the unexplained behaviour experienced at work? Ella did comment on how the relationship between her and the subordinate was strained for a period of time but resolved itself over time – but clearly without explanation. This experience illustrates how interpersonal competition is possibly the most complex dimension because it is loaded with behaviours, attitudes and emotions which can operate on a multitude of levels. It is often overt and yet hidden, distorting a picture which with some better communications could be managed effectively.

Working as middle manager for a newspaper publisher in London, Clem has been in her position for three years. She remembers with anger the circumstances surrounding her promotion and transition into management. The company had new owners who brought in their own senior management team. Clem was promoted to her first management role, placing her in a peer group with people who had previously been her superiors. She explains how unfriendly the middle management team were, having been very friendly when she was in her old job. Clem's anger came from the way she was isolated at a time when she wanted to enjoy her achievement. Feeling isolated or, as Marshall (1995) describes, 'in an evacuated relational space' illustrates how internal promotion can be interpreted as interpersonal competition. While Clem's disappointment is easily understood it does not account for the disappointment the managers felt who had to accept the status quo in their positions. However, another level to this discussion is whether there is reflected glory in seeing subordinates progress. Mergers and acquisitions are likely to accentuate the imbalance between been pleased for subordinates and disappointed for oneself.

Clem: When I was promoted internally to this management position one of the other woman managers was very hostile

towards me. But the team that I managed were predominantly women and were very supportive of me. My previous
boss, who was now on the same level as me, tended to try
and keep me below him and to be honest I did feel undermined and isolated.

These stories show how chain reactions resulting from ill-defined
interpersonal competition can originate in a number of ways while
increasing the risk of misinterpretation. A chain reaction started at one
end of a hierarchy can be felt all the way down the ladder and this
makes it difficult to predict, leaving managers potentially having to
respond to the fallout.

Measuring performance

In the original cohort of managers I interviewed, the majority had a
tertiary qualification and about a quarter held a postgraduate qualification, reinforcing the benchmark that managers need a formal
education. Benchmarks in all areas of business have become popular-
ised in management practices. This is often extended into the creation of personal benchmarks promoted in the language of professional
development courses. One manager takes this a step further when he
suggests that his perception of competition and competitive relations
has changed over time as the requirement for professional comparison
has been replaced with individual benchmarking. As careers progress
and hierarchies are climbed it becomes increasingly difficult to find
peers for direct comparison.

> David: I look at competition I guess both personally as a bench-
> mark for improvement, I see competition with yourself as
> important always striving to be better. I am less concerned
> these days about being better than somebody else, I am more
> concerned about being better than I am.

Amy's approach to benchmarking is similar to David's, where the role
and the person are the key factors for goal setting and are intrinsic in
achieving satisfaction and stimulating passion.

> Amy: I'm not particularly individually competitive. I'm very
> passionate about being the best at what I do and my team
> delivering all of those kinds of things but I'm not especially

competitive amongst my peers or individually in a sense of bigger jobs and more promotions and those kinds of things.

Amy has recently been assigned an executive coach to assist her in developing her skills in relation to managing her team better by delegating and coaching them more effectively. Her superiors suggested to Amy that she needs to develop her team management skills. She comments how she uses the 360 assessment to ensure she never has 'blind spots', but agrees with the assessment. This is a good example of how assessing and interpreting weaknesses is productive when supported by the resources and personal motivation to develop.

> Amy: My challenge is actually to learn to be a stronger leader in a non-instructional coaching style with my people. Although I thought I was doing that, I'm incredibly impatient. I would coach them for five minutes and say, now, just get on with it. So the executive coaching is excellent for getting me a better grounding around enlightened self-interest and why it's important to deliver results by developing other people.

Sandra publishes a monthly magazine, primarily for women subscribers with the audience in the 35 to 60 age bracket. Growing the subscription base is important for this niche product. Sandra sees personal competition as a means of motivation to push forward the business and her own skills.

> Sandra: Competition is just about trying to do things better really. I try to be competitive with myself, especially after each edition.

Like David and Amy, Sandra sees the benefits of personal competition in delivering better performances, both personally and professionally. Discussing personal competition comes easily to the managers interviewed and, judging by the stories, consideration of this dimension is active across their careers. However, personal competition rarely operates as a single dimension no matter how much we may think or want it to. Managers don't exist at work in isolation; they have subordinates, peers and superiors as well as an organisational culture to which they belong and which in turn is part of a marketplace.

Organisations as friends and foes

An organisation operates on two levels; the first is the public profile driven by its purpose and the second a people element, including internal and external people. For those individuals who join an organisation, the transition from the disembodied business to the complex system of relationships which operate can be difficult to navigate. Acker (1990), in her article 'Hierarchies, Jobs, Bodies', argues that until a person occupies a role, the role is merely an idea. It is in the process of employing someone to embody a role that their values and beliefs become entwined with their position. Similarly, organisations may change and transform influenced by the people who populate the management hierarchy.

In thinking about how an individual's relationship with the organisation develops, a number of variables emerge from the managers' stories, including loyalty, rewards, job satisfaction, career objectives and length of service. Halford and Leonard argue that 'the pleasures and dissatisfactions from working within organisations are complex and multiple, and may cut across gender' (Halford and Leonard, 2001, p. 92). This sentiment underpins the experiences of the majority of managers I spoke to. What I found was how aspects of pleasure and satisfaction were running concurrently with more difficult and challenging aspects crisscrossing their role as part of the organisation.

Amy is a rarity in having been with the same organisation for over 20 years, but as she says, she has had more than one career. Over the course of her tenure she has developed a keen sense of what the organisation demands, how it demands it and what the key measures of success are. Such insights highlight how potentially difficult it can be and how long it can take to work out the subtexts operating below the surface of an organisation. For Amy, time and experience has served her well. While other factors may influence understanding the organisation's expectations, good line managers are crucial. Amy makes it clear that she has learnt to deal with the frustrations of her relationship with the organisation and has come to expect them. She has learned an important tactic which has lessened her frustrations. Networking in a wider context than her immediate environs, categorised by Ibarra and Hunter (2007) as important strategic networking, is a new development. Extending relationships in this way has become a useful tactic for Amy to increase her support network of trusted colleagues.

Amy: This organisation is results driven...they kind of lead you to a certain point until you're quite close, you know, you've done quite a lot of work and stuff and then they'll say that's good but I want the results delivered in this way. I can't say I don't find it irritating but I've learnt to roll with the punches of it. And the reason why I've been here so long is that I fully expect them to happen.

There are no surprises now and what I've learnt to do is to spend a lot of time networking outside my region. So I've learnt to reach out for those kinds of people whose views and judgements I trust and send them loads of stuff in draft before I go to our Board.

As seen in Amy's experience, individual organisations over time become embodied with the values and attitudes of those at the top. Even after her 20 year career the organisation is still personified as 'they' – being those without name but with the power to challenge, change their minds and to surprise. The identity of the contemporary manager, as Reich (2000) and Wajcman and Martin (2002) agree, is one which accepts responsibility for balancing their career trajectory and commitment to an organisation, aware that in a free market nothing is certain or totally predictable and contradictions constantly prevail.

Managing a relationship with an entity is likely to be fraught with potential difficulties around issues of expectation and loyalty. While an organisation chugs along it is the individual who must resolve their role in the relationship, which is often complicated and changeable. Understanding the dynamism of competition is important in enabling distinctions to be made between believing the organisation always wins and seeking to establish a more controllable relationship where there can be more than one winner. When a manager takes up a new role the opportunity to further their career, learn and develop new skills, meet useful individuals, be promoted and of course be paid more is available. How a manager develops their relationship with the organisation will determine the outcome. For Amy, it is obvious that she has worked out a relationship which serves her personal ambition and in turn serves her role.

Matt works for an organisation which he explains is deliberate in stating how staff are measured across five core competencies. This is a structured framework which outlines to staff at the start of their employment how the relationship is going to be directed. Again, while this may seem to favour the organisation, it actually allows staff to challenge areas where the organisation does not provide the infrastructure to deliver the objectives. For example, an individual is supposed to be assessed in terms of technical excellence so the onus is on the organisation to provide the equipment and training to enable the desired outcomes.

> Matt: We [the organisation] measure success against five core competencies which the company believes are essential for success and those competencies cross all the different roles, but that is how we define success here. The five are: technical excellence; people, teams and culture; management; client experience; and commerciality.

For managers in Matt's organisation I would conclude that people, teams and culture is the most critical and the most difficult to define. Before being able to measure performance in this area some more information is clearly required. What is the culture? Is the culture intended to remain static or is it able to be disrupted on the journey to future success? How are individuals measured in terms of their participation in teams?

> Matt: Our organisation is all about excellence and, ah, while you've got people striving to show themselves to be the one worthy of promotion, you've got five people striving for that and five people displaying excellence hopefully all the time, so that sits nicely with what we are all about.

I do wonder whether the inclusion of such a category responds to the trend for organisations to be more transparent about their culture in a world of diversity and inclusion. When I asked Matt about promotions protocol and practices in relation to the five stated core competencies he said that if the competencies are achieved then the demand for excellence would be achieved and rewarded. Matt said the competencies made it clear what was expected in the contract between the organisation and an individual, which helped both parties work out whether the match was right and had potential. I did conclude from Matt's remarks that his organisation had a number of dimensions of competition working both covertly and overtly, and how this balance is managed is likely to be an indicator of whether the right people like the values and decide to commit to this organisation.

Perspectives on external competition

'Negative and positive' is how one interviewee initially describes competition, before expanding her view to encompass the responsibility she has to her team and the organisation in terms of external competition. The language she uses in terms of threats, passion and beating the competition certainly illustrates her recognition of something energetic and dynamic about the concept. However, this does not appear to extend into the thinking or discussion which she suggests she gives other subjects such as power, hierarchical relationships, market dominance and success.

> Amy: I think competition is both negative and positive. I think you need those kinds of styles or attributes; you can overdo it or under-do it. You know if you're not competitive at all then you could be letting one part of your organisation do a better job than another part when you should be challenging them to get up to the same kind of standard. If you're not seeing where those blind spots or competitive threats are and if you're not passionate about getting into those quickly or beating the competition in that sense then you're not going to perform very well either.

Deferring to the organisation, Matt, in a similar way to Amy, is reticent to engage with competition as a general concept dominated in the scarcity model. However, he is active with external competition. Matt is in his mid-thirties and changed industries and careers with the appointment to his current role three years ago. He defines competition as zero sum with winner and losers, and for him this outcome is only acceptable in external marketplaces. Matt suggests that for him competition operates in opposition to co-operation. The co-operative nature of his team is likely to be an influence on this approach; he suggests that within his team individual ambition is subsumed by team ambition and drive. He tells how his boss is retiring next year and he finds it inconceivable that anyone from the team will be involved in a promotional race. How this plays out over time would be interesting to observe to assess whether Matt's predictions are accurate. Many sceptics may not be so accommodating.

> Matt: When I think of competition I think of people striving to win, perhaps meaning someone will not win. In one sense, look, I think competition is good in certain contexts and not so good in others. For me sitting here if I am representing [the organisation] I think it's important that I am competitive and try to win for them. But if I sit here as part of my team and think of being competitive, well, as part of

> a team then no I don't want to be competitive. I want to be supportive and helpful for the team, so within that context I don't think competition helps.

We witness the tensions and breakdown of teams in some fairly public aspects of society, such as political parties and sports clubs. Changes in leadership are often at the centre, as is the retirement (forced or voluntary) of key people. The impact on teams of such changes is not easily predicted, especially as new visions and objectives are determined. However, external competition is one dimension where individuals, teams and organisations can bind together through transitions as the focus remains one's position in the market, league or the environment of operation. External competition is a key element of the psychological contract individuals have with an organisation and what is left unspoken are the other dimensions of competition. The competition cage is difficult to construct and use unless competition itself is seen in multi-dimensional ways.

Conclusion

Relationships in any working environment are likely to be complex and the managers' stories are no exception. Breaking down the different relationships into layers can be useful in identifying the value of people in terms of mentors, line managers, peers, subordinates, associates and friends. As is human nature, it often difficult to step back to work out the roles individuals have within the organisation and team, and as an individual. In examining the managers' stories, two broad aspects emerge in terms of important relationships.

First, there is a group of managers who identify one or two relationships as proving crucial to building their confidence, encouraging their career development and pushing them towards achieving successes. While often described as mentors, it transpires that the other people in these relationships are managers who have a mentoring style, which has a pay-it-forward effect on the managers, developing their own work identity and style. The second group identify information as being the main driver for identifying the people to have relationships with. While such relationships are necessary within organisations, the informal networks attract individuals who are seeking to broaden their information base.

Gender becomes an obvious factor in discussions of relationships. This is no more prevalent than in networks and the constant citing of old boy networks as a barrier for women. To counter this institution the women's network phenomenon has emerged since the 1920s and grown at a rapid rate since the 1980s, which has coincided with greater numbers of women entering management. While many women's networks offer a range of supportive and advisory offerings, which undoubtedly assist many women, questions remain over whether there are too many networks and whether there should be more lobbying from networks on wider societal issues. Because these networks can operate formally within organisations, across industry sectors or within some other category or interest as well as functioning as either an open, online or exclusive network, I would suggest that finding common ground among the networks would be difficult, except perhaps in admitting that power for many remain elusive.

External competition is the most visible dimension managers actively acknowledge and engage with in their relationship with the organisation. In this dimension the rules of engagement are broadly agreed, bound by external market forces and governed by the organisational positions and their associated contracts. Personal competition is also widely understood and utilised by individuals to challenge themselves against previous levels of accomplishment. While both these dimensions are widely recognised and used by managers, lesser numbers of managers positively respond to other dimensions, resorting to the comfort of competition stereotypes such as winning and losing. The negative aspects of competition in relationships at work prevailed when there was a perfect storm between a lack of confidence in one's work and positional identity which led to misunderstandings in the actions of others. The purpose of building a competition cage using the knowledge gained from the dimensions of competition is to enable clear links to be identified between functional, learning, teaching, peer and quasi-social relationships. Alongside this strategy it is important to note that all relationships change over time and require important and constant adjustments.

5
Language and Images

I was asked to join the so-called 'Equality' Committee when I first joined the BBC – it had been set up to make sure that women and ethnic minorities got promoted ... I said I was sorry but regarded signing up to an equality agenda as a backward step ... women must not be treated as a special category if we are to compete and succeed in the workplace.

Janet Street-Porter, 2008

Assembling different standpoints is the bedrock for social scientists driven by the process of researching questions through the qualitative collection of experiences. For me the question 'Is competition gendered?' has led to building this anthology of managers' stories which I draw on throughout this book. One could describe such research as the opportunity to explore the insights of individuals as a collective, finding commonalities and unique perspectives. During this project it has become clear that competition in the lives of managers is usually left to its own devices and yet, on closer examination, exists in many aspects of individual identities. Like any dynamic, if competition is left unchecked it is an opportunity missed.

In this book any number of the managers could be described in the following way: senior or middle manager, married, in their forties or fifties, tertiary educated with two school age children. However, this profile paints quite a flat picture and whatever mix of demographic material I used a similar outcome is likely. Without probing for details it is impossible to capture the simple and sophisticated angles of any manager. This might include insights such as how to create a good balance between authority and responsibility, how to navigate through stagnant periods of work where job satisfaction is minimal and how to embrace the ebbs and flows of ambition over career. What this approach shows is how the language of management, like any subject, can be static or with some thought can provoke insightful discussion. Too often we read management reports or books where the language is descriptive and analytical which, while informative, does not necessarily take the reader to new places to discover new thinking.

The analysis of competition in this book is primarily concerned with assessing the role of gender in management. Broadbridge and Hearn (2008) argue that in identifying organisations and management as gendered, some trends emerge: first, the priority of work over home commitments and second, the gendered division of authority in management and gendered processes in sexuality, reproducing dominant heterosexual cultures and practices. In this chapter three themes will be discussed: perceptions of gender and competition, the development of healthy competition as a dominant discourse and finally how the tentacles of sexuality remain far reaching in the lives of managers. In each of these themes the language and imagery of my interviewees will be offered to add texture to how we think about some of the prevailing issues.

Access to competitions

The participating managers shared their own perceptions and experiences, enabling an examination of their relationship as managers with gender and competition. In conversations I had with different people throughout the process of my research and writing this book I found the first response to interacting with competition was centred on men as being the main practitioners. References to competitive men were made with associations to egotism, winning and the desire for external validation. The sense projected by some people was that being competitive is not an attitude or trait which is viewed positively.

Zoe begins her assessment of competition with the essentialist perspective of it being a male tendency. Yet what is interesting is that her first response appears robotic as she starts to think more deeply about her own relationship with competition.

Zoe: So, I think competition is innate and it's...I think it's more of a male tendency than a female tendency.

Int: So, if I asked you if you were competitive what would your answer be?

Zoe: Yeah, I think I am deep down. I think I act like I'm not, but I think I am probably.

Int: Do you think there's probably other people like that?

Zoe: Yeah.

Int: Would you say that you're not quite sure how to channel your competitiveness?

Zoe: Oh absolutely. Yeah absolutely. So I think it kind of comes...it manifests itself in different ways. Particularly where guys can play sport or in their work. Whereas women...it's not viewed negatively that they are competitive whereas for women, it is a bit more viewed negative if they're competitive. But I think I must be good at it.

So why does Zoe respond in the early part of this conversation with a mainstream response? Perhaps, like many women, Zoe knows women are not rewarded or encouraged to be competitive at work or more generally in society. Recognising how discourses can influence how we think is what Zoe is struggling with in this instance. She has become susceptible to the idea of competition being a male trait, supported by images of men in sporting or powerful poses which represent this notion.

The other aspect of Zoe's thinking is making the connection that men have greater opportunities to practise competing, whether as active participants or observers. This can happen in many sporting contexts of playing or supporting which, as discussed in Chapter 2, is a global trend accessed via television, attending or playing. The opportunity to practise any skill set with willing participants in multiple settings is likely to enable an increased understanding of not just one's own performance but that of others within the tactics and strategies devised. For women who want to challenge the fundamental discourse that competition is for and about men, it is difficult and isolating because there are so few platforms to explore the concept with like-minded individuals. This is also the juncture where it is useful to revert back to the importance of competitive sport in childhood experienced in team and individual capacities. Without this foundation it becomes more likely that competition remains something which women believe is not supposed to be active in their lives. For some this can lead to feelings of frustration, while for others they are arguably being duped by a discourse which disadvantages them, particularly in the workplace.

Butler (1999) argues that discourses can be important for maintaining scripts and behaviours which regulate and reproduce the dominant cultures found in organisations and their management hierarchies. The discourse which proposes that competition is a negative trait in women can limit their engagement and as a result negate the opportunity to freely participate. The distinction Zoe makes between feeling competitive and being competitive suggests she has found covert ways of practising her version although she is unable or unwilling to articulate these in any detail. How individuals perceive competition in others can be an influence on how they experience and engage with it themselves. Another interviewee, Martha, suggests that women lacking in confidence are competitive as they strive for acceptance at work. She points out that the gap between being good at something and having to prove it to others can become a site for internal conflicts.

> Martha:　I think there is competition, especially from women who are not confident; I mean there is a difference in being good at something and proving you're good at something. I think a lot of women still try to prove they can do a man's job even though it's the idea that most jobs are men's jobs. This sort of attitude says to me that more maturity and personal growth is needed. I should know, I've been there.

Martha thinks there are two common competitive situations, first between men and women, where women try to prove they are capable of delivering their positional responsibilities, and second, where women have to build their confidence just to do their job. The type of competition to which Martha refers describes an overlapping number of dimensions: personal, interpersonal, positional and symbolic. This overlap can certainly make for complex encounters which are difficult to unravel without a framework. Leonardo da Vinci says that 'simplicity is the ultimate sophistication' and I would argue that those individuals who effectively navigate their way through the dynamism of competition are likely to have a sophisticated approach which recognises competition as an interdependent relationship between multiple dimensions. For many women, to achieve this requires a rewriting of the scripts which have gendered competition.

Gendered approaches

Analysing the experiences of male managers is an important aspect of understanding the perceptions of gender differences. Sinclair argues how the two identities of man and manager fit together – hand and glove – in ways where 'work accomplishes masculinity' (Sinclair, 2000, p. 84). John doesn't believe men and women are any different when it comes to being competitive. Yet he suggests that men are usually more open, visible and aggressive about competition.

> John: I think statistically there might be more males who are outwardly aggressive in a sense of competitiveness, and outwardly aggressive – not in a nasty way – it is probably just be more visible. I also think there are plenty of women who are driven and competitive and my gut tells me there's no difference between men and women.

Connell (2002) argues that society has gendered arrangements in education, work and politics that we take for granted and view as the norm, and which are embedded because we do not challenge them. In examining John's comment that men and women may both be competitive, it is the visible aggression of male competitiveness with which he appears to be more familiar, which resonates with the concept of hegemonic masculinity as a component of gender order. Connell says, 'People construct themselves as masculine or feminine. We claim a place in the gender order – or we respond to the place we have been given – by the way we conduct ourselves in everyday life…Most people do this willingly and often enjoy the gender polarity' (Connell, 2002, p. 4). Re-examining masculinities at work and in management is an important step in disrupting the traditional gender orders which still dominate many organisations.

During the process of testing how well the dimensions of competition worked as a model for thinking about competition, I had the good fortune to meet and talk to Zoe Dryden, the owner of 'Second Base' a leadership programme which organises trips for corporate managers to Nepal. The unique element of the programme is the core activity of getting the managers or group involved in a local village community project. There is a leadership team from the village who run the project, providing a unique opportunity for the managers to walk in some else's shoes, along someone else's road. Zoe's observations were revealing of her own experiences as a manager and coach. Leaders who are highly individualistic and competitive, Zoe suggests, want to work with similar types so they have someone to compete with. But taking this one step on, competition is likely to be predictable because of the limited input given by the finite number of people involved. (This type of competition is based on the scarcity or zero sum model and in this aspect is better recognised as being the gladiatorial version.) She asserts that there are gender scripts for men placing competition on a one dimensional plane, which is often exhibited or interpreted as being essential to their ego. This process, she suggests, begins for many boys particularly in the education system and rolls into the workplace. But, as Zoe continues, competition is not necessarily bad: 'It has an effective time and place but when it becomes an automatic default pattern for behaviour or an implicit organisational culture, it is limited. An over-reliance on competition is extremely limiting and there are more effective ways which can lead to creating higher levels of performance from your team.' Such observations fit well with work on hegemonic masculinity which has become increasingly valuable for developing discussions around identifying and understanding the frameworks some men utilise to build their social profile at work and in society.

Hegemony describes a process where dominant group values are subsumed into wider society and are viewed as commonplace. In terms of assigning men, and particularly leaders and senior managers, with traits such as competitive, egotistical and aggressive, an image is drawn which is then embodied by those men who enjoy such distinction. The association of leader and competitor embody hegemonic mascu-linity and honour this version of being a man, setting it as a standard from which other men can position themselves. Connell argues that 'Inequalities define interests and those benefiting from inequalities have an interest in defending them. Those that bear the costs have an interest in ending them' (Connell, 2002, p. 142).

By claiming competition as a masculine trait and assigning that trait to successful male managers, an unequal access to practising compe-tition can result. This can certainly raise the question as to whether gender inequalities in the labour market and in management have a connection with competition. It could be suggested that it is in the interests of some men to perpetuate the gendered script that women who compete are 'iron maidens', or honorary men, stripping them of the choice of how to construct their gender identity.

Mark, a senior manager, comments that men and women compete differently. Yet immediately he focuses on a trait widely categorised as feminine: empathy. Mark interestingly uses the term 'skill' rather than 'trait', which positions empathy as something learned rather than innate. In making this point he suggests that feminine and masculine skills do not need to be bound by the gender orders which govern the roles of men and women in society. But they do need to be challenged and re-engineered so the traits can be more fluid and less predetermined by the comfort of stereotypes.

Mark describes the behaviour of the men in his team using images which strongly suggest masculinities based in a dominant heterosexual language of guns blazing and bulls in a china shop. Working in binary opposites, Mark presents interpretations which appear in one sense to accept the role of women managers and simultaneously continue to accept that men dominate the organisational culture. Wilson observes the influence of masculinity as central to the structure of organisations and yet in terms of analysis this influence is 'hidden, taken for granted and unexamined' (Wilson, 1996, p. 828).

> Mark: Certainly men and women compete differently. I think, funnily enough, having described that to you, I thought oh my God, the skills you need for this job is empathy and on the whole women have the capacity to display empathy or feel empathy considerably better than men do...I try and teach the younger guys here exactly that, that they can't be bulls in a china shop. That they've got to pause and take a breath and you know, discuss the weather, don't go in all guns blazing.

The language Mark uses to describe men is quite different when compared with that another interviewee, Felicity, uses. Describing women and competition in the terms 'subversive' and 'covert' directly contrasts with Matt, who talks about the openness of men. From Felicity's point of view, she identifies the main objective for women as gaining, having or protecting power using tools such as gossip and withholding information. The relationship between information and power is one which suggests that women have reached a point where they have identified an important element of organisations and utilised tactics with which they are comfortable.

> Felicity: I think where women are concerned issues of competition are under the wire, subversive, covert. With women it happens with gossip and withholding information, because knowledge is power. Control of knowledge, who has it and who needs it.

Suggesting that women are under the wire about their competitive behaviour is an observation also made by Martha, who describes men as being more honest about competition than women. The distinction Martha makes between women and recognition and men and achievement is expanded by the comment that women actually want recognition from men. In common with some of the women managers I spoke to, other studies (Cockburn, 1991; Charles and James, 2003) found women managers sharing experiences of feeling uneasy as if waiting to be welcomed in from the outside. The unfriendly environment which continues to impact on women managers could have an influence on them believing that the only way to engage in and practise any type of competition is in a covert manner, which will in turn skew the situation. This is in contrast to the repeated observations that men are more open and honest about competing and competitions. Simply put, this effectively marks the historical nature of men being the owner–occupiers of management.

> Martha: I think men are more honest about it. I think, like if they say I'm going to get this sales target, they're just thinking about that at that level. A lot of women compete with me for recognition. They do it to be recognised by men. Men do it because they're more competitive between each other, they do it to achieve but I think women do it for recognition.

Eve, in suggesting that competition is about temperament, reflects how the layers of experience contribute to how a manager handles situations. Although she does not discuss gender per se, it is likely that the experiences a manager has will be influenced by their gender, thus affecting how they construct their temperament. Eve makes the comparison between an emotive and a more considered response which can be interpreted to mean how with experience also comes less emotionally based reactions. Whether this is because emotion is not considered appropriate in management per se, or merely a domain from which women managers should steer away, lest they be typecast an emotional female, is unclear. While we may like to claim we live in modern times it is only in recent months that David Cameron, the British prime minister, was castigated for telling a member of parliament to 'Calm down, dear,' in what can only be described as a patronising tone. While this is a disappointing episode in broader terms, it motivates concerns because the Prime Minister lays out for us unconscious thoughts which betray his policy positions and projected identity as a modern man and a modern thinker.

> Eve: Competition is about temperament. I think you have layers of experience and I think those things affect people and

how you handle it as an individual, and this determines the
outcome. You can be emotive or you can take a step back and
in ten seconds work out what you need to do.

These stories reinforce the concept that organisations are not gender
neutral and the behaviours and attitudes which govern how social identities develop at work are influenced by the existing gender order and
all challenges to it. How men and women experience similar situations
and yet present different perceptions highlights the tension between
the fluidity of gender and the fixed ideas about who should do what in
the labour market.

Distracted by healthy competition

Exploring different dimensions of competition in relation to day to day
work experiences provides insights into how competition is rationalised as a behaviour and an attitude by managers. During my fieldwork,
'healthy competition' repeatedly emerged from the women managers
as a popular way of describing competition. Notable was that none of
the men made any reference to this description. Healthy competition
articulates for some managers an acceptable and accessible means of
thinking and engaging with competition. As a gateway to gendered
competition this description uses an interesting image of health and
wellbeing. Such a discourse rationalises a widely accepted means of
making sense of experiences and perceptions of competition, allowing
people to frame what they consider acceptable and unacceptable
competitive behaviour.

But how and why does using the prefix 'healthy' construct competition as acceptable or good? For example, in governmental reports, business and market analyses, sporting commentary, child psychology and
education, 'healthy competition' is used without specific clarification or
agreed definition. Colin Powell, the first African American appointed
US Secretary of State (2001–05) and to serve on the Joint Chiefs of Staff,
claims that the 'healthiest competition occurs when average people
win by putting above average effort' (Powell, 1996). While this is probably the way many people would interpret the words, the description
is arguably still quite vague and intangible. Another more literal take is
found in the Healthy Competition Foundation. This organisation was
established in 1999 by Blue Cross and Blue Shield, the two main sponsors of the American Olympic team, following media stories of doping
in athletics. The sponsors wanted to bring attention to the issue of

educating young people on the use and misuse of sport and drugs and keeping both sport and athletes healthy.

Another aspect of healthy competition is how this idea is visually conceptualised. When we look at media pictures of sports men and women, is the version of women what might be considered healthy? In the run up to the London 2012 Olympics the media in the UK have certainly added to this with their glamour photo spreads of women athletes they profile. Two instances came to light in the week of newspapers researched for sports coverage ratios as discussed in Chapter 2. While the *Observer* was considered as a Sunday paper to replace the now extinct *News of the World* following the phone hacking scandal of 2011, it was not used because of the different position in the market. The *Telegraph* (Sunday, 8 January 2012) had a feature on cyclist Victoria Pendleton, styling her as Audrey Hepburn in one set of photos and in a ball gown in another. While these might be a preferred look for Victoria out of her sporting role it is difficult to believe that this is how she dresses on a day to day basis. The images of health become distorted when sports women particularly allow themselves to be represented as film stars rather than successful athletes. In the same week Rebecca Adlington was pictured in the *Sun* in her swimsuit, with full make up and her crotch front and centre. Continually we are confronted with these contradictory images of sports women who perhaps need to have more media savvy advisors who push for an image connected with their skills, allowing them the courtesy of being projected as authentic.

In a sport blog entry for the *Guardian* it appears I was not alone in noticing the increasing number of athletes buying into the media frenzy of self-promotion by any means. In the entry, titled 'Cricket drags feminism back from the future', the blogger Marina Hyde brings attention to what she thought was a press release from the 1950s:

'Whilst the girls' motivations may be different,' it goes on, 'they are all united by their dream to see women's cricket become one of Australia's most recognisable female sports.'

'Each year,' trills one of said girls, who are apparently all dolled up to the nines, 'we spend a day being pampered, scouting through racks of amazing designer clothes and generally feeling beautiful...We love the opportunity to showcase to Australia what makes us tick as individuals.'

Sadly though, the date was 16 January 2012. The reinforcements of mixed messages communicated in such a piece are too many to mention and would simply take us back to the many debates which many women thought they would not have to take up again. The position of women in society continues to present challenges without having to go back over old ground – yet in this instance and others like it, sexuality remains potent. For all those sports women who have tirelessly campaigned for respect and reward it must be disappointing to see this unhealthy version of sport, competitors, and editors who think readers want to read this and, like the blogger, must feel as if they are caught in a time warp.

In the following section healthy competition will be unravelled to show the array of how individual managers understand healthy competition in their working reality. A love of competition is for Pat an important element of her approach to work and management, seeing the role of competition as a means of motivation to be better than before. Pat is in her forties, divorced with no children, and has been living in Australia for the past six years having moved from New York. Her change of country and career direction from the 'cut-throat' world of media advertising to publishing and communications was a strategy to find more personal time, accepting the financial implications of less money as the trade-off. Pat's perceptions of healthy competition illustrate the interplay between the dimensions of personal and interpersonal competition.

> Pat: I love competition. I think it's important and whether that competition is even just with myself to try and get more articles out than last year. So I like those little kinds of targets, you know, bets to win or one up someone, as long as it's what is considered to be healthy competition.

Pat admits to enjoying winning and shares how this fuels the desire to be best or first, although this is tempered by the reference to little targets within the boundaries of what is considered to be healthy competition, using the term without further clarification. The initial passion Pat exhibits in relation to competition is increasingly diluted as she moves from discussing just herself to the involvement of other people. Other managers I interviewed also found discussing interpersonal competition more difficult than personal or external competition. The discomfort highlighted by Pat and other managers around the different dimensions of competition continues to appear in the stories.

For Sandra, healthy competition is a comfortable position and she admits that being competitive is something she is working on resolving within herself. She suggests that 'healthy competition' is generally not well defined and finds this limits her engagement. She explains how she struggles with her relationship with competition and making money, suggesting that in the past she viewed making money as a negative aspect of competition. She suggests that making money can make women 'feel guilty' and comments how this experience is shared by other women in business and management whom she has met in the course of her work. Sandra's version of healthy competition involves accepting the concept and renegotiating her existing negative relationship with earning money and success. This contrasts starkly with Pat's view of money as being an important measure of success. Sandra's perception of competition can offer an insight into explaining why some women managers find negotiating their salary difficult.

Bowles and Babcock (2007), in their investigation into whether women encounter more social resistance than men in negotiating contracts, salaries and bonuses, found that male evaluators penalise women more than men for wanting more money. They argue that if men are more welcome at the negotiation table for resources in organisations then an advantage exists which may contribute to explaining the continuation of gender pay gaps.

> Sandra: Healthy competition, that's one of the internal things that I've got that I'm working on with myself, that it's OK to be competitive. I think a lot of women, you know, I talk to a lot of women and when you come out with it they say the same thing, some of us feel guilty if we make money, you know what I mean, or we think of that money as the negative side of competitiveness or whatever.

The role of money in competition is not a theme that is raised in any depth by the managers I spoke to. This could mean a number of things: first, equal pay may be viewed as an issue separate from competition; second, money may not be a key motivator or driver for managers with salaries negotiated periodically and accepted as the commodification of time and skills; third, without transparency on pay it can be easy to fall into thinking that equal pay is largely already achieved. However, with such a big part time workforce operating it is difficult to work out who is underpaid and by how much. Furthermore, there is legislation in the Equal Pay Act, and a minimum pay award.

Rules of healthy competition were often referred to in the discussions with managers. Eve is one such manager. She outlines below her requirements of respect, responsibility and accountability as the three key tenets of healthy competition. However, alongside this Eve admits that whenever there is competition she is suspicious of other people's motives. She suggests that her interpretation of the rules of healthy competition are generally accepted by people. However, in reality this is clearly not the case. People enter competitions with different versions of what healthy is, and perhaps some do not consider 'healthy' to be part of competing at all.

'Healthy competition' is a term widely used by managers, including Eve, who uses the description in direct relation to interpersonal competition. The emotive responses are therefore not unexpected as interpersonal competition is found to be filled with tensions, expectations and disappointments. However, in unravelling the different meanings and interpretations of healthy competition I would argue that the eight dimensional model of competition outlined in Chapter 3 provides a better framework for managers to engage with the practice and could aid the discussion of competition at work.

> Eve: I think competition is good as long as it's kept healthy and it makes everybody accountable and responsible. Now, there's always a motive behind competition to me, and it's about who is initiating that. If it's good and healthy, everyone is respected and is clear about what has to be done. I think it's not healthy if you are lifting someone up by putting someone else down, I don't believe you have to do that.

The description of one person rising over another suggests that Eve has witnessed the opposite enactment of her version of healthy competition. This may be an influential factor in how she constructs her version of the term. How competition is experienced by an individual or observed in others at work can have important contributions to how it is practised.

Eve highlights how when her expectations of competitive relations are often not met she does nothing more than passively accept the outcome. This passivity perhaps exposes the lack of engagement with competition and all its dimensions and continues to keep it invisible in management hierarchies. Communicating healthy competition as good or positive seeks to distinguish the concept from competition which is bad or negative. Accepting that these two concepts are binary opposites presupposes only the existence of only the scarcity and challenge models of competition.

As a framework for understanding competition, healthy competition is limiting, as illustrated by Eve's story. Not discussing dimensions and actions of competition disables its dynamism, preventing the opportunity to explore and practise the multiple dimensions potentially at one's disposal. Felicity shares her story; she is certainly an exception in the labour market, and for me this was the first time I had ever come across the claim from someone who has already had and moved on from her perfect job. At 26 years of age she was appointed to a position where she thought she would be now, aged 40. Felicity admits to not having given competition any thought beyond viewing it as a necessary evil involving threatening behaviour that can be extreme in terms of one person's position over another.

Felicity: I've never given an enormous amount of thought to the word 'competition'...I think competition is a necessary evil. I mean how could it be seen in a positive way?

Int: Have you experienced competition at work?

Felicity: I always think...there's always people who have been threatened or feel unstable and that causes extreme behaviour, but I've never really thought about what's driving that behaviour and what issue competition has.

Int: What do you mean by threatened?

Felicity: By threatened I mean someone else is trying to take over their job or they are not feeling empowered in the way they should be.

This view is included for its contrast to healthy competition, as it highlights another aspect of unhealthy competition. What emerges in this discussion is how descriptions of unhealthy competition are actually more easily defined, allowing for great examination. It does make me wonder whether healthy competition has been harnessed by people to counter the negative aspects they may observe and experience in connection to unhealthy competition. The difficulty with these two concepts remains the visual representations and language associated with them, for as long as the reference points come from sport in its broadest sense there are limitations in trying to use them in the workplace. This situation only increases as careers develop and yet ideas about competition remain stuck in a transitional state while other managers may have created and enact a more sophisticated and adaptable version of multi-dimensional competition. In such terms 'healthy' and 'unhealthy' become inadequate as descriptions.

Words with multiple meanings

As the only part time manager in the study, Zoe is in a unique position to understand the limitations of working two days a week in relation to competition. She explains how her new work schedule has meant a reassessment of her working persona, including how she directly views personal and interpersonal competition. Zoe shares how she needed to lessen her professional objectives and goal setting in line with what was realistically achievable. Further to adjusting her own ambition, she quickly recognised that she had to build a different type of relationship with her colleagues. Being reliant on peers to cover your clients when you work part time means having to develop layers of trust which has implications on how competitive one can appear to be. Zoe's experience examines how being aware of competition and how it can be interpreted differently at work can enable a more strategic approach to engagement, especially when there are other limitations.

> Zoe: I slot in and out and I'm deliberately not competitive because I couldn't score more runs on the board. I only work here two days. I think if I worked five days I would be more competitive. I mean, I'm competitive on other things. I don't think I'm not a competitive person. [The sporting reference to 'runs on the board' is an active part of the language of competition and refers specifically to the game of cricket.]

David observes how like competition, stress can be seen as something which is simply there in different societal environments – existing as an implicit part of life. As someone who is actively reflective of his own behaviour and those around him, David offers some considered insights. He thinks both concepts are similar in how they are practised at work, with positive and negative elements highlighted according to different experiences. David suggests that some people seek out stress as a means of challenging themselves to perform better, to seek a promotion or play a sport, in similar ways to which personal competition is practised.

> David: I think a lot of people talk about stress being bad; I look at it and think people go looking for stress. Why do people play golf or run marathon? They love the adrenalin rush that comes from the stress of it. Why do people seek to get promoted in companies? They seek out stress. They say, I want that stress, I want that opportunity, I want that pressure. So

when people talk about it as a bad thing, it is if you get more
than you wanted, it's a bad thing if you don't manage it well,
but actually most people go look for it.

The comparison of competition with stress is a useful illustration,
showing how different concepts are engaged with in similar ways.
Using terms like 'good' and 'bad', 'healthy' and 'unhealthy' for both
stress and competition highlights the lack of time devoted by individuals to understanding the range of dynamics operating at work. What
we find with David and Zoe is the use of sporting references to make
their points; the difference is the rationalising of their positions beyond
the words they use. This certainly presents a strong argument for challenging discourses which can be useful by way of illustration rather
than explanation. Whether it is curiosity that drives one's thinking,
which is where David appears to come from, or a change in circumstances which requires reassessments of how work is constructed, as
found in Zoe's stories, the point is that progressive thinking is borne out
change – social or structural.

Rules of the game

The managers' individual accounts generally support the idea that
competition in management is usually ill-defined, largely unarticulated
but widely understood in terms of the scarcity and challenge models.
There are three main streams of thought emerging from the managers I
interviewed which highlight the spectrum of ways individuals engage,
often unconsciously, with elements of competition and competitive
relations. The first group report that they do not engage with competition at work beyond what is deemed necessary to carry out their jobs.
For the second group (mostly women), who have a basic consciousness
of competition at work, the discourse of healthy competition dominates their approach. The third group is distinct from the other two
as managers (mostly men, and the smallest group) who consciously
interact with competition. What this group reports is how sport is their
foundational framework of experience from which they understand
and develop competition at work.

   The role of competition, as revealed in the accounts of these managers,
is not always visible and can lurk in the suggestions of games and
rules which are often referred to without specific location or definable
guidelines. This was also referred to in Blackaby et al.'s (1999) study of
senior women and in J. Oakley's (2000) study of gender based barriers

to senior management positions. The reference back to sport where the scarcity and challenge models are found, as discussed in the early chapters, confirms my hypothesis that competition is generally understood within the confines of sporting scenarios. This is reinforced by one senior manager I interviewed, David, who strongly argues that learning about competition comes from playing sport or being part of a team activity in childhood and early adulthood. This view is shared by the former British prime minister, Sir John Major, who has been a patron for organisations including Cricket for Change. What is instrumental to making any sport successful are rules and regulations which, however you interpret them, are governed by an umpire or referee. What becomes difficult to understand in the workplace is the references made to rules which are often inexplicable, unarticulated, vague and yet somehow vital.

References among the participants in this study to management as 'the game' suggest the existence of these rules and that identifying and defining them may be revealing. Beth is responsible for managing a number of sales teams which keeps her active and at the coalface of the business. She is a confident individual who knows her job and her industry, and is commercially experienced. Beth makes it clear that she views the marketplace as a battleground that favours men more than women. She suggests that the rules of the game are more often undefined for women, placing them at a disadvantage. Beth suggests that men and women compete differently in terms of the rules, who sets them and who knows what they are. As a manager, Beth believes it is important to teach subordinates that these rules exist, explaining that although sometimes indefinable, they will be at least equipped to recognise when they are active. McDowell (1997) and Marshall (1995) report similar instances in their studies of high achieving woman who attributed their success in part to senior women managers who shared with them basic guidelines of how organisations operate. Although Beth describes the rules as not being rocket science, she says you do need someone to tell you as they are very difficult to work out by yourself.

Beth: Look, men and women compete differently; men can put one over you as they know the rules better.

Int: What rules do you mean?

Beth: Those undefined rules that are all around us. I tell my teams to be careful because competition is not the same thing to everyone. Some people see it as negative and may not be able to stand up to it. But whoever and whatever, you have to always be looking to see what games people are playing on the inside and the outside.

Accepting there are rules in organisations and management often referred to as unspoken and as part of the culture underlies their covert nature and highlights inequalities in accessing the same information. The value of a manager's experience repeatedly suggests that recognising sites of tension and prejudice can result in a measure of knowledge allowing for more informed strategies to overcome, bypass or merely accept situations.

The managers I interviewed were keenly aware of external competition and their role in representing the organisation to deliver a performance which contributes to its on-going success. External competition was found to be intrinsically embedded in a three way relationship between the manager, the organisation and the wider commercial world. While this outcome was readily shared and communicated by the managers in this study, similar outcomes with the other dimensions of competition did not result. The relationship between external and personal competition is keenly felt by the managers, who repeatedly describe their personal sense of responsibility to the organisation and their position. The further up the hierarchy one goes, an increased sense of responsibility is found, superseding other considerations such as being concerned with the judgements of peers and subordinates. The ease with which managers spoke of 'doing their best, securing more business and commanding market leader type positions in their industry' demonstrates how when competition and competitive relations are disembodied a comfortable relation with competition is experienced. The currency and practice of external competition was generally agreed by the managers as being somewhat separate from other competitive dimensions, whether or not these dimensions were consciously acknowledged.

The first level response of managers sharing their perceptions of competition often described a general concept which centres on a dichotomy of winning and losing. This highlights how considering competition as dualism is limited, and confirms the proposition that competition is largely invisible and inarticulated among managers and across management hierarchies. The grounded theory framework used for building accounts of competition gained depth and breadth throughout the interviewing process. As the managers, with some probing, moved past first level responses to competition they often enacted a process of exploration and interpretation from which their own rich and diverse experiences emerged. This process was further informed by a small group of managers I interviewed who did engage with multiple dimensions of competition, demonstrating how the dynamic can be motivating and challenging. However, it remains that clarity in defining multiple dimensions of competition is rarely addressed by managers, regardless of whether or not they are engaging with one or more dimensions in their working lives.

Personal competition is the most frequently identified dimension by the managers after external competition. Through the examination of accounts of personal competition it was found that not connecting one dimension with another presents limitations for managers in considering how and in what ways competition may be practised. For Pat, Sandra and Eve, who engage with personal competition as a means of self-development, a sense of understanding that competition is dynamic is apparent. However, despite reaching this point, Sandra and Eve remain fixed on only developing this dimension, appearing unaware of or unprepared to engage in any further dimensions.

Pat is different, with the majority of her career spent in the cut-throat world of advertising, where competition operates across multiple dimensions. She consciously decided to change environment to lessen the dominance of competitive relations. She has reduced her engagement with the dynamic, although it is evident she misses the fast world of advertising, albeit momentarily, as she shares the value of having time to experience other activities. It became apparent that the managers who identify and use personal competition as a means of benchmarking their own progress do not necessarily consider how they would answer the question 'Are you competitive?'

Each of these issues highlights the importance of analysing the breadth and depth of managers' encounters with superiors, peers and subordinates at work and externally with the clients and other organisations. The use of sexually loaded language and imagery, for example, which objectifies women is often found in male dominated sectors and highlights how accepted organisational cultures can determine how relationships at work are constructed. Women who are confronted by such behaviour appear to either accept the situation and remain isolated or seek to become honorary male members (Kanter, 1977). Whichever course a women takes, it does not allow the full development of their professional identity and can subject women managers to criticism from other women across all hierarchical levels. In this chapter the managers have shared an array of relationships they have or have had at work.

For many managers, good managers and mentors have been influential in offering positive learning outcomes which have been beneficial to building confidence and ultimately career development and success.

Overt and covert sexuality

Since women entered management it is well documented how as a group they have been marked by men as distinct and different based on their sexuality. Pringle argues, 'Far from being marginal to the workplace, sexuality is everywhere. It is alluded to in dress and self-presentation, in jokes and gossip, looks and flirtations, secret affairs and dalliances, in fantasy, and in the range of coercive behaviours that we now call sexual harassment' (Pringle, 1989, p. 162). How sexuality at work plays out in the informal and formal practices of managers is the core of this section, which examines what role this has in how different dimensions of competition are understood and experienced. The influence of sexuality at work on how some women construct their social reality of being a manager is an important element to understanding the different environments which exist at work. How such an element may override the capacity to engage with competition and competitive relations is also found to have some traction.

Sexuality is not just about biology, reproduction and sexual orientation; sexuality, as Martin suggests, is 'sensed, expressed and interpreted within very specific socio-political conditions' (Fleming, 2007, p. 241). As with gender, sexuality responds to different situations and as a result influences how sexuality is understood and practised. Segal suggests that 'what one becomes is always ambiguous with only some signs of "woman" to the fore, some of the time' (Segal, 1999, p. 72). Separating gender and sexuality is difficult and I agree with Richardson (2007) who describes the relationship between sexuality and gender as 'patterned fluidity', pointing to a mix of complexities which can be influenced by any number of predictable and unpredictable social, cultural, political, legal and economic situations.

Introducing sexual harassment laws in the workplace is a good example of how over the last three decades the issue of sexuality has been made visible in organisations and also in the wider public sphere (Hearn and Parkin, 2003). This is supported by the introduction of legislative and judicial processes now in place across Western societies to serve and protect the workers from unwanted sexual behaviour. However, as Halford and Leonard (2001) argue, definitions of sexual harassment range across a spectrum, making it difficult to identify, as what one person may deem harassment another views as part of the organisational environment. This highlights the complexity of sexuality and the fluidity of its influence on individuals.

The body of work that investigates the role of sexuality in the workplace is comprehensive and continues to influence policy developments and their implementation (Himmelweit and Sigala, 2001). In my research sexuality at work emerged as a theme comprising a mix of experiences and concerns about seemingly old issues such as dress codes and language, which continue to fuel tensions between men and women and, interestingly, between women. This included scenarios of women actively using their sexuality to gain advantage at work with men and over other women. Also discussed is how some young women workers and managers hold particularly high expectations for senior women managers in terms of their behaviour and attitudes to being a manager, and an unspoken demand for loyalty to the sisterhood. Such attitudes continue to set women managers apart from their male counterparts and can contribute to additional tensions in gender relations. Additionally, new issues such as women managers having to negotiate around their gender and sexuality with partners of their male colleagues were discussed on a number of occasions. This was found to be particularly prevalent in the scenario of travelling with male peers and colleagues in line with positional duties which needed to be conducted.

The behaviour of some young women which one interviewee encounters in her management role is a major concern. She reports increasingly witnessing the use of 'girly charm' as a mechanic to meet work based objectives, a tactic she believes to be inappropriate. She recognises that such behaviour used to be prevalent in the workplace but the fact that it is appearing again is a situation she finds unacceptable. When she has directly addressed the issue with several women subordinates in her organisation she says they are simply bewildered by her concern. The idea of using any tactic available to get the job done illustrates how some women see their femininity as a weapon which, although it may be intended for use against men, can also be used against women.

> Amy: I see a fall back on this very girly behaviour as a way of getting through conflict or getting what you want. I've had a couple of people who worked in different parts of my organisation that I've spoken to about it. Their reaction is bewilderment.

They are, you know, if it gets the job done, you know, then it's part of my arsenal of tactics. I go back to them with it's not working for me, honey; things get done on the merits of your arguments, on the cleverness of the proposals, on the smarts of you working well with the organisation.

Grace has a similar view to Amy on women using their sexuality, commenting that it is a game which at best has short term gains. She is adamant that other women do not encourage or support this approach and suggests that as a game plan there is no evidence that it even works. Women who use their sexuality explicitly to gain an advantage are often demonised by their women colleagues. Abramson (1975) was early into the debate on identifying the tensions between women as their place in public and private sector organisations was established. This began the discourse of queen bees, which we still see being used as a catch-all phrase for women who are being judged on success and the tactics they may have used to attain their position. Concurrently, queen bees are often accused of stopping the pipeline from developing which generates anger and frustration from those women in the pipeline. While queen bee syndrome is a great marketing tool for collecting attention, it must be firmly positioned as a discourse which serves no constructive purpose but to make women, generally, the problem.

> Grace: Watching some women use their sexuality with male bosses does them no favours amongst other women – I was not prepared to play that game, it's like selling your soul for a few pennies and I always thought it was naive because in the long term they never got ahead, they just seemed loaded down with work and responsibility.

Making distinctions between women who do and do not overtly use their sexuality at work highlights a gendered practice which can indicate a blurred line between intentional and unintentional practices and produce negative perceptions. As a site of tension the issue of some women actively using their sexuality is potent and suggests that progress made in one generation does not mean it carries over to a new generation of women entering the labour market. The terms used by Kanter (1977) and McDowell (1997), including 'pet' and 'seductress', show how sexuality continues to influence women's attitudes towards themselves and others.

The continuing experiences of women managers still finding dress and language an issue which marks them as being different to men should cause some shock and dismay. But throughout my research assumptions of progress have been found to be erratic in reality. The double whammy now, as Esther explains, is that it is not just men but also women who practise the use of gender as a tool to secure control, power or advantage. Esther is in her early thirties, is married with no children and is a young manager who has been in her current position and organisation for only a year. In this new organisation she finds herself being judged for unintentionally practising her sexuality at work. She was told by a female peer that the only reason she got the job was because of the way she looked. Esther says she takes pride in her appearance but in her current position is made to feel conscious of her sexuality and gender by a male colleague who displays discriminatory behaviour towards her as a woman, reinforced seemingly by her boss's attitude.

> Esther: One woman who is always trying to compete with me said that the only reason I got this job was because of the way I looked. Funny though, another colleague who is a man, and started here after me, thinks all women should be pregnant and at home and who I would say does not get on with me at all, or me with him. He only ever talks to me when he wants something and then dismisses me. He only ever deals with the male reps and never the women. My boss though takes him more seriously than me even though he thinks he is social misfit.

Esther's story illustrates the difficulty in explaining or challenging gendered practices because it is the little comments and behaviours which on their own can be passed off as ignorance. But as the continuum of attitudes and behaviours increase they illuminate the underlying unconscious biases which operate in the workplace. To take unconscious bias and move the concept into thinking about practising gender is I believe a useful progression. Practising gender is important for reflecting on our literal activities, as Martin (2003) describes – the doing, the speaking, the gesturing and the asserting. Unconscious bias training has been gaining ground in the corporate world for some years now. While I do accept it has value, I think not making gender and the practice of gender central to how we think and act is a missed opportunity to engage men and women in the subject of gender as fundamental to understanding society. The influence of gendered practices at work can have a wide ranging effect on how managers as individuals develop. To a young manager, organisational hierarchies can be intimidating and adding gender into that equation can exacerbate any feelings that may arise, such as isolation and a lack of confidence. While Esther describes her female colleague as competing with her and using Esther's sexuality as a tactic to undermine her position, Esther finds the behaviour and attitudes of her male colleague out-dated but still effective in their outcome. The experiences Esther describes are good examples of the difference between practising gender and gendered practices.

For Esther the repeated behaviour she experiences from her peers and superiors appears to cause her degrees of discomfort around her gender, role and identity. While, as Martin (2003) argues, the comments and actions may not be recalled because they are subtle, a part of everyday work life and happening in real time, this can also mean that when they are verbalised they can be interpreted as minor hiccups which one should expect in gender relations. However, this view can reinforce the idea that issues such as sexuality at work are largely resolved, leaving managers like Esther fending for themselves. Developing and defining a competition model enables fresh perspectives to be taken on identifying gendered practices and for the game to be better understood. Strategies and tactics used by subordinates, peers and superiors at work can potentially be more transparent to more people, whether as participants or bystanders, enabling responses to be more effective and productive.

The long-standing gendered practice of setting a dress code for women can be an affirmation of a gender order within an organisation or hierarchy contributing to maintaining attitudes and behaviours where gender is actively reinforced and certain types of gender performance are predetermined. As found in the experiences of women managers in my research and in other studies (Coward, 1992, Franks, 2000), Acker (1990) argues that gender hierarchies can be maintained by organisations who use sexuality as a means of ruling women's bodies out of order. Again, if we look at the media interpretations of sports women, the process of glamourising them is a way of suggesting, perhaps, that they would better fit the world of beauty than of sport, or that portraying women outside of beauty is too difficult and disruptive. While I certainly appreciate the fun of being pampered and treated like a film star and given beautiful dresses to wear, the lasting image is one of misplaced sexualistion.

Esther: Women were not allowed to wear trousers or short skirts. This didn't seem to bother the other women who were older and seemed to think it was right and proper. We also had to call all the directors 'Mister' which I found a bit off in this day and age.

The embedded nature of sexuality intertwined with gender relations recognises a relationship which can change and transform in response to organisational attitudes and behaviours. Moving away from an acceptance that organisations can be gender neutral to accepting gender as a dynamic in organisations continues to be an important transition in management hierarchies. While I show that dimensions of competition are largely operating below the surface at work, I also find that, similarly, gender in some organisations also operates this way. While I would like to be able to define and examine practices of gender and competition in management, it is clear that seeking to compile a finite list would be counterintuitive, as practices are continually changing and adapting according to circumstances.

Lois and Liz both call attention to a new situation which now confronts them. Travelling for work with male colleagues has brought into sharp focus their position as women managers with their colleagues' wives and partners. Being called to account for perceived sexual attraction between them and their male colleagues has required them to take pre-emptive measures to lessen unnecessary stresses. These experiences are aligned with Wajcman's (1998) argument that women managers who want to be successful need to negotiate their sexuality, which is what Lois and Liz are actively doing. However, Wajcman made her comments referring to people inside the organisation whereas this scenario of travelling for work steps outside this structure to include men's partners. As women managers have increased in number, populating all levels of organisational hierarchies, combined with many organisations operating beyond their local geography, the demand for travel as a required component of working life is accepted as a necessity. However, this appraisal, as the managers' experiences show is not so simple, with gendered practices active and reaching beyond the organisational structure.

Lois suggests that building some trust with the partners of male colleagues is an important tactic, making it clear that while you are not attracted to your colleague, you are not suggesting that he is unattractive. Negotiating around one's sexuality, as Lois explains, highlights the additional pressure women managers can encounter in merely undertaking their positional duties. Blackaby et al. relate in their study that some senior managers were unwilling to go on business trips with women colleagues because of the 'suspicions of

their wives and they resisted working with senior women as a result'
(Blackaby et al., 1999, p. 75).

> Lois: Something else I have come across lately is how women are
> leery about their man taking business trips with women. I
> hadn't really thought about it as I have always tried to make
> a point of talking to wives and girlfriends so they know I
> am not interested, without trying to make them think their
> husband or whatever is a prat who I wouldn't touch with a
> barge pole. You really have to be careful about that one.

Liz agrees with Lois that having to resolve other people's issues around
sexuality at work is a burden that is tiring and has no benefit other than
simplifying potential complications. Having your gender thrust into a
work related situation from outside can be an isolating and tiresome
experience where resolution is not easy to navigate.

> Liz: Travelling with the job is difficult because you are away
> from home and it requires always being on duty. The other
> problem is wives who automatically assume that because
> you're not married, going away is a chance for you to get
> involved with their husbands. It's a pain really and does add
> an edge to what is already an exhausting experience.

This study shows how cycles of words and actions which encourage
attitudes and behaviours in management can continue and morph
both in and outside of organisations. Sexuality at work is diverse, with
examples of conscious and unconscious behaviours varying alongside
changes in organisational structures and cultures. Although legislation
and education have succeeded in providing the basis for policy design
and implementation alongside a system for complaint, the on-going
reality of women's sexuality being used and abused at work remains a
site of confusion and conflict. Continuing to portray women's sexuality
in management as different to men's sexuality and consequently prob-
lematic indicates the on-going need for this old issue to be reconsidered
alongside other examinations of gender and work.

Conclusion

Throughout this discussion the sense that women remain outsiders
in management is persistent and this is evident in the descriptions of
competition shared by the managers in my research. Whether through
the use of language like 'bulls in a china shop' or references to being

outwardly aggressive, men appear more comfortable across competitive environments, explaining why they may be described by women as being more honest about competing. The taboo of competition particularly for women, as discussed by Coward (2000) and Miner and Longino (1987), also had some resonance with the managers I interviewed. The gendering of competition is evident in the perceptions and experiences of managers. While there is value in having role models to illuminate achievements in areas which may seem remote to certain groups, a lack of role models who actively engage with competition remains a void.

Understanding specifically how the dynamic of competition operates for managers is, as I have argued, important to assessing how it influences gender equality. The reliance on healthy competition as a framework used by a significant number of women managers is an important contribution for explaining how competition is gendered. The process and outcomes of healthy competition I have discovered are flawed for two reasons. First is the generally communicated assumption that healthy competition is widely held and understood as an approach to competition. The second reason comes from its practice, which is reported by some managers in this study as resulting in varying degrees of isolation and disappointment. Finding that healthy competition is at best an idealistic notion of doing the right thing means that individuals need to start understanding that competition is a multi-dimensional dynamic. Breaking down the taboo of competition by using healthy competition as a framework for engagement is an inadequate response.

The quote at the beginning of this chapter from Janet Street-Porter, a successful editor and media contributor, is helpful to highlight the view that when it comes to discourse the gender scripts we are comfortable with are probably the ones we should question. In her role at the BBC Street-Porter openly uses her voice to back away from what she sees as a process which is going to box women into the position of being a special category. Bucking against the equality agenda is certainly one way of opening up the space for discussions which can move more freely in different directions. What becomes apparent in exploring the language and images which are associated with a subject like competition is how limited they are in really digging into the energy of this dynamic. There is certainly enough evidence to suggest that despite progress for women in management, the road ahead is still a bumpy one.

6
Confidence and Success

Why individuals work has not changed for centuries – they are primarily fuelled by financial need. How individuals work is, by contrast, complex. McKenna (1997) suggests that, 'Every woman entering the business world soon finds that, contrary to her academic experience, how well she performs is only one factor in creating a future for herself. Instead, an unwritten set of rules directs her fate – a Darwinian system that weeds out those with no stomach for politics, competition or mono-focused ambition'. The intersection of the how and why of working is at the centre of this study, using gender and competition as a lens to examine the behaviours and attitudes of managers. The thread which this study finds weaving through the practice of being a manager is the traditional career model which, as Edwards and Wajcman (2005) argue, remains intact in many organisations while it is becoming more flexible in others. How gender intersects with management careers is highlighted most acutely among men and women who have dependent children. The collisions across work and home environments are difficult to navigate and can lead to decisions about how much time from the household is available to sell to the labour market.

Crompton's (1999) work on patterns of employment and gender in the banking and medical sectors found, like other sectors, that women often work part time to meet the family's needs. This of course has a profound effect on career progression, especially within traditional organisations and professions, an example of which is women doctors who work part time as general practitioners rather than taking up expensive time in specialisms such as surgery. As Edwards states, 'The developmental trajectory of a career is still designed to fit men's life course. Women's careers, which are generally "broken" or "interrupted" to have and to care for children, are thereby rendered not just different but deficient' (Edwards and Wajcman, 2005, p. 77). This conclusion certainly transmits the view of women being likely to find achieving career focused success more difficult and will have direct impacts on confidence levels.

Interpretations of success

Notions of success emerged as a recurring theme among the managers as we explored competition. The connection between these two concepts resonated particularly with senior managers, who need to have a keen sense of understanding organisational strategic objectives while motivating team performance. How some of the managers motivate and measure their performance within this business framework requires thinking about the different interpretations of success and how it is to be managed. Success means different things to different people and is a subjective area for discussion. While there are clear markers in terms of sales targets and market share, this is only one way of thing about success. While organisations are usually clear about how success is measured internally, with position and salary being the two main elements, the transformation from linear to more multi-directional careers in the Western world has been influential in identifying more varied measures of success. Sturges (1999) found that how superiors define and manage success can be a strong influence on how their subordinates think about it.

Mark, David and Beth are all senior managers with more than ten years of experience at this level. Beth is in her late forties and has been in her current position for ten years, lives with her partner and has one independent child. The three managers each eloquently present the portfolio of skills and qualities they believe are important characteristics of a successful manager. Drawing a picture of success with successful managers is an insightful process to explore what qualities they identify and positively encourage in subordinates.

> Mark: Point of reference. I think in no particular order of significance you need a pretty high intellect, a very strong work ethic, a healthy streak of ambition, healthy dose of humour and I think because it is a very people oriented business, you've got to be able to show empathy.

Beth: I think to be successful you've got to have tenacity, I think you've got to have a lot of energy, I think you've got to be curious and I think you've got to have empathy.

David: You have to have integrity because you can't lead people who don't trust you…I think you have to be innovative, you've got to have lateral thinking and you've got to be decisive when it's needed and listen when it's needed. You need passion, you need to have an element of empathy. But I also think you've got to have a certain amount of perfectionist desire and you have to also have a certain amount of impatience. If you are too patient things will never get done.

The role of empathy is the only quality all three managers cite as being important, suggesting a significant strong and human component in the relationship between managers, peers and subordinates. For Mark, a strong work ethic and ambition indicate a manager who works long hours – he works over 60 a week. Beth, in citing tenacity and energy, suggests that her management career has endured a long hard process to reach her personal and professional goals. David produces a range of qualities which appear to hinge on being passionate first followed by having the ability to know when to be decisive and when to listen, but always focusing on achieving the objective. Notions of success and management styles together compile a layered cake of managers' experiences accumulated over the period of their career. Although this stratigraphical (ice core drilling provides a stratigraphical method of dating; this term is used in this study to describe the layers of experience which occur over the period of a career) method of analysing data does not provide the detail of individual situations, it does enable conclusions to be drawn about those management practices and approaches which are successful.

For a number of managers in this study who had either changed career direction, re-entered the labour market after leaving or had moved from the private to the public sector, their criteria of success had expanded. However, whatever the personal measures of success, such as less stress, more time, increased variety or new challenges, the managers generally agreed about some of the skills required to be successful managers and leaders. While the need for empathy is important it may also reflect that, increasingly, a more engaging management style is being practised. Mark views empathy as a learned skill and what is interesting about this view is that, before women entered management all skills, including empathy, were available to male managers and in many ways this has not changed.

Yet when women began entering management in numbers there was a shift in thinking and research where traits were claimed as masculine or feminine (Schein, 1975). In making such distinctions the misunderstanding around sex and gender became visible and began the process of setting up binary opposites. Some men as managers seek to be successful by accumulating all the necessary resources they require to achieve the goal, excluding nothing which may be relevant. Tenacity and energy were cited as important by some women managers, highlighting a sense that greater degrees of commitment are often required to overcome obstacles and barriers not always experienced by their male peers. As the landscape for careers changes in such turbulent economic times skills like tenacity are likely be a key currency for staying motivated.

What became clear in the different accounts of the mangers I spoke to was the changes which occurred between middle and senior management in relation to values, attitudes and behaviours. Middle management, often referred to as the clay layer of an organisation, is a battleground of different agendas. For some middle managers this is the step towards the next rung on the ladder, for others it is a comfortable place which satisfies their career, lifestyle and financial expectations. Pat recognises how the spectrum of people in middle management equally have a spectrum of personal pictures of success. While the reasons are all different, these reasons can change over time, which is what Pat experienced herself about five years ago.

> Pat: I've seen far more people here who I consider to be very ambitious and extremely capable, but because of having young families or because of health reasons...they've chosen not to purely do the corporate ladder climbing. They're able to make that choice, that they're this level and they work these hours and that's the choice that they've made, and that, that is success.

Pat's definition of success is measured by the choices an individual can freely make about how they work. She cites examples of people with families or health issues choosing not to climb the corporate ladder as being successful because they have exercised choice. There are two critical issues here. First, stepping away from measuring success in a singular way is increasing as we live more complex lives in a more complex world. Second, choice is not always as freely available as it may appear on the surface. For some people it is the constraints of time and money in relation to social, professional and familial roles and responsibilities which govern the decisions made which can be perceived as choices (Crompton and Harris, 1998a). Choice and constraint is a useful mechanic and probably underused in terms of thinking about success, ambition, care and career and what is important in individual decision making processes. Discourses of choice certainly exceed those of constraint, projecting unrealistic pictures of what is really going on at the intersections of public and private spheres.

Within the organisation middle management is likely to feel pressure from the top on its way down and the bottom on its way up increasing the need for these managers to be effective and efficient. So to find three managers who had only in the last couple of years found themselves promoted was an opportunity to explore the transition. Ella, Amy and James, at the time of being interviewed, were establishing themselves as senior managers, a process which seemingly takes some time. In the move from middle to senior management, what takes place is a shift from manager to leader in terms of positioning and as result one's management style needs to adapt and shape to include a leadership style. Like many parts of management, there are no rule books and even after a couple of years this process was still being fine-tuned, indicating the time, effort and dedication required to succeed in corporate hierarchies. The other aspect of this transition is a re-examination of working relationships to establish the right balance of authority and responsibility with subordinates. For managers this is the point where succession planning and mentoring pay off as the pipeline is ready to deliver the next group of junior and middle managers.

Personal competition was noted by Mark and David to become in senior management a tool for self-motivation and on-going self-assessment. Both spoke of how personal competition becomes more important the higher up the hierarchy one goes. They agreed that this happens in direct response to recognising that social and professional comparison becomes obsolete, leaving a reliance on the individual to continually benchmark their own performance. This certainly highlights how, despite a lack of visibility around competition generally, personal competition keeps appearing as important at different points in a career journey.

Having spent her career in advertising, Pat experienced a change in the way she views success, from only money to one where personal achievement and more leisure time became the key measures. This change came with a complete reformatting of her life which included leaving a New York advertising agency and moving to Australia and taking a public relations role for a media organisation. In making these conscious choices Pat had her claims of changing her financial success challenged by needing to accept a financial trade-off to meet her goal.

> Pat: Success can be measured in so many ways. In the early days of my career, I could tell you that my success was probably almost solely measured in dollars. You paid me more, I went and worked for you. Simple as that.
>
> Now I really base my personal success on primarily knowing that I've done the best I can for that day with what I have and the circumstances. One of the trade-offs I made in deciding to move away from advertising was a clear decrease in salary in exchange for measuring my success in having a fuller and richer life.

Notions of success as defined by individuals can be fluid and subjective whereas organisations are more likely to have fixed measures. Pat's story highlights how organisations are often inflexible and do not accommodate change in managers' attitudes or circumstances.

Symbolic competition

Symbolic competition was previously defined as the ability to impose one's own definitions, meanings and values on situations or processes. This dimension is most often found in the practice of management styles which connect with an individual's professional identity. The tension in this space is the degree to which a person believes they can be authentic. This is the point where the intersection of gender, ethnicity, social class, age and sexual orientation can be challenged by the dominant organisational culture. Bowen and Orthner describe the relationship between work and culture within organisations, highlighting the influence of leaders in shaping and directing how open the culture is to diverse values and perspectives on management and leadership styles. They state that 'Work organizations have cultures – rules and expectations for behaviour... that arise through both the deliberate actions of leadership and the on-going interaction of group members. Typically unwritten and often unspoken, this culture gives the organization a certain style and character and may have considerable impact upon the values, attitudes and actions of employees in both work and non-work domains' (Bowen and Orthner, 1991, p. 190).

How the formal and informal practices of managers are experienced can be found in their working styles and their attitudes to superiors, peers and subordinates. Potential areas of conflict can arise when expectations for themselves or for others are not fulfilled. The mismatch between an individual's values and that of an organisation is often undervalued in terms of losing managers and more attention should be afforded to this issue. While women have dominated the research in this area, organisational cultures continue to be styled by white, educated, men. Gordon (1991) argues that successful women have diluted their values to ensure they fit with the prevailing values of the dominant power base and in so doing becoming bound by an inauthentic persona. For some women managers the issue of having to be the face that fits in order to progress chips away at the façade they create until the only option is to leave to reclaim their authentic persona. Ten years after publishing *Women Managers: Travellers in a Male World* (1984), Marshall took a second look at women managers, collecting 16 stories of women who had left their roles with an overriding theme that they wanted be 'less defined by other people. They especially wanted senses of self – which – however multiple and relational...– they could validate internally...' (Marshall, 1995, p. 321). Being authentic is a difficult challenge for all of us to achieve and I think becomes harder the more complex environments we juggle.

Management requires a broad and flexible skill base which develops through the experiences gained from doing the job (Mintzberg, 2004; Peters, 1997). How a manager develops a style to work across the multiple relationships and situations encountered allows an examination of how symbolic competition can be brought to light as a useful way of thinking about organisational cultures. The managers in this section articulate their interpretation of the management style developed within their career journey. Accounts of positive and negative relationships with colleagues are shared and discussed within the framework of this dimension of competition. What emerged in some of the managers' accounts was the how tenure in an organisation allowed the boundaries and expectations to be clear. Establishing this knowledge enabled managers to create some space to fine-tune their style without disrupting their duty to the organisation.

The relationship a manager has with their organisation changes over time as hierarchies are climbed and markets challenge new ways of working. As individuals take on a much greater share of the responsibility for their own career planning and development, the relationships fostered in working scenarios can be very important in achieving the opportunities required to reach identified goals. Wajcman and Martin (2002) use and define the term 'market narrative' to describe how managers understand and explain their career paths and to account for their future choices. As Reich states, 'Now you owe your career to yourself. Financial success depends on how well you sell you. Selling yourself can be a full time job' (Reich, 2000, p. 133). He recommends connections as being crucial to meeting a person's working objectives and definitions of success. The majority of managers in this study have been with their current organisation for between one and five years which suggests some stability and commitment, although loyalty in the traditional 'job for life' sense was agreed to be a past way of thinking.

Management and leadership styles

The managers were generally agreed that amassing a rich tapestry of different experiences as individuals was important to creating a career which could withstand both predictable and unpredictable events and trends. Martha's account is a good illustration of how this study finds managers drawing upon their own observations and experiences for wisdom and direction. What also emerges is how important instincts are, often overriding analysis.

> Martha: In my experience with some adversity in business also comes some blessings and to overcome it you need to make sure your head is on right and definitely work the management part with your team because you can't do it solo, there's just no other way, so a good business has to have a good manager. I've hit the wall a few times about management things but you know we all do.

James is a senior director in a European publishing company based in London. He has climbed the corporate ladder in the publishing industry over the course of his career and has held his current position for nearly two years. James leads a team of about one hundred people and is responsible for the organisation's activity in the UK. Discussing his management style, it is clear that James has considered his position and persona in terms of his own performance. James' description contains the major hallmarks of a stereotypical masculine style of leadership, including the expectations he has for his team.

> James: If I was to describe my management style I would say I am antagonistic, ruthless and competitive, balanced with a good

dose of positive encouragement. I am competent at my job and I expect those that work for me to be competent at theirs.

Du Billing and Alvesson (2000) argue that understanding and evaluating the components of a feminine style of leadership would be more beneficial to debate than promoting the style itself. Distinctions between masculine and feminine styles of management need to be deconstructed to enable a more integrated approach that is not gender based. Like James, Amy describes her style as being a leader, which comes from being responsible for multiple teams in different countries. However, unlike James, Amy comments on the concerns she has about how, as a leader, she is perceived by her staff, a worry countered by a staff member who tells her that she is viewed as successful and knowledgeable. Her use of language, such as 'ruthless' and 'my way or the highway', suggests that, at times, Amy struggles with the balance between her position within the organisation, which she is clear about, and her approach, which fluctuates in terms of clarity. The organisation makes judgements about leaders and their value to the business and it is apparent that James and Amy are clear about this being the ultimate measure of external success.

Amy: One member of my staff said that people like working for successful people and they don't actually see me as ruthless, they see me as knowledgeable, and that I get people out when I need to. So I guess one of the things I worry about a little bit is, you know, am I going to be seen to be a – my way or the highway – kind of leader but ultimately there comes a point where that's actually what I am paid to do.

Ella has moved up the hierarchy from middle management to her first senior management position, which she has been in for 18 months. She notes a change in the aggressive element of her style, once intentionally practised to give her an edge, but one she considers not as necessary at this new level of senior management. However, she is happy with the legacy of being regarded as a bit scary. Ella's experiences of middle management could be interpreted as subscribing to a masculine stereotype of being competitive and aggressive as a means of being accepted alongside the men, trying to survive and progress. Having been with the same organisation over the past decade, the culture Ella describes appears to be demanding of its managers, especially those who are ambitious. Styles which include aggression to meet expectations and deliver results are rewarded with promotion, as Ella had found out, and in reaching a threshold in the hierarchy, different approaches and management styles can be enlisted.

> Ella: I have actually stopped beating desks to get things done, but I know that some people think I am a bit scary and I don't mind that because it gives me an edge.

The team Mark leads comprises men only and although he purports to have a consensus style of management, which he believes is best suited to his team, he does admit to ultimately being responsible for performance. In contrast to James, Mark is arguably more reflexive about his style, adapting to the demands of the situation and the people involved. This suggests the greater amount of experience in senior management roles, the greater the chance of being confident enough to be an engaging rather than a heroic manager, as Mintzberg (1973) describes. Mark retired once and took up his current position because, as he says, the challenge was too tempting. This suggests a degree of experience the other managers interviewed do not currently possess and may reflect in the more adaptable approach Mark describes. Unlike the other three managers, he does not use the language of aggression and although eager to succeed, appears to rely more acutely on his solid and underlying confidence as a leader.

> Mark: I ceased work a few years back and wasn't really going to go back into my profession. I was done with that, but this job is rather a unique sort of situation and opportunity and I made a decision that I'd probably live to regret it if I didn't give it a crack. So I will see this through to a certain stage and then I will happily go back to university to study the Classics.
> Int: How would you describe your management style?
> Mark: Consensus.
> Int: All the time?
> Mark: No, ultimately somebody has to make a decision but it's a small group and we operate a very flat structure. These are very bright, very intelligent people and a very hierarchical structure would not be one which would encourage their growth. So a more consensus approach is appropriate, but ultimately someone makes the call.

The hierarchical ladder of organisations tends to operate differently once a senior level of management is attained, and arguably the roles of leader and manager become much more entwined. However, degrees of experience at this level continue to influence how managers work and how over time they adapt to their new positional environments and the ensuing demands as shared by James, Grace, Ella and Mark. Understanding how each level of management works highlights how managers have to repeatedly reassess their styles to reflect their position. Concurrently with leadership comes a responsibility to be confident and, like many other human experiences, confidence is something that comes with practice and success.

The art of experience

Martha, who started her career at 18, has a wealth of experience beyond her years. She is matter of fact about the role of a management style, suggesting that hers responds to the demands of staff by assessing the most productive means of extracting their best performance. However, to achieve this Martha says it is important to be attuned to the people in the team and the organisational culture, quickly working out tactics to achieve the necessary work outputs. For Martha the goal is managing staff effectively by practising a style which is personally and professionally satisfying. Although Martha is confident in her style and her current level of middle management, this may change. She acknowledges that her style required having different tactics for different people, which includes, as she highlights, 'doing the fluffies' with some staff, as the means of getting a desired performance from them.

> Martha: I am very black and white in how I can process a lot of things and that works great with my current employer, but with other members of staff we have to do all the fluffies and we talk and it's repeated and it's more on the emotional side. That's part of management, you know, it's what process they need to get down and get their work done. People are all different, different upbringings, different cultures, different processing of the brain.

In contrast to Martha, Eve is confronted by her lack of a defined management style. Yet the essence of what she describes as important for her in terms of managing is similar to that of Martha. She accepts the differences between people and the need for managers to understand and work with a variety of personalities. These two women have similar career histories, working from the bottom up to the level of middle management where they are both now positioned. Eve, however, is very clear about the importance of combining her personal moral code with the demands of the job to ensure she sets a good example as a manager.

> Eve: I don't really have a particular management style and that is something maybe that's been a negative thing. I don't know, but we were always taught to have different management styles and have different hats because of the different personalities we're dealing with. But you do have to be above reproach and it is really hard to manage if you're not. You have to be honest.

The ranks of middle management are populated by potentially the most diverse group of managers. Within these ranks are the frustrated and ambitious like Angela, the experienced and content like Martha, and those seeking to develop a style which allows for the authentic person to be the authentic manager, like Eve.

> Angela: I would describe my management style as supportive and encouraging and adversarial in a positive way, being constructive.

Dopson and Neumann (1998) argue that middle management has become more generalist in many organisations in response to the scaling down of this level over time. This has resulted in the demand for a more flexible and adaptable style of management responding to the changing needs of the organisation. Middle management can provide an interesting and challenging environment which satisfies the current career needs of some managers, such as Eve and Martha, but can become a battleground for unfulfilled ambitions, as in Angela's case.

Building confidence and ambition

> There is a subtle way in which we are never given quite the full authority, never quite the full credit, never quite the full respect.
>
> Coe, 1992

While investigating how women can be more effectively incorporated into management structures, Coe (1992) found that only two thirds of the women she interviewed felt they received adequate respect from their male superiors. So is there a link between being given respect as a manager and building the confidence to become a more successful manager? Kanter says that 'power begets power' (Kanter,

1977, p. 168) – those who have it get more and those who have none continue to have none. Exploring how confidence is an important factor in becoming successful can inform strategies to help build it. Women working in management sectors appear to make more trade-offs than men, often in direct response to the additional responsibilities they carry in terms of care and domestic work (Schwartz, 1989; Still and Timms, 2000). This fundamental point of difference may be important in examining how men and women managers perceive competition at work and what effect this may have on building confidence and enjoying career success.

Martha has a confident attitude to work and motherhood and this is projected in her language in explaining her priorities. From the outset family comes first and having made this decision, Martha is in a strong position to maintain a satisfactory boundary between work and non-work. Confidence is a key factor in constructing relationships at work, particularly with superiors, and in the exemplar of Martha's story it is difficult to believe that she has not communicated her priorities to her superiors to ensure that there was an understanding from the start. Women who are not encouraged to be confident or who are driven by the fear of what might happen if they challenge the dominant culture are at a disadvantage on many levels, including negotiating working terms and conditions.

> Martha: I've got a daughter, you know, and making sure first of all that I'm a great mother to my daughter – the rest can take a hike. That's sort of my thinking … I would never compromise my family for a job because at the end of the day it's just a job.

Ella shared some thoughts about why women do not reach the top of organisations and although she too concludes that confidence is a factor, she also suggests that ambition plays a key role. In terms of ambition, Ella observes that in publishing, creative women only want to create and are therefore not interested in moving outside the discipline into middle or senior management. With an editorial background herself, Ella understands that in order to join the higher management ranks of the organisation it is important to demonstrate ambition in conjunction with displaying confidence. Ella has struck an interesting insight with the creative women who want to create. This is a conundrum which we have probably all experienced in some way or other, trying to understand why some people are ambitious and some people simply are not. Do both parties see ambition in the same way? For Ella, ambition is clearly about promotion and climbing the ladder to reach some place near the top, and for someone sitting in the creative department this might seem like madness. They may wonder why anyone would want to sit in meetings all day, work many hours and travel when they could be designing fantastic new products. It is the psychological contract with an organisation where ambition and confidence sit and by its very nature it has multiple interpretations. In an article in the *Guardian* (Steiner, 2012), a collection of regrets of the dying recorded by an palliative care nurse in Australia revealed that most of the people wished they had not worked so much. Should be shocked or scolded? It's a tough call because, as many will respond, it's not as simple as that. Perhaps it should be.

Ella: There appear to be two reasons why women don't reach the next level: firstly they are not ambitious enough and secondly they lack confidence. In my company the ambition thing is because women work in creative and editorial areas and they just want to create so as long as they do that they are happy. The confidence thing applies more to women like me at my level.

The trade-offs people can make to ensure they meet their own personal life requirements are often measured by the financial sacrifices made to secure more time, but they may also be measured by reductions made in personal and career development opportunities which may or may not limit their ambition and confidence. Felicity is adamant that a manager should be accountable for not providing feedback and acknowledgement to staff, suggesting its strong connection to building foundations for confidence and success.

Felicity: Success, that's about a hunger for acknowledgment. Crap managers don't give positive feedback to staff so everyone is hungry to do something that is noticed. Personal success is about acknowledgment.

Furthermore she suggests that when managers promote acknowledgement as a fixed or limited resource it can make staff 'hungry' for attention. The idea of hunger as a basic human need can result in behaviour that could be interpreted as a zero sum competition when it is more likely to be rivalry. Felicity's description presents a scenario which places the successful manager as one who encourages confidence in their subordinates as the gateway to success as opposed to the poor manager who is unable to enlist empathy of any kind. Uhl-Bien and Maslyn (2003) suggest that reciprocity between a manager and subordinates is an area which can measure the value and quality of the relationship. They observe negative reciprocity resulting in lower levels of performance and conscientiousness, with the opposite being true of positive reciprocity.

Acknowledgment for managers can be experienced directly from superiors or indirectly through the undervalued process of reflected glory as subordinates' efforts are recognised. John combines success and satisfaction as the key factors important to him. Both John and Felicity see the relationship between success and recognition via acknowledgment as integral for themselves as individuals but more importantly as managers responsible for a team.

> John: I am always trying to gain personal and reflective satisfaction from my peers and staff. I do compete with myself but not necessarily to improve who I am and what I do but to get more recognition. Success for me is about recognition for the work I do and the work my team does.

As the layers of a manager's experience are unpacked, it becomes increasingly evident that some practices at work which are unintentional or unchallenged can persist throughout a career causing negative effects on workers. Making a connection between the value of acknowledgement as a management tool for building confidence in subordinates is important and this requires more attention to be placed on the social skills desirable in a good manager.

Esther is new to management, with only two years of experience in her first and current role. Esther draws on the negative aspects of being a subordinate to challenge her own approach to developing a management style that is fair and reasonable. This raises some questions over the performance of her former manager who was unable to exercise authority in a measured way, and suggests that when a subordinate feels they are in some unidentifiable competition with their superior the relationship is likely to deteriorate.

> Esther: My first boss was a woman and she was always competing with me to prove that she was better than I was. She only ever communicated the negative stuff, never the positive and always did it in front of others. She saw subordinates

as mud on her feet and treated them the same way. She certainly made me aware of everything you shouldn't do to staff and how you should treat subordinates as it is very easy to lose their respect.

Esther continues to share her experience of this relationship and becomes angry at her former manager who as a woman appears to have let down – not just Esther, but women managers in general. How this experience influences Esther's conclusion about wanting to work for men is difficult to ascertain but she is not alone in stating this preference. In a Gallup poll conducted annually since 1982, men continue to be preferred as a boss year on year, but change is being recorded. In 2006 the poll indicates that although 37 per cent prefer a man and only 19 per cent prefer a woman, 43 per cent have no preference. Powell et al. (2002) conducted studies in 1979 and 1984 hypothesising that a good manager would be androgynous (high in masculine and feminine traits). In both studies they found that a good manager was defined in predominantly masculine terms. In 1999, repeating the study for a third time, they found that good managers were still perceived to possess more masculine characteristics, although the margins had lessened. They argue that stereotypes continue to hinder the development of women by restricting their behaviour. Stereotypes, as Schein repeatedly observes (Schein, 1975, Schein and Muller, 1992 and Schein et al., 1996), are a barrier for women as they seek to overcome entrenched views of a manager being male.

> Esther: My boss made me angry because she was confirming to everyone that women didn't make good managers. I had thought that having a woman boss would be good and thought she will do things that are not 'a man's way' but now I prefer to work for men.

As this study shows, the scrutiny, often hidden, which some women managers face from their female subordinates can over-emphasise their gender in their management role. Do women managers experience a double bind of stereotypes: those that seek to constrain them by comparison to men and those that seek to judge them against unrealistic expectations by other women?

Lois, in a similar way to Esther, expects women managers to have learned more than she thinks they have. The combination of anger and disappointment which pervades what both these managers say is concerning. Perhaps when we see a wider range of men and women having successful long term careers that are not boxed into a traditional career model, we will also see less idealist expectations of women by other women.

> Lois: Women bosses tend to take two views, either support or no support, but with both it is on their terms and is often driven by personal attitudes. There isn't one woman who I can look at and say, yeah, I would like to be like her, they don't exist and if they do I never come across them.

The disillusionment Lois shares in discussing women managers may suggest a lack of role models which show a spectrum of authentic career options for other women. I would like to argue that what Lois and other women are suggesting is that there has been a societal seduction about firsts. For example, we have countless examples of the first woman to become a CEO of a multinational, the first woman to be president, the first women to become a millionaire and so on. Every time there is a 'first' story it becomes too easy to believe that there can be a second and a third, which increases expectations for women. I cannot recall a story which starts – 'Today for the thousandth time a woman reached, was awarded, was promoted etc.' I would also argue that until we have both variety and a critical mass of women across management hierarchies, bad women managers will be held to a higher standard than bad male managers. Mavin (2006) comments that whether stated or not, the 'blame or fix women' position can become a default mechanism which continues to marginalise women in management. The indication that some women managers are unable to meet the expectations other women set for them can lead to conflict within working relationships. This is difficult to resolve because of the personally held, and often hidden, views of the individuals involved.

Amelia works a flexible schedule to accommodate school hours twice a week and periods of school holidays. She finds in the employment process there is a noticeable distinction between the behaviour of men and women and often the 'best man for the job' gets it because of the confidence he demonstrates.

> Amelia: I have had to employ a good few people over the years and I still find that generally women are much less able to negotiate for more money and benefits and sometimes appear to just be grateful for the interview. Men on the other hand

come across as ambitious and available for a price that they set, which gives you the impression of confidence and in this business that's important.

This is a situation Amelia would like to see changed so that competition for positions is based on a package which includes skill, talent and confidence; a combination she believes is important. As for herself, she maintains that getting her own levels of confidence right is difficult and an on-going process. So why do women managers find developing confidence at work seemingly more difficult than men and what impact does this have on career trajectories?

Amelia: At times I want to shake some of the women I see and tell them to be more positive about what they have to offer. There are a few though that do stand out as confident and self-assured, and they teach me a thing or two in that area. I have learnt that there are many shades of confidence and how you portray it is an important part of what you offer to an employer. I think men are just so up front about it that it's just over the top, but it does work although I couldn't do it like that.

Why women managers can be perceived as not exhibiting enough ambition and confidence may be a result of the definitions used in organisations, which portray male versions of confidence as the norm. Blackaby et al. (1999) found in their study of senior women managers in Wales that women's confidence was easily undermined, and that this marked a difference with men, who often have much more support in developing confidence through mentors and networks. Early successes in a career can build the confidence repeatedly referred to by the mangers in this study as necessary for longer term career progression.

Taking stock of confidence

Exploring how managers assess their people development requirements is often overlooked, probably because of a lack of time – yet taking a measure of what young and inexperienced subordinates need in terms of guidance is important. The connection between early experiences and creating a foundation for a career which is based on confidence, curiosity and commitment should be a successful formula. When I interviewed Zoe, the only part time manager, she was in the midst of inducting three women graduates and was obviously shocked by their lack of interpretative skills. The qualities Zoe cites as important for successful progression she found lacking in the graduates, raising the question of how and where those skills are learned and from whom. The wake-up call of coming face to face with young and inexperienced graduates underlines how important the teaching aspect of management is.

> Zoe: I can't believe their lack of interpretative skills at this stage. They're just check listing things. They don't think – and that's really important if you're going to be successful, you've got to be on the ball. You've got to be time focused and driven and you have got to understand the scope of the job and what your role is in it. You have to have attention to detail, be energetic and focused on that end result.

Furthermore, leaders expect their managers to admit their weaknesses and compensate for them by delegating or appointing the appropriately skilled people. Having a manager such as Zoe, who is aware of the level expected, can be an important process for graduates to begin identifying and shaping their own strengths and weaknesses. However, many women managers are sensitive about their weaknesses and may be more likely to avoid this step with their subordinates.

The perpetuation of not laying the foundations for confidence may be an area which also should be highlighted for discussion. Some women managers want to avoid any message around weakness which may suggest they are not good enough for the job. Addressing this response is complicated and predicated on a prevailing environment that is not welcoming to women managers. Confidence is required to stake a claim to being a full citizen of the labour market and when enough women do that then it won't really matter about being welcome, because the space will already be shared.

While confidence is shown to accelerate when it is supported and nourished with acknowledgement and guidance, the most effective way to achieve this is to have more good managers who recognise their influence on their subordinates' futures. The observations made by Ella and Grace suggest that managers presenting themselves as confident leads to them being perceived by peers to be confident. In a similar way to Kanter's argument that 'power begets power', I would say that confidence begets confidence. However, there is no right or wrong way of acting or being confident. But as a cycle – however one views it – it is self-perpetuating. As Grace suggests, it also supports the argument that women managers largely remain uncompetitive.

Elaine shares her experience of how passive men can be when confronted with gender and the opportunity to openly confident about her position. The situation many women managers face in meetings, when they are or see themselves as the token female, is repeatedly said to be isolating. For some men this type of situation can provide the platform to be sexist, rude and antagonistic, claiming the spotlight for themselves and marginalising not just the women but the men who sit on the side-line doing nothing. Some people might describe this as confident behaviour but it is clearly better described as uncivilised. But what of the men who are too uncomfortable to challenge the situation?

> Elaine: I was often the only woman at management meetings and this was at times quite intimidating and I had to put up with the snide comments that floated around and the roving eyes that always seemed to land on my boobs. Some of the men were great and were supportive of some of the things I had to put up with but they never supported me in public, only when quietly walking back to the car park or whatever.

Does the presence of a lone woman accentuate the desire by some men to perform their gender more overtly? The answer to this question is important to understanding gender performance and the fluidity of gender. Whenever there is an accentuated gender spilt in terms of a numerical imbalance, the likelihood of some individuals behaving in stereotypical ways such as being sexist indicates a discomfort with the group make-up. As Elaine explains, some of the men offered support (albeit not openly) and this exposed their discomfort. However, while this tug of gender war is being pushed and pulled by the men, Elaine is left recognising that she is still isolated in such a situation. Should this situation result in an attack on Elaine's confidence or should she just accept the isolation of this event and move on? There should be some consolation in recognising that no one was confident in their attitudes and behaviours apart from Elaine, who walked in and out of the meeting as the same person and the same manager.

Women managers are increasingly taking their place within management hierarchies of organisations, and for some the road has been smooth. For others it is a story of structural, attitudinal and behavioural impediments gradually negotiated over time. However, the male manager norm found in many organisations continues to contribute to the gendered experiences of management hierarchies. Acker (2000), in her own experiences of managing an equity project, admits to her frustration of having a colleague go on maternity leave and compromising the project timeline. What is important to note is that without the honesty of frustration there cannot be the rational thinking that follows which can effect change. Women perhaps need to be more honest about the human condition in terms of their roles as managers. Acker is just as likely to be frustrated if it was a man who went on extended paternity leave, so it is only a woman problem if people make it one.

Although women and men managers in many situations exemplify the progress made in working together, some women managers, as cited in this project, continue to face the same barriers and experiences found in the glass ceiling, glass walls and sticky floor debates. Concurrently, women managers appear to be increasingly adroit at analysing and understanding their position in their management environment. Negotiating difficult situations when work is not always a hospitable place to be, as argued by Davidson and Burke (2000) and Horlick (1997), is without question a challenge and while many women can identify with this there are also many men who can make the same claim. However, in undertaking my research it would have been easy to spend time and energy repeating the analysis already evident in the body of work which examines these issues. My aim is to present competition and competitive relations as a dynamic which can illuminate new thinking about old and new issues around gender, management and into wider society. While external and personal competition as dimensions of the concept were accepted by women managers as a necessary element of doing business, they were less likely than the men in this study to have spent time and energy considering and practising some elements of competition as a dynamic.

Women in the workplace

Being a manager and a woman can result in being judged by other women in terms outside the parameters of their positional role. This is evident in the descriptions of the relationships between women managers, their women superiors, peers and subordinates. Some women in this study shared experiences where they felt disappointment and anger at the behaviour of women managers. Such behaviours include a failure to act as role models, being openly ambitious and having heroic management styles. The expectations held by some women in my research suggest a sisterhood exists which is perceived in the same way by all women. When the realisation emerges that not all women managers are good at what they do, or that some have bought into the dominant masculine management culture to succeed, or simply don't want to have a career, they are often demonised.

Why women direct expectations onto other women in the labour market is possibly a phenomenon responding to the newness of seeing women in society succeed at work, be financially independent and well educated, and have choices about how they live their lives. Yet for me the question is how long until the newness has dulled and the reality of women in society doing lots of different things well is accepted as the norm? Women who look directly to senior women managers for guidance on what is possible in terms of balancing a career and a family and an authentic persona did not in this study find any positive results. On the other hand this suggests a need to recognise multiple versions of having a career, a family and a life and that life is about compromises. More often when we judge people and their life package we are judging the compromises they have made without necessarily understanding the context of choices and constraints.

Casting women managers who demonstrate ambition and the will to succeed as somehow behaving in an unacceptable manner continues to foster different standards for men and women. This can have a negative effect on junior managers who begin to realise that on the journey up the management hierarchy they too will become subject to the expectations they project onto their superiors. There are suggestions by some managers that such observations did act as a deterrent for them entering middle and senior management. What was surprising. however, is that there was no mention by the managers of wanting to become a manager in order to make changes and be part of the continuing transformation process.

Sometimes it is difficult to avoid thinking that it is easier to believe that women are equal in the labour market, because this lets men and women off the hook. Having worked in the gender and management space for a while it is worth mentioning that come August every year most people I know who also work in this arena sign off in order to sit in the sun, drink cold beer and talk about sport, books, holidays, cooking and anything other than women or gender. But for as long as we witness the continued re-emergence of queen bee related discourses there is a stark reminder that women as a group still have to resolve the obstacles which are enforced by women based stereotypes around ambition, commitment and success.

Elaine's reference to some women squashing those who stand in their way illustrates how the queen bee syndrome continues to be perpetuated. There needs to be some widespread recognition that the sisterhood is not about solidarity in management styles. It is about girls and women having access to health, education, dignity, financial independence and the choice about how to live one's own life; the same as boys and men.

> Elaine: I have come across some women who are very open about
> wanting to reach the top and who make it very clear that
> you don't want to cross them or you will be squashed. This
> attitude I have always found quite sad because they end up
> looking petty to their colleagues and just plain intimidating
> to their staff. They do often have pretty high staff turnover
> which is hardly surprising really.

While it is likely in any organisation that some individuals will practise management styles which are considered by some as innovative, others may consider them single-minded and cut-throat. While the gender of the manager should not be part of judgement this is sadly not the case. As long as women managers continue to be held to account for their actions in ways that men managers are not and are singled out as a problem, especially by other women, queens bees will continue to distract women from bigger and arguably more important issues like challenging the power base which privileges only a few. Schein (2007) argues that equality at work will not be achieved while current organisational structures (where there is often one major site of power) are accepted.

So while the sisterhood is a convenient cover all for women casting judgement, it is the feminists who emerged as strong and successful women in this study, proud of what they achieved because of the women that went before them. While feminism continues to attract controversy, often without foundation or based on a stereotype, it is also rejected by many groups of women, young and old, who subscribe to not being politically active. The pity with such a position is the dismissal of the contributions feminism continues to make in the areas of business, academia, education and social justice. Rindfleish (2000), in her study of senior women managers, found four types of perspectives on feminism: conservatives, moderates, reluctant feminists and definite feminists. The decades of supporters and critics, who together have assembled a wealth of knowledge on gender, offer invaluable resources as we face new struggles in our world such as population growth, ageing generations and emerging economies growing at exponential rates. What the feminists in this study have reminded me is how the younger generation, who appear to be taking choice and freedom as a right, need to grab that opportunity, but not without recognising the right to be an active citizen.

Policies, projections and propaganda

For at least the past 30 years discussions about the future of work have taken place in human resources (HR), business, government and academia. Research on the value of flexible working has taken centre stage, quickly followed by government policies in the UK which now offer the opportunity to request flexible work arrangements. While some issues facing women and men with children have progressed, as seen in extended maternity, paternity and paternal leave legislation and policies, the issue of combining work and family continues to reinforce stereotypes that working women are a problem – unable to fit into the rigid organisations and their equally static temporal structures.

In my interviews with this group of managers and wider conversations with individuals who work in variety of ways, some aspect of temporal competition was identified with by everyone. However, there was some predictability about temporal competition being keenly experienced by women with children or those thinking about starting a family and wondering how to plan a future combining care and career. While the focus around work and family has centred on children, the future impact of the ageing population is beginning to gain some air time. In a UN report, 'World Population Ageing 1950–2050' (2002), the number of older persons is cited as having tripled over the past 50 years and is predicted to triple again over the next 50 years.

While the developed world currently has the most older people, this trend is expanding into the developing world where the numbers are growing year on year. When this report was written the global banking crisis had not happened and so pensions and welfare systems were not threatened in the way they are post-crisis. Two interesting trends emerging are the decrease of older males working in contrast to the increasing share of the older workforce being taken up by women, and the general increase of literacy rates across men and women globally. What is a societal challenge is how to prioritise the needs of the old and younger populations when there are so many struggles in breaking down the structures which discourage women from joining and remaining in the workforce. The UN report draws on an earlier statement to summarise the future challenge, which is 'to ensure that people everywhere will be enabled to age with security and dignity and continue to participate in their societies as citizens with full rights'. At the same time, 'the rights of older persons should not be incompatible with those of other age groups, and the reciprocal relationships between the generations must be nurtured and encouraged' (United Nations, 2001, paras 9 and 14). How this will impact on women's lives at work and at home is something that is still only quietly being discussed and will no doubt become more evident as the impact of government austerity measures, falling pensions values and unemployment dig into Western societies. While women have increased their labour market participation rates over the past 50 years, in a response to inhospitable working patterns, women have taken up part time work as a means of balancing the time clashes between work, home and school hours. The UK and Australia exemplify how attempts to reorganise working patterns have not fully resolved the issue of women working and having a family and it is easy to see this situation exacerbating as elder care increases in the mix.

The hidden brain drain is the phenomenon where women are found to be working below their skills base in part time work to juggle the intersection of family and work. This loss to the labour market is unquestionably wasteful and is detrimental to a career path which can lead to building confidence and achieving success. Hakim 's Preference Theory (2000) suggests three classifications for women: work centred, home centred and adaptives. Making up the largest category, adaptives reflect the transient nature of many women's careers as they move between full time, maternity, part time and full time working patterns or opt for self-employment. Part time work in the UK is dominated by administration, care and customer service sectors, which lend themselves to flexible shorter hours or unsocial hours which enables some juggling with childcare. In these scenarios it is arguably impossible to be thinking about ambition, career development, skill evaluation, further education or full time work. Whether adapatives would be better described as survivalists is a question which perhaps provides some insights into why women more generally struggle with confidence. Having the capacity to state one's career ambitions publicly is not easy when there are so many variables to consider before actually making such a commitment, and even then changes can still happen, as McRae (2003) found in her study with first time mothers. There are instances when a lack of confidence in women in management is viewed as something too broad and does not pick up the more subtle issue of being confident to make a career commitment knowing that one is actually able to deliver.

Then there are questions such as what happens if my children are sick? How much time will there be to enjoy my family when I am not working? How will I manage to travel overnight when we have no extended family nearby? How will we pay for additional childcare while I am still proving myself on a lower wage? What happens when the trains are delayed? How soon do I have to get to after school club? Will my children suffer because they don't have any freedom after school and can't join a team or go to gymnastics? I think women are more prone to recognise that they need to cover the potential of failing, not because they are not up to the job, but because they are not capable of a constant work rate coupled by the double whammy of not earning enough money to buy in the domestic services. The rate of managers working part time in the UK is about 4 per cent of management roles. These positions are usually, as Tomlinson et al. (2009) found, existing roles which were negotiated down in terms of hours rather than the creation of new part time managerial jobs.

Conclusion

The replacement of linear careers with portfolio careers, as predicted by Baruch (2004), has made less impact on society than expected. While there has been a rise of small business enterprises, particularly among women, these can range from contracting and freelance contracts, to product or service based businesses. When I think of the people I know who would fall into this category I can name someone who makes and sells herbal remedies for horses, and a few who do PR, media and marketing, cleaning and ironing, and catering. Not all these women have gone down this route because of children. The reason is similar to what Still and Timms (2000) found in what they describe as a 'do it yourself' response to finding a job and career that is lifestyle proof, profitable and anti-corporate. When we think about managers it is the traditional picture of a man in a suit, working for a big organisation which dominates – when in actual fact all of the women running the businesses mentioned above are managers, and seemingly pretty good ones at that, judging on their sustainable business models and the quality of their holidays.

While linear career models continue to dominate the management sector, what has changed is that workers generally no longer expect a job for life and also no longer see the corporate world as the only option for pursuing a management career. This results in an increased demand for individuals to ensure they continue to develop their skills and stay engaged with how they want to be perceived by the labour market, depending on what choices may lie ahead. In such an environment of individualised career development the role of competition would be expected to increase, as Beck (2002) suggests, making building a competition cage a useful asset.

One of the key assets for managers is to build an authentic persona which is flexible enough to make compromises when necessary but strong enough to withstand the provocative behaviours of others in the workplace. While some women appear to have navigated around the judgements, others remain locked in supporting queen bee discourses which only serve to weaken their position as authentic, confident managers. Moving away from stagnant debates around women in management could positively serve a platform where confidence and success in whatever format are complimented and encouraged. The recurring themes in dominant discourses and the motives behind keeping these discourses relevant, reminds us all of the importance of challenging them. While there may be a cost in disrupting the status quo, a better understanding of the dimensions of competition and the behaviours of the competitors could allow calculated and risk neutral strategic disruptions in organisations.

7
Collisions with Time

Introduction

Thinking about time as a resource, a currency, a constraint and/or a competitor requires time. This may appear a cruel irony given the challenge many people face on a daily basis to complete a range of tasks at work, at home and across an array of other circumstances and environments. But for as long as time equates to money and is used to measure productivity and commitment, battles will continue between individuals and organisations to control the ownership of time as a resource. Selling one's labour to the market inextricably binds the individual to the static temporal structures governing many aspects of society, including the workplace. In this way temporal competition activates the pendulum of choice and constraint, locking individuals into a spiral of seemingly endless dilemmas of finding the right type of time in the right place.

The tensions surfacing around the concept of time tend to focus on it as a resource fixed into globally understood segments of hours, days and weeks. The general population divides a day into two main streams of activity: work and sleep. What time is left can include a multitude of other tasks and activities such as domestic responsibilities or leisure activities. The private sphere is where frustrations and conflicts are often acutely experienced, driving the popular comment that there is never enough time in the day. The rhetoric of work–life balance has gained ground over recent years, giving rise to debates focusing on women and their role as working mothers. While there are certainly issues for this group, such discussions project working women as disruptive to the workplace and deviate away from challenging the way society values time.

Temporal competition is defined as the ways and means time, as a fixed resource and a commodity, directly or indirectly, becomes a competitor with an individual in all aspects of their life. Unlike the other dimensions, temporal competition interacts with all the other dimensions, yet is probably the most invisible, because of its subliminal integration into our lives. Temporal competition is a useful lens to examine the behaviours and attitudes practised by managers, consciously or unconsciously. How managers compete for and with time presents new ways of understanding how organisational relationships for managers, their peers and superiors remain tied to static temporal structures which can limit attitudinal shifts towards flexible organisations.

This chapter seeks to release time from the constraints of work–life balance discussions by defining the concept as a dimension which can productively engage and support the development and maintenance of an effective competition cage.

Paid and non-paid work

The tensions between paid work time and non-paid work time are fluid and not easily resolved. Literature and policy on work–life balance, family friendly workplaces and flexible working is comprehensive in the areas of maternity/paternity and the process of returning to work. However, there is less evidence of a wider focus which should include the life stages of children, multiple maternity/paternity leaves, elder care, family sickness and sabbaticals. Temporal competition has its roots in the working culture whose premise is that time is money, which creates the situation where time that has no economic base is diametrically opposed to time that does. So leisure activities, holidays, family activities, voluntary work, domestic and care work all operate outside the time is money zone. Placing one side of life (working) against another side of life (everything else) is difficult and suggests that trying to unpack this conundrum is simply going to be too time consuming. However, this could arguably be considered an easy opt out and an avoidance of the issue that society as a whole needs to re-evaluate the different issues faced at different stages of the lifecycle.

Gerson and Jacobs (2004) argue that social change in America over the previous five decades has borne five interconnected dilemmas or time divides: work/family divide, occupational divide, aspiration divide, parenting divide and the gender divide. As a summary this analysis is a sound contribution to the role of time in connection with work, leisure, parenting and gender and outlines how temporal competition can be a useful category for explaining these divides. How and where individuals perceive they are competing with time can result in a zero sum game where time, or the perceived owner of time, always wins. However, if the terms of perception change, and the competition is viewed differently, then perhaps multiple relationships with time could be subsumed into working and living cultures.

Work–life balance, married to the company, greedy organisations and quality family time are examples of discourses managers can find difficult to address adequately. Whether from a personal perspective of juggling work and home or managing the various demands of subordinates and their changing situations, hard choices may ultimately need to be made to meet the demands of the organisation. Starting a family may personalise the shortcomings of family friendly policies and attitudes to maternity and paternity leave. Deciding not to have children may also change a manager's view on how the demands of working parents should be met. Retirement plans, outside interests and other care responsibilities beyond children can all impact on how the attitudes towards policies are held and implemented by managers. Do junior members of staff see the way their superiors are treated and question how their work and home needs will be accommodated in the future? Organisations which profess to encourage family friendly policies to support workers and managers to fulfil interchangeable roles in their lives often have limitations. These restraints are likely to originate from within the organisational culture, which in turn influences the managers who are at the front line of implementing different work patterns. How this translates into meaningful take up of policies by managers and their teams remains scattered, with a mix of progression and stagnant responses to levels of cultural encouragement and support.

Holidays and leisure

Holidays are an opportunity to step outside the routine of daily work and have benefits for managers and organisations, as it is increasingly accepted that all work and no play is neither physically nor mentally healthy for people, even if the level of work satisfaction is extremely high (Massey, 1995). How managers cope with holidays is not always straightforward in terms of letting go of work, which in fact is complicated by the availability of 'keep in touch' technology. Only recently I heard a senior manager of a financial services organisation say how holidays were now possible because of technology because you can be with the children on the beach and available to clients. While I accept that some clients are demanding, relinquishing the relationship to a colleague or team member for a period of time should be feasible in most cases. The situation where technology makes and allows managers to be available 24/7 is as much about curbing a perception of being invaluable as enforcing disciplines which limit the invasion on non-working time.

David is a managing director of a transport based organisation and makes the claim that holidays are an important opportunity for managers to assess different roles and to break the routine of working practices.

> David: Holidays are a different story because if you can't take your holiday then someone isn't doing their job. It's important for staff to get a fresh perspective on their job by having others do it while they are away. Holidays are also a useful management tool for assessing a role and how it can be improved.

While David's view about holidays is a valuable contribution to the discussion and makes a good case for time away from work for managers and workers, individual circumstances can complicate the holiday intention. Bittman and Wajcman (2000) argue that leisure time has become more fragmented, with unpaid work being a dominant feature. They argue that although men have more pure leisure time than women, the difference between parents and non-parents is as marked as that of gender. For women and men with children, leisure time can be a combination of domestic and care work and entertainment, with holidays similarly composed. The value of this break away from work can be different for managers, as they have to spend the majority of time in what is often only a part time identity, as compared with their dominant management identity. In some cases the clash of identities can be difficult to resolve. Some managers, as Hochschild (1997) found in her study, admitted that working long hours was a viable way of escaping the chaos of home which they perceived as out of control. The often intense situations managers may face can be further complicated by the on-going changes which come with different life stages.

Amelia, a senior executive, shares her struggles to define the boundaries of work adequately.

> Amelia: I tend to work on Sundays rather than Saturdays and my husband will watch the football while I work. Then he doesn't feel like I've stolen quality time off him. I've thought about it and not just ignored it because otherwise it does kind of build up, and it's taken a bit of trial and

> error, that's for sure. On holiday I have a ten minute rule,
> started by my husband, which is I'm allowed ten minutes a
> day to check my Blackberry, so I have some time manage-
> ment techniques around to restrain myself.

Juggling home and work time by intentionally identifying practices that
enable both zones to co-exist illustrates the often dominating nature
of organisational time over leisure time. Recognising that the boundaries, no matter how loose, between the personal and the public space
are important to maintain has, as Amelia admits, taken some time to
achieve. What is often missed in achieving a balance is the conclusion
that in order to maintain the balance the need for adjustments has no
expiry date and is continuous. Balancing working time with the impact
on personal relationships is for some managers too difficult to reconcile
and there are plenty of sad stories of broken families. Other managers
may be more open to accepting their weaknesses in achieving a balance
and rely on the intentional practices of their partners and families to
remain grounded in life outside work.

The competition between work time and family time is often a battleground for managers which can be presented in different realities. Mark
is in his late forties and came out of early retirement a year ago to take
on his current business acquisitions role. Mark suggests that the answer
to how many hours a week he works would differ between himself and
his wife. However, he admits that with his return to the workforce he
is better at taking holidays and enforcing this for his staff, even if it
is referred to as 'grabbing two weeks' which suggests a rushed or last
minute approach to taking time away from work. Mark's relationship
with time remains dominated by work, and, like Amelia, he is reliant on
his partner to encourage time away doing other activities.

> Mark: How many hours do I work? Well there's the answer I'd give
> and there's the answer my wife would give you. But it's 60
> to 70. In terms of holidays I have actually I've got pretty
> good at it in this life; I was terrible at it in a former life but
> on the whole yes. Mostly we're pretty rigorous about trying
> to enforce staff taking holidays. Over Christmas and New
> Year it's pretty slow so it's comparatively easy to take time off
> then and grab two weeks.

David admits that for him working time and leisure time often co-exist.
He identifies the least definable aspect of work, thinking time, which
cannot be confined to prescribed hours. For managers who already

work long hours, being distracted by thinking about work can increase the likelihood of conflicts at home as the boundaries encroach upon one another. Finding space and time to think is not always easy and for many operates alongside leisure activities, as David explains. Probably one of the greatest challenges we face as the lines blur between so many aspects of our lives is confining our thinking to the appropriate environment. This becomes more blurry as our workplaces often extend into our homes. While working from home is one feature of flexible working practices which more people are utilising, there is a cost. The option of home working has the obvious time bonuses by removing travel time to an office. What one does in this additional time may vary from school runs, exercise, visiting elderly relatives or some other activity. However, working from home does continue to break down the boundaries between the public and private space and can actually result in working longer hours – just in a more fragmented way.

> David: When does the work stop and start and where do you include the thinking is an on-going dilemma for me. Finding the balance of self-time is also hard. I was swimming this morning and all I was thinking about was work; it's hard to shut that off sometimes.

In a similar vein to David's experience of thinking time is the question of where travelling time fits in the space between work and home. If an average working day is eight hours with an additional one hour round trip, this can negatively impact on perceptions of long hours at work. Defining travelling time as work time rather than non-work time is difficult, as for some people it is an opportunity to relax and read the newspaper or listen to music and move comfortably between the sectors of work and home. John is a senior publishing manager in his mid-forties and commutes to work every day, an experience he defines as a necessary evil. However, he does claim the time as his own and suggests that his fellow commuters do the same. On the surface this may appear a time luxury but, as all commuters know, the unpredictability of public transport can be stressful as indeed can the constraint of timetables. So perhaps the necessary evil position which affords some space for thinking is the trade-off on the choice and constraint pendulum.

> John: I catch a train every day and I am committed to timetables, especially in the morning, but once I walk out my front door I do enjoy the prospect of having an hour to do the cross-word and read my paper. Like most of my commuter friends

we rarely do work, using the time for ourselves. There has to be some perk to this necessary evil.

Temporal competition intends to challenge our perceptions and experiences of different aspects of time in relation to work and home. The inference of the work–life balance proponents suggests on one level that work and life are different. Taking this language a step further suggests that if we could compartmentalise work and life then we would also be able to correct any imbalances more easily. By exploring time away from the workplace it becomes obvious that every stage of life brings different challenges and joys, some of which we can predict, others which are beyond our control. However, finding time to simply be and take a moment, often described as getting off the bus, cannot be prescribed for holidays, commuting or leisure activities as the components of life are fast moving.

Working practices of temporal competition

How time for an individual manager is structured within an organisation during a working week is influenced not just by the tasks they need to undertake but by those tasks which involve interacting with subordinates, peers or superiors. Across the spectrum of practices some managers use to exercise authority over others' time, the scheduling and duration of meetings is probably the most popular. However, for middle managers particularly, time is a resource over which they can have limited control as the impact of superiors, peers and subordinates can dominate daily schedules. Liff and Ward (2001) found in their study that senior managers reportedly enjoyed the opportunity to manage their own time, using their position to make meeting times which suited their diary, having previously been dictated to by superiors.

Lois is in her early thirties and a middle manager; she has found herself powerless in some meetings because of the combination of her position and gender.

Lois: I was in a meeting the other day and it went on for five hours. The guy who was running it would just not even look at me because I was a women and I am managing the project. He is ringing me all the time and I know it's going to be a nightmare. Meetings are so often unnecessary and just a power trip for men.

A manager may be required to attend a meeting but have little or no control over the agenda or manner in which meetings are conducted and may experience the frustration of what is experienced as a zero sum temporal competition. The use of meetings can reflect prevailing organisational attitudes which are difficult to challenge within the management hierarchy.

Jake is a number two in a publishing company and raises the point that meetings are often run by senior managers who are not always skilled in running meetings to an agenda. As temporal competition interacts with positional competition the process of conducting a meeting is governed by how experienced the manager is in utilising this mechanic. Jake has a different experience to Lois as he uses his position to actively take on the role of his superior, replacing him and his meeting style with a more efficient and effective practice.

Jake: I have 45 minute meetings now and in the last month we have not run over this time limit. People are arriving better prepared to contribute and they are arguably more productive. We have a GM who is prone to meetings without agendas or time limits and some of them went on for hours and people didn't contribute and generally got bored and then had to work late to meet our deadlines. Over some months I have persuaded him that it is more effective for me to run the meetings which he is now pleased to not be responsible for.

For Clem the experience of meetings was dominated by subordinates in her team which created a major barrier to being able to do her job and eventually resulted in her leaving the organisation. Responsible for a team, Clem became the point of contact for all problems for all the team and found herself experiencing the fallout from being too available. The specific fallout was incremental increases in her working day to get her own tasks completed after spending too much time with her team members. Clem perceived this experience as a zero sum competition with her subordinates and by default, with time. By asking for more guidance, personal support and problem solving her subordinates were increasingly taking control of her time and becoming powerful dictators of how Clem's day was constructed. As many managers will testify, the art and practice of managing staff, like other management skills, is often only learned through experience. Without guidance and support for managers such functional responsibilities can be mismanaged, get out of control and result in detrimental and costly outcomes personally and professionally.

> Clem: In my last job I left because of the people managing – do you know how sick and tired I got of managing people and thinking for them? You know, I would get one staff member coming to me with an issue and then I'd have the whole bloody lot of them lining up outside my office so all day all I did was solve their problems.

Meetings are a good example where the differing meanings and practices in relation to time can present some managers with an opportunity to communicate effectively with their colleagues, while others are subjected to the frustrating power plays of superiors operating a zero sum competition. Making a connection between time and the power to demand it from others can reinforce meetings as a site for accentuating hierarchical positioning and power. As a result this feeds into reinforcing an organisational culture which projects overtones of traditional male dominated versions of management.

Perceptions of busyness

'I'm so busy' is part of a popular discourse used by managers, especially the most time poor, as both a statement of fact and a tactic which offers some of protection from essential or emotional requests. However, like many terms, the more often we hear it, the less impact it has. Using 'I'm too busy' as a reason for not being able to do something is understandable occasionally. However, as a default position questions around different interpretations of 'busy' usually emerge, creating potential rivalries among people to see who is the busiest. Rivalries which often lead to interpersonal conflict are viewed as interpersonal competition which distorts the dimension which is actually most relevant – temporal competition.

Felicity is a senior communications manager who has recently discovered how her perception of time is influenced by the attitudes and behaviour of people who dominate her working environment. This observation was triggered by a new role in a new organisation. She comments that throughout her career, working over and above the hours of nine to five was regarded as normal and relative to how she described her own sense of busyness. In her new role Felicity has noticed an organisational attitude to working hours which has re-defined her own sense of work time. In this new organisation colleagues, she says, are markedly less frantic compared with her experiences of other organisations. What is interesting is how quickly and positively Felicity responded to this new definition of 'busy' and the prevailing culture of leaving on time, and not taking even a moment to feel guilty about working only the prescribed hours.

> Felicity: In this job busy is just not busy, I am horrified by what they think busy is – but I do like their version. Unless there is something on, people down tools at 5.25 ready to walk out the door at 5.30 and no one appears to feel guilty; in fact it is more like their right to do so.

Putting 'time management' into a Google search and getting over 1.3 million pages highlights how many different versions of telling us to think about time and task allocations consciously there are. One might suspect that as a society we have not learnt how to do time management sustainably. While I have never been on a time management course, I have read a few books on the subject and usually find a common focus on making 'to do' lists from which priorities are made. While this logic is sound, being busy is more complicated than being simply about making lists. Being busy captures for many people a life filled with complex responsibilities in multiple environments. The working element of being busy is another layer of complex responsibilities and demands, particularly for managers generally and especially women managers with dependent children. One question worth asking managers is how effective they are at delegating up and down the hierarchy and, if they are not, whether this is one key to resolving some time issues. Too many times I hear managers tell me they are too busy to delegate because by the time they explained the task they could have done themselves. This may be true but taking the time once to delegate means the task can be repeatedly done by someone else and can be embedded in their role.

Hochschild (1997) found in her seminal study that time is often experienced as a constraint for managers. She found both men and women using work as a refuge from the chaos of home life complicated by an inability to see how to resolve work and non-work conflicts and simply choosing to avoid them. Matt is a middle manager in a large organisation and also subscribes to this theme of constraint, commenting how he feels he is a part of a large group of people for whom not having enough hours in the day is the norm.

> Matt: Probably like lots of people time is one of my biggest constraints; there are just never enough hours in the day to get everything done.

A manager's relationship with time is influenced and developed by organisational practices and attitudes which can advocate a constrained sense of time in relationships. Felicity, in reviewing her distinct experiences, does not suggest that in keeping to regular hours the organisation she works for is any less competitive, nor is productivity anything but satisfactory. Miller (2005) published an article which featured a number of senior managers from large American companies who addressed their work roles questioning the trade-offs and sacrifices they make to do their jobs. These managers (predominantly men) were reorganising not just the way they work but the ways their teams work to reduce their hours and allow for weekends and holidays. Time and work is a tension filled relationship, not helped by the 24/7 mantra which has taken root alongside globalisation. In real terms 24/7 should relate to businesses, and not people.

Twentieth Century Fox now employs two presidents who are jointly responsible for the company. This position emerged in response to the demands of the organisation, the industry and the realisation that one president could not do the job. The recognition that some roles have become too big for one person suggests that more thinking and research is required on how to accommodate the needs of businesses and the people working in them. Adam (2003) argues that change in how working time is understood and experienced is unlikely to see transformation in organisations until time is considered by senior managers beyond merely outputs (profits) against a fixed resource (time). The problem in waiting for transformation is that the lives of many senior managers do not resonate with the lives of the people who populate their organisations. Male senior managers who dominate this upper part of the hierarchy are likely to have a wife/partner who does not work, releasing them from the daily responsibilities which most other people experience in any number of different combinations. The idea of a human sized job is probably a concept which should be given more thought. But in order to think about job redesign, cultural redesign is also necessary. For as long as success and ambition fit into a package which has a perceived co-relation with face time, temporal competition will continue to exist in the background. Howard Schultz, chairman of Starbucks, points out that 'The problem won't be solved by working smarter or tinkering at the margins to add flexibility.'

Miller (2005) shares the story of Gregg Slager, a senior partner in Mergers and Acquisitions at Ernst and Young, who had two young children and worked 80 hours a week. At a time when he was reviewing his own work pace, the young professionals working in his team said they were not going to put up with the work pace year on year. In response Slager set about changing the way he and his department worked. Over a period of six months he and his team rethought every job and real-located tasks to the point where holidays are now taken and weekend work is not the norm. The team discovered that by rethinking time and work they could deliver better business performances and improve their own lives. This example supports what Schultz is saying and suggests that disembodying jobs would be a useful process to evaluate how jobs should be designed to fit with the needs of the business and of workers.

Discourses of double burdens, double shifts and double days reflect time for managers – particularly women managers who have depen-dent children (under 16 years of age). How women managers experi-ence time may be influenced by the performance they believe society demands of them. The residual influence of the 'having it all' (which I think must be past its sell by date) has been replaced with a reality of 'doing it all'. Zoe is a middle manager in her mid-thirties and is honest about admitting that she uses 'I'm so busy' as a tool to navigate certain areas of her life. She says that because it is widely understood this makes it viable to use to justify decisions and behaviours to different people at work and at home. Concurrently Zoe struggles to resolve the conflict between work and motherhood, accepting the on-going diffi-culties of being in the right place at the right time.

> Zoe: I think I like the persona of being busy or frantic. What I do is I complain about it to try and use it…you know what it's like. Oh sorry I couldn't see you, I was so busy, and it's like an excuse to try and justify why I haven't spent time with people. And then everybody thinks I hate my life because I'm always justifying…I'm saying, I'm sorry for whatever. I'm always busy. But I don't actually hate it. I mean I do hate it but I don't want to be totally a mother and I don't want to totally be a worker and I just don't know how you get that balance.

Fran is a middle manager, married with two school age children in her mid-forties. She has been in her current position for three years, returning to full time work when her youngest child started school. Like Zoe, Fran would be categorised as falling into the time poor group of working mothers yet she admits to being frustrated by the 'I'm so busy' discourse. Fran thinks people should relax and stop trying to compete with the clock, because it is a zero sum game. By focusing on time as a hold all for issues around work, career, family, childcare, eldercare and stress, time becomes a distraction. How in each of those elements of life society considers the value of time is where the thinking needs to be directed. To assist this process I would argue that using the different dimensions of competition and placing time in the middle would allow a visual map which marks the points of intersection. Establishing this picture allows individuals to see pathways which suit their needs and also illuminates the alternatives for others, which, it is hoped, would generate some wider thinking about society.

> Fran: I get really tired of people saying they are so busy; it is such a cop out. I work and have children and sure I don't get everything done but then it does come down to priorities and time management, which I think has lost favour as a skill at work and at home.

I certainly think that people should just relax a bit more about trying to be the busiest or whatever; it has just become so repetitive and makes me feel like I am in a competition or something, which is just futile. I say put your feet up when you can and don't be afraid to admit you spent the evening watching TV and not spring cleaning the pantry before writing a strategy document for work.

Temporal competition challenges the status quo of the way we think about paid work. This requires looking at why the breadwinner model still dominates the labour market even when two people from a household are economically active. For as long as the breadwinner model is predicated on a combination of time and availability within a traditional model of work and home, the static structures of many organisations will preclude equal access to management careers for men and women. Society increasingly recognises the many varieties of family which exist but has not managed to change the way we think about traditional notions of work.

Women and working time

Time as a catalyst has led to debates over the gendered nature of time and the barriers this places on individuals, particularly women who have a family. Dex and Bond (2005) identify 48 hours of work per week as the marker over which stress dramatically increases, and that women aged between 36 and 45 years are the group which on average are the most time poor. The manifestations of work and time can present a number of scenarios where too often prevailing male dominated norms of organisational structures, behaviours and attitudes dominate the labour market landscape. The assimilation of women in large numbers into the labour market, particularly women with dependent children in dual or single earning families, has not generally been supported by changes in temporal structures.

Couprie (2007) reports that on average single women in Britain spend ten hours a week doing chores, while single men spend seven hours, women in a couple fifteen hours and men in a couple five hours. Chores are defined as being confined to the house and are an additional element to the working day. This puts pressure on key parts of the day and dictates how days are constructed. For example, childcare and education facilities generally offer pre-defined daily schedules of up to 12 hours, from, say, 6.30am to 6.30pm. However, the homogenous approach by childcare and schools to a manager's day being 9 to 5 does not often meet the organisation's approach to a working day which is frequently arguably longer. Second, although we are reportedly told by the media that we live in a 24/7 society, this is not strictly true. Many services, such as doctors and dentists, are not available outside of working hours except in emergencies and this can increase the pressure on time to fulfil the needs of children and extended family. I would argue that gendering time at work and at home has resulted in creating a complex site of tension for women, particularly as they juggle between the two spheres of care and career (Siriani and Negrey, 2000). However, to focus on women managers with children should not be taken to suggest that this group are unique in their experiences of gendered time and it is important to continue exploring a spectrum of experiences from men and women over demographic profiles.

Serving the long hours culture

A culture of long hours in organisations continues to create barriers for some women managers who for a variety of reasons do not or cannot offer the same degree of visual commitment as their male counterparts. Accepting overtime as an implied daily demand for managers should be challenged across organisations. However, it is unquestionably difficult to do this as a single voice, further complicated by economic downturns in global markets. But what can be challenged through visible performance and productivity is why, for reasons including career progression, job enjoyment and job security, some managers succeed without using presenteeism as a tactic to demonstrate unconditional commitment to their work (Massey, 1995; Simpson, 1998; Blair-Loy and Jacobs, 2003). Presenteeism is defined as the extent to which managers remain at work when the demands of their job do not require it. Simpson's study found that men are more likely to subscribe to this activity. She argues that as a competitive element presenteeism is prac-tised and developed down an organisational hierarchy, embedding itself in the culture. Rutherford (2001) observes that some organisa-tions use long hours as a fear tactic to motivate managers, potentially leading to internal rivalries between managers to see who can work the most hours.

The managers I interviewed were sensitive to the long hours cultures pervading the organisations they work for and generally agreed that men were more likely to use time as a tactic against peers and subor-dinates to secure additional power. Jill, a manager in her mid-thirties, lives with her partner and has no children although she is very open about the fact that she wants to start a family soon. She has been with her current organisation for five years and in her current senior manage-ment position for a year. She finds the compulsion to present a working persona based on always being available for work difficult to resolve. The situation Jill shares demonstrates an example of a colleague using an intentional working practice to meet a real or perceived expectation by an organisation of being available at all times.

Jill: I know one guy who writes all his emails and then sends them from home at 11.30 at night to make people think he is working late – that is very sad.

Jill is certainly resolute about not having signed up to being available without reason on an unlimited basis. Her attitude to working time does not appear to have disadvantaged her career progression given her recent promotion. While the managers interviewed largely accept the culture of long hours, they did not accept, as Powell and Graves (2003) argue, that non-compliance would result in career suicide. What becomes relevant is the purpose for long hours which, if important, is considered part of the contract as distinct from the long hours associ-ated with face time.

However, what is interesting is that when motherhood is the reason for increased adherence to regular hours, a different set of rules and responses begins to emerge. This implies that organisations are oper-ating multiple practices in regard to time and temporal competition, perpetuating the importance of presenteeism to some, often young men, while making mothers feel isolated and underperforming. When organisational cultures target different groups with different messages the managers and workers as a whole are purposefully fragmented, making challenges more difficult as they are perceived as single issues.

Julia is in her early thirties and a middle manager in a publishing company, is single with no children and, like Jill, sees long hours as a tactic to lever potential progression at work, impressing superiors by committing time to the job. However, Julia also suggests that men, particularly, use long hours as a tactic to get support at home from wives, especially those wives who do not work. The scenario Julia describes conforms to a notion of maintaining a management model where senior managers have non-working or part time working wives at home supporting their career. As Wajcman (1998) describes, the dependence of men on women to provide their domestic and caring functions is predicated on the norm of men being managers. Julia, in identifying the scenario and the gendered nature of time, has, like Jill and the women managers in Simpson's (1998) study, made a clear association between organisational attitudes, time and men's behavioural outputs.

> Julia: I think with long hours it's a power thing, trying to impress the bosses, and also men are using work as a way of making their position seem important to their wives or whatever, making out they have had a hard day when they get home.

Proposing that some men use long hours as a means of avoiding domestic and caring responsibilities and activities presupposes that within some family units the man's working status is considered more important than the woman's. This position perpetuates the breadwinner model and creates a bubble for those managers who are protected from all the other work involved in running a house and a family, whether immediate or extended. This bubble is possibly the greatest barrier to equal access to management for men and women because it is rare to find a person who can step out of their position and see that their road was easier to navigate because of their privileged position. Bradley, whose work on gendered power I have drawn upon in my thinking on dimensions of competition, argues that, 'It is harder for those in receipt of privileges to accept they have attained these because of their gender, class or ethnic attributes, rather than because of their own individual efforts…If women are indeed to be equal competitors, then men see their own chance of promotion and economic advantage weakened' (Bradley, 1999, p. 74). While this can be hard to accept because it requires personal reflectivity and open mindedness, it reminds us all about the value of transparency within systems so there is some leverage for those without privilege.

Elaine is not convinced by the idea that men work harder than women. She relates back to her childhood and seeing her father describe the hard day and long hours he worked, covertly comparing his day to her mother's as somehow more important. Elaine is a relative newcomer to middle management, having been in her current role for less than a year. She is single with no children and works on average 41–50 hours per week which she considers the norm for her position. As more women enter middle and senior management they become privy to the workings of organisations and the illusions that have been perpetuated in the past but again are being exposed to the transparency of insights.

> Elaine: I remember when we were kids and dad worked all hours and
> we were made to think that he was having a harder day than
> anyone else, especially my mother. Now I am in the business
> world myself I know that a lot of times it was just a façade
> and an excuse to be looked after when he got home.

The projection of men's work and women's work being valued differently continues to be broken down as more women become managers and traditional social roles are disrupted along with the thinking that has supported their maintenance.

Juggling commitments

Suggestions that the relationship between long hours and the organisation is like a marriage indicate how strong the cultural bind may be for some managers. Susan observes how some women (she does not mention men) have found the expectation of long hours impossible to commit to, leaving to find other more culturally compatible alternatives. Those alternatives, as research shows (Marshall, 1995), are a combination of enterprise, competitive organisations and different industry sectors.

Susan is a middle manager in her early thirties, living with her partner, has no children, and has been in her current position for four years. She likens her work to a marriage between the organisation and manager, suggesting a level of commitment which goes beyond a contract to deliver a set of tasks in return for a fixed financial reward. The discourses surrounding work and time are filled with emotive language, such as 'marriage' and 'commitment', 'workaholic', 'work to live' and 'career suicide'. The impact of such terms is a persuasive influence and can make it difficult to be pragmatic about finding ways of managing the varying components of a manager's life.

Susan: I know some women who have left because they found the responsibility of long hours and being married to the company too much to deal with.

Ella is a senior manager in a European publishing company. She has worked there for ten years and in her current role, three years. She is in her mid-forties, married with a preschool child, and comments on the positive experience of maternity leave. However, now having been back at work full time for quite a while, she recognises how her options are governed by dominant organisational attitudes to commitment. She remembers a colleague who left after having a baby because the culture did not support her new life package of early motherhood and management. Like Susan, who spoke of being married to the company, Ella talks about the organisation being a family. Such emotive terms as' marriage' and 'family' underpin how much some organisations demand from their people. It is difficult not to question whether the degree of manipulation is perhaps extreme. Even if in a family, it would be reasonable to expect support in times of need and patience for lifestyle changes. However, the danger for organisations in failing to accept change in the people who work there is the potential and inevitable loss of valuable skills and contributions. Continued myopia in demanding one-sided commitment and loyalty will surely become a competitive disadvantage in terms of retention for those organisations who fail to have a more flexible approach to the lives of managers.

Ella: There was recently a woman who had been with the company for years and she was responsible for revenue generation of £100 million and she went off to have a baby. When she returned life was not easy and she left two months later. Although they stay well within the law there is an attitude at the top that you must be fully committed to the company, it's like a family, you work and you socialise together. You live to work is the philosophy and women need to keep children in the background. Work must come first.

Fran has two children and shares a positive experience of her organisation who supported her role as a manager and mother when she separated from her husband. The loyalty her organisation demonstrated in this highly distressing situation allowed Fran the opportunity to work and be at home without the pressure of defined hours while she put together a new structure for her and her children. By agreeing with her boss to remove the pressure of time Fran was able to meet her work responsibilities and rescue her life without major disruption to either. For this manager having the capacity to do some damage limitation was certainly, in Fran's view, of immense value. An additional bonus was how she unknowingly acted as a role model to a younger woman who was struggling to work out how to work and have a family. Fran suggested that the key element for the young woman was the honesty which Fran had demonstrated at work, highlighting that an organisation cannot support their staff if they don't know the problem.

> Fran: The last company I worked for were very supportive of me having children, especially when I separated from my husband – the younger women with children were very generous in their admiration and said they found me a role model. One woman especially who found herself pregnant and single told me that seeing me organise my life meant she felt she could too and returned to work after the baby was born.

Liff and Ward (2001) found that junior managers – especially women – found it difficult to rationalise how they could combine a family and a career and stated that a lack of role models in senior management did seem to make it less likely. The combination of career and motherhood is fraught with issues, highlighted by a lack of sustainable and growing numbers of women in senior roles. The issue of sustainable numbers is one which should draw more attention than it does because when talking about ratios of men to women at c-suite level, a merger or acquisition can skew figures both positively and negatively. In the discussion of quotas for women on boards this is one issue which might be resolved with some formal targets. My point in an earlier chapter, that we are still reading media stories about the first woman for this, and the first woman for that, should be worrying. But while in some quarters change is slow and painful to watch, it is worth looking for some bright spots. Standing in a school yard dropping off kids there is real life evidence that attitudes are progressing. There is a mix of parents, there are stories of compressed hours, home and office working, four-day-week jobs, self–employment, stay at homes mums and stay at home dads. I think sometimes it is important for all of us to reach outside of our social bubble and take stock of what is going on around us to get some flavours of reality. I think it is also important not to judge managers and organisations based on the global corporates alone as the labour market is a mixed bag. While such evidence is anecdotal, I can say that I have stood in school yards in Australia, London and Yorkshire and the observations are similar. Sceptics who think this may be about one-off football matches or school plays should know that this is not the right impression because week after week it is the same people with the same stories.

Decisions and consequences

The decision to choose a career instead of a family is for some men and women quite clear cut. For others it is a much more sensitive issue and a difficult decision to reach. Society ultimately places the decision making process of having children, and as a result the care requirements, with women because of biology. But taking care out of the equation, having children and a career remains an ambitious and financially demanding task for women. At this junction in the life-cycle, men and women expose their different socialising experiences, revealing actual, not spoken, beliefs and values. For example, it may seem reasonable for other women to work and have children but when it becomes personal the process is more complicated. With gender relations intersecting on so many levels around the children question it is no wonder that we spend so much time talking policy, practice and preference. The other issue which emerges in this discussion is that what happens when there is one child is often quite different to when there are two or more children.

Hewlett (2002) argues that women who want to combine career and family need to be presented with the 'gift of time' by employers. I would extend this to say that women need to be extended the gift of time without limits and restraints to truly allow for the opportunity to participate in the labour market. However, as proven, time is not available and nor is a societal wisdom and foresight to think about women's career models in different ways thus ensuring the hidden brain drain is not the final resting place for the careers of women with children. The hidden brain drain has been identified by the Equal Opportunities Commission (EOC) in a study of flexible work. The research shows 5.6 million part timers in Britain working below their potential (EOC, 2005). Connelly and Gregory argue that managers are the highest group of people who on moving from full time to part time downgrade their position by giving up managerial and supervisory aspects. They found that '29% of corporate managers downgrade mainly to clerical positions and 47% of other managers usually in smaller businesses downgrade usually staying in the same sector but in lesser roles. For example a salon manager goes back to being a hairdresser' (Connelly and Gregory, 2008, pp. 71–2).

Grace's experience of a change in the relationship she had with her boss after she become pregnant suggests how sacrificing a career for motherhood can be presented as a fait accompli by superiors who cannot consider a subordinate having more than one major priority. Grace is a manager in her early forties with two children one, of whom is a preschooler. She has worked in the publishing industry for the majority of her career and has been in her current role for three years. She has spent some time being self-employed as a consultant, allowing her to have children and work at a pace she set for herself. Her current role allows her to work flexible hours, which she comments does have a financial implication, but at this stage she accepts she is not a strong negotiating position.

> Grace: In terms of my career I did have a job where the boss saw me as a younger version of herself and was helpful in building my career. But once she found out I was pregnant the relationship changed completely – I actually resigned prior to giving birth.

Fran, who earlier described the positive support she received from her organisation, also observed an incident which exposed her experience as being unique or at least not widespread across the organisation. A managerial colleague returned to work after having a baby and was openly penalised for not being readily available to the organisation. Not only was her new role as a mother regarded as unacceptable, it was openly tested in a way which isolated her from her peers, showing her to be a token, not just as a woman manager, but as a mother.

> Fran: I worked with one woman who had a baby and when she came back to work her boss changed all the management meetings to breakfast meetings. It was certainly perceived that he was trying to make life difficult for her knowing she had to take the baby to childcare in the morning.

Himmelweit and Siagla (2001) identified matching childcare and working hours as a constraint faced by mothers, arguing that attitudes of employers and government need to change to acknowledge this crucial area of constraint. The competition to control the time resource of others is demonstrated in this example where a senior manager is using their power to reinforce their own position. This type of response to a perceived change of priorities could be based on stereotypes of working mothers being unable to commit fully to their jobs. Using time as the mechanic to test commitment makes it almost impossible for the woman manager in question to counter as she is constrained by the combination of childcare hours and employer attitudes.

Flexible working or just family friendly

Adam (1995) identifies that part of the problem with time is that people generally do not give it due consideration and yet continue to have days dominated by work. In this way an individual sells time to an organisation which then controls it, often beyond the terms of the contract. At the extreme end of the time and work spectrum is work addiction, where work becomes all embracing. The term 'workaholic' has been widely used for some decades now and, as Killinger (2006) explains, the difference between a hard worker and a 'workaholic' is that a hard worker maintains a balance between the private and public spheres of their life. She suggests that 'making a resolution to save 25% of your energy to bring home every night and putting fence around your weekends to protect yourself from temptations are both good ideas' (p. 62).

Gerson and Jacobs (2004) argue that when cultural messages simultaneously stress both the work ethic and family values people feel torn because it is difficult to enact conflicting values at the same time. They say 'competing values cannot serve as a roadmap for action' (Gerson and Jacobs, 2004, p. 61). Exploring temporal competition shows how flexible working has become caught in a stereotype of applying to predominantly women with children. To fully explore flexible working it is necessary to move beyond the rhetoric of family friendly policies and place it at the centre of working practices which are available to all. Flexible working should not be stuck in discourses of maternity leave and part time working because all this does is embed the process of fragmenting parents from the non-parents.

Policies and legislation which seek to address the needs of pregnancy, birth, preschool children and, to a lesser extent, older children or extended family are referred to as being family friendly. 'Family friendly' is defined by Callan (2007) as a formal or informal set of terms and conditions which are designed to enable an employee to combine family responsibilities with employment. How well such policies are embedded into organisations remains an issue of debate. Research suggests that take up is not uniform and that pregnant women are often targeted with redundancy (EOC, 2004).

Sarah is a manager who works on average 50 hours a week, is divorced and does not have children. She views the focus on supporting parents as a burden which she and her colleagues without children, rather than the organisation, carry. This can make it particularly difficult for managers without children to implement and support policies with which they have adverse personal issues.

Concluding that those workers without children should work longer hours to cover those with children is difficult and contentious. However, discourses around flexible working and family friendly policies contribute to underpinning opinions which suggest that the needs of only some people are considered. Although this may be true, the difference in how organisations deal with parents shows the glaringly opposite effects on managers. Demonising parents, particularly mothers, and the relative time they commit to their jobs and their family is a good example of how the issue of temporal competition can operate negatively. Accepting time as an invisible but constant presence can distract managers from considering time in any other way than work time or clock time. One of Hochschild's respondents describes a 'clay layer of middle management' (Hochschild, 1997, p. 31) where family friendly policies often remain unimplemented. Sarah is an example of how this is embodied in a hierarchy and in the attitudes of managers and workers.

> Sarah: They force the burden too much on those seen as not having families, i.e. children. We lose leave entitlement and have to work longer hours.

Liz is a manager who has been in her current position for four years. She is in her early forties, lives with her partner and has no children but does have a number of horses which are an important part of her life. She takes a broader view of family friendly practices and discusses what she describes as a dilemma for women. She sees mothers in a no win situation. Whether mothers want or need to work, society criticises them and makes the workplace pretty unfriendly. Liz sees getting policy and practice right for working mothers as being the key to getting work and life practices right for workers generally. The observations women managers make in relation to other women acknowledges their differences and, as discussed in earlier chapters, can fuel excessive personal judgements. However, Liz suggests that as a feminist it is important to remember that it is always about the bigger picture, not just the individual at a certain point in time. But taking the temperature on how policies, discourses and practices are operating within an organisation can be constructive for everyone. Meyerson and Kolb (2000) agree with Liz's observations when they argue that a bridge needs be made between feminist theory and everyday practices to push forward with societal transformation.

> Liz: I think that although much has changed that drives society, society has also created a dilemma for women. If they don't work they are criticised, if they do work and have kids they have to manage and not be seen neglecting their kids. It's difficult and I don't see much changing on this issues which does seem to be important to all the other issues about work and life.

The approach Martha takes to managing a work–life balance for her team is people oriented. She presents scenarios where staff are able to work flexibly to encompass activities outside of work, including those associated with children. Her experiences of individuals calling in sick to avoid asking for time off reflects the pressure some organisations, managers and peers can place on staff is judging these situations as unacceptable. Although Martha suggests that the association between family and flexible work is strong, she does not agree that family is just about children.

> Martha: We very much promote if you need time off for something with your family to let us know so I can plan it rather than ring me at six in the morning to say you're sick when I know you're not. I have one member of staff who has a son with a disability and she has to attend progress meetings, and I have another who has a really sporty daughter and so she wants to go off to some of her events. We factor this in and each of the staff covers others to get that flexible environment and I really think it works. I would be concerned if somebody was here and was so work focused because it shows their life is out of balance.

How a manager defines their style in relation to flexible working arrangements is a key area in assessing why some organisations are more progressive than others, and why some departments have distinctly different views and actions on implementation. Martha, in her account, shows that she has given the issue consideration and has taken the approach of fostering the positive outcome of workers having a balance between work and non-work. Callan (2007) found that organisations predominantly left the application of policies to managers, who in turn felt constrained by them, anticipating that full implementation would leave them under-resourced to fulfil the objectives of the organisation. In Callan's study, it was primarily the women managers with dependent children or those thinking about starting a family who discussed this issue. They suggest that there were few instances of seeing family friendly polices work to enable family and work to be combined to the satisfaction of all parties. Managers who themselves may be in conflict with work and non-work responsibilities are likely to assume that if the policies are not going to work for their team, it is unlikely they themselves with be able to use them successfully. This is a double edged sword which is fuelled by management stereotypes which set the ideal worker as male and available because he is supported at home by a female.

Liz is an exception. Openly describing herself as a feminist, her insights into the changes occurring in the workplace add weight to the work achieved in terms of equality in the labour market. She shares how she has seen the dynamics among women in management change as policies and practices have enabled realistic choices to be made by women to have a career and a family without having to aspire to the hollow 'having it all' package which has never been helpful in this area. Hewlett (2002) found some women who felt cheated out of the family choice by leaving it biologically too late. It was inferred that some were falsely seduced by thinking that technology would solve any biological problems surrounding conception. Sadly, this scenario is a trade-off which can leave women feeling that their career is all there is and, as Liz says, this can feel like a monumental sacrifice.

Senior women managers, as Liff and Ward (2001) found, describe the downside of their roles as trying to maintain two roles of manager and mother, whereas their male counterparts merely express regret at not having as much family time as they would like. However, for the women who have chosen career over family their reality is likely to be dominated by work, and like men, they have no experience of living in a double shift of work and care.

Liz: There seems to be a noticeable change with women, particularly in senior management, as you get older. These are women who have sacrificed their ovaries for the company and I don't know whether you would call it jealousy or envy but they seem to be very negative about women who supposedly have it all. It's almost like they worked for women to have better working conditions and opportunities but they don't want progress to be right under their nose.

Unfortunately Liz appears to be in a minority in terms of her socially focused thinking. This is partly because she is a senior manager who is still in the minority and who is aware of how many of her colleagues and peers have full time wives at home. It is still rare to find full time house-husbands, which is something that should concern society if we want to achieve equality at home and at work. The erratic nature of organisations and their approaches to temporal competition continue to impede the development of a workplace which satisfies the lifestyle needs of men and women managers.

Conclusion

Temporal competition does not have to be a zero sum game but, as found in the experiences of many managers, this is too often the dominant perspective. While time and money remain locked in a relationship which conforms to a mainstream way of doing business, managers also remain locked in a job design which allows for one kind of almost constantly available manager. Acker argues that jobs become embodied with the values and attitudes of the people who do them. While she is examining the gendering of jobs and hierarchies, I would further argue that in a similar way temporal values become embodied in jobs depending on who is doing the job. The connection between job design and temporal competition is a critical relationship which should provide new ways of thinking about how we work in terms of a broader framework than simply morning to late afternoon, five days a week. Evidence shows that when managers cannot see a way to navigate through the living archives of organisational cultures which perpetuate success in terms of serving long hours and keeping distinct work and home, they leave. Time is the currency which differentiates the privileged and powerful managers from the majority who live in a reality where breadwinners are from a bygone era, where parents work and look after children and family as well as striving to succeed as managers.

The value of using temporal competition to examine how we work enforces the importance of recognising that time is owned by individuals and although it is for sale to the labour market, ownership needs to be retained by the individual across all the aspects of their lives. Managers particularly need to reclaim the notion of time as a resource which they are charged with utilising effectively and efficiently for the good of the individuals in their team and, as a result, the organisation. To evaluate how we can work in different ways to achieve the desired results is a challenge but one which should be exciting and adventurous as we acknowledge a changing world.

8
Beyond Winning and Losing

> You cannot go on 'explaining away' forever: you will find that
> you have explained explanation itself away. You cannot go
> on 'seeing through' things for ever. The whole point of seeing
> through something is to see something through it.
>
> C.S. Lewis (1978)

In this final chapter I want to do three things. First, I want to return
to the five questions posed in Chapter 1 and briefly answer them.
Second, I want to introduce the social theory of communities of practice and discuss how this can contribute to expanding the knowledge
of competition. Third, I want to look at what happens next.

In this book I have shared the process by which the managers I spoke
to related their experiences and perceptions of competition. The first
level response often described a general concept centred on a dichotomy
of winning and losing. This highlights how considering competition as dualism is limited, and confirms the proposition made in this
book that competition is largely invisible and unarticulated among
managers and across management hierarchies. The grounded theory
framework used for building accounts of competition gained depth and
breadth throughout the interviewing process. As the managers, with
some probing, moved past first level responses they often enacted a
process of exploration and interpretation from which their own rich
and diverse experiences emerged. This process was further informed
by a small group of the managers interviewed who do engage with
multiple dimensions of competition, demonstrating how the dynamic
can be motivating and challenging. However, it remains that clarity
in defining multiple dimensions of competition is rarely addressed by

managers regardless of whether or not they are engaging with one or more dimensions in their working lives.

Is competition gendered? This question challenges us to find new way of looking at the environment of gender and management. This book is a contribution to that challenge. To identify competition as a lens shows how a concept largely accepted by managers as inherent in markets and in organisations does not translate into a body of knowledge or experience which managers understand beyond the dualism of winning and losing. To find that competition in management is gendered is to support and add to the large body of research and debate which finds organisational structures, behaviours and attitudes are gendered.

How and in what ways do men and women in the workplace perceive and experience competition and competitive relations differently?

The taboo of competition in society is more potent for women than for men. This potency may lie dormant in some sections of society but becomes dynamic when women enter the workplace where careers are a package of ambition, promotion, performance and success. Achievement of such a package is certainly accentuated on entering management, and competition on some levels become unavoidable. Hearing managers refer to competition as a necessary evil illustrates the vehemence which competition attracts, and yet external competition is intrinsically embedded in a three way relationship between the manager, the organisation and the wider commercial world. While this outcome was readily shared in the managers' stories, similar outcomes with the other dimensions of competition did not result. The relationship between external and personal competition is keenly felt by the managers who repeatedly describe their personal sense of responsibility to the organisation and their position. The further up the hierarchy one goes an increased sense of responsibility is found, superseding other considerations such as being concerned with the judgements of peers and subordinates. The ease with which managers spoke of doing their best, securing more business and commanding market leader type positions in their industry demonstrates how, when competition and competitive relations are disembodied as found in external competition, a comfortable relationship is described.

The currency and practice of external competition was generally agreed by the managers as being somewhat separate from other competitive dimensions, whether or not these dimensions were consciously acknowledged. The two main frameworks used to guide further interactions with competition at work are limited. For some managers (mostly men), drawing on sporting contexts of competition is the main point of reference. While this foundation is undoubtedly solid, it is weakened by a lack of discussion about the distinct differences between sporting and working arenas. However, experience and knowledge of sport and competition are advantageous in driving a fundamental recognition of competition and its dynamism. Managers (mostly women) who refer to a concept of healthy competition in the workplace are also limited on several fronts, such as by a lack of definition combined with mixed messages of what 'healthy' actually is, and no evaluation or discussion following the repeated failure and disappointment associated with the description.

But I think it is important to take the question back a few steps and point out the importance of recognising that, with or without competition, men and women experience the workplace differently. As the broad and deep body of work on women in management research has found, women are still considered outsiders in the labour market and in management. While women may have accessed education with diligent and impressive results as a group, they have not achieved the same outcomes at work. Yes, there has been progress on many fronts and women are now found in most occupational sectors, although they are still clustered in traditional roles such as caring, teaching and administering. The workplace has as yet been able to achieve a proposition where women and men can seamlessly have children and work and not at some point in that process be financially dependent on the other unless that is the choice they make. This is further complicated by women who can achieve independence until they have children, when the stereotypes come raging to the surface, illuminating the social issues of who should be looking after the children: the mother, the childcare provider, extended family or the father? While women cannot discard the traditional caring role which society has assigned them for generations, the workplace is likely to retain and be influenced by the shards of this living history.

But all around, at big and small organisations, women are there working and achieving varying degrees of success. What this picture misses, though, are the faces of women from the top to the bottom of the pyramid of workers and managers. At the top women are often still tokens and below the top tier, women are smaller in number than they should be if the pipeline worked. What tends to happen is that women look up the pipeline and see how difficult it is to achieve the top positions without significant sacrifices in other areas of their lives. However,, many if not most, men at the top usually have a wife at home and operate a traditional breadwinner model which makes such sacrifices less significant.

Such a complicated picture of the workplace is one which women navigate often without support or knowledge and this can help us understand why competition is often not given consideration. In talking to the managers, the question I kept asking myself is why these smart and savvy people had not worked out more of the competition picture, especially the women. The male managers all led busy lives and yet, whatever their personal opinion, communicated some rationale of thinking which at least enabled some analysis of where the experience stopped. But management is a hard world where the demands to perform tasks, lead others, think tactically and strategically are often never ending. This is most acute for middle managers who sit at the crossroads of organisations where what goes up and what comes down the hierarchy has to pass through their position.

How do competitive relations at work affect relationships between individuals of the same gender and those of different genders?

This question is loaded with personal attitudes and values which influence relationships and the perceptions of those relationships. Men certainly struggle to break down the perception that they are not a homogenous group and this is reported in the stories of men who manipulate their values to be accepted. Whether it is the suppression of sexual or cultural preferences, men in organisations suffer from having to accept that they do not fit the norm if they bring their authentic identity to work. The difference between this situation and that of women is that women's bodies are marked as different from the norm before even beginning the process of confronting the other aspects of their identity. The relationships at work when mapped are complex across superiors, peers and subordinates, and within these complexities are strands of gender, role models, networks, friends, colleagues and associates. Notions of women in the workplace are loaded with stereotypical behaviours which are trawled out in queen bee syndromes, negative role models, un-feminist feminists and female misogyny.

While I think it is important to address attitudes and behaviours it is sometimes easier not to challenge the people whose judgements are reported, accepting that they have some right to make those assessments.

While women continue to operate a tick box evaluation of who should be elevated as being a good woman in the workplace and who should not, the discourses grow powerful in their destruction. There are certainly explosive headlines on the behaviours women seemingly exhibit in the workplace, especially as they climb the ladder and become more visible. But there is a danger that the 'tall poppy syndrome' prevails and that we give credence to attitudes from inexperienced sources who on many other subjects we could dismiss. Some perspective is required in the space where women are judged by other women in ways men are not and some responsibility needs to be assigned for contributing to sustaining a culture which is unwelcoming. The misconception by men and women that such judgements and attitudes are the bedrock of interpersonal competition and the creation of anxiety should be unfounded.

How managers manage can produce pivotal experiences for members of their team. In many examples the relationship with a manger can be transformative in terms of learning how to assess and conduct wider organisational relationships. A good manager is repeatedly referred to as being critical in gaining confidence and building a foundation for a progressive career. On the other hand there are the bad managers who are negative and, while they may be useful in working out what not to do as a manager, do not support the learning elements of jobs and functions. Managers, especially middle managers, are both the instrument and barometer for influencing how competition is understood and experienced by their teams. Good managers will be equipped to direct different dimensions of competition into forums where co-operation and interdependence can work in a three way relationship.

Being a manager and having a multi-functioning relationship with their team was cited by the managers I spoke to as important and some managers spoke warmly of the respect shown to them, particularly in difficult situations. While 'wisdom' was not a word found in the repertoires of the managers it is apparent as an observer that good managers are often also wise and instinctive. Subordinates, while showing respect to senior managers, commented on how important it was to have a manager who was able to execute the tough decisions because it instilled confidence in their ability to stand up and be counted when it mattered. The notion of symbolic competition is one which offers individuals the opportunity to develop an authentic image and identity which outwardly positions their values and beliefs. Of course, in any organisation there are likely to be times when those beliefs will be compromised, but this is more acceptable if the authentic image is believable. The transition from middle to senior management is identifiable as a point when such authenticity is challenged and evaluated in the context of moving to a leadership rather than a management role.

What is the relationship between competition and success and/or failure in terms of career development/pathways/trajectories?

How success is measured operates on both an organisational and personal level. For the organisation, a mix of transparent and opaque benchmarks – salary, bonus and position – are the determinants of success. The personal measures of success can be as varied and include elements such as less stress, more time, increased variety and new challenges and international opportunities. When it comes to exploring those skills considered by the managers I interviewed as important to being successful, the top three were empathy, tenacity and energy. What was interesting in the commentary which came with the list was a view that these three skills are learned, and not inherent traits which might be labelled masculine or feminine. The discourse that men as managers and leaders can exhibit any combination of masculine and feminine traits and be judged on their leadership is still illusive for women managers who continue to be criticised for not demonstrating the right mix of traits.

Length of tenure in an organisation can also be useful for accurately interpreting the standards an organisation sets for measuring success in terms of managers and staff. While these measures are obvious in job descriptions and key performance indicators, and are judged in relation to promotion and pay, there is another area of success which is determined by organisational culture – how individuals fit within that culture. The unspoken practices and rules which are often referred to by young managers are often difficult to access, and yet being provided access is a clear way of measuring cultural success. Mentors and networks are also useful platforms for building relationships which can help navigate some of the cultural nuances that speed up career progression.

The choices of the types of relationship managers consider as important in career development appear to be governed by their availability. Markiewicz et al. (1999) looks at how different friendships develop over the early stages of careers. For men who occupy positions horizontally and vertically the opportunities to form relationships with other men in similar and more senior roles is much more apparent than for women. The role of same gender relationships in management has historically been the domain of men and this continues and is seen most visibly in old boy networks and social/business networks which operate on the golf course. For women, replicating successful male only relationships is not easy given their perceived newcomer status and the existing power base of their male counterparts. Women's networks visually illustrate how many women are active in the workplace but still do not carry the weight of power for change that I believe is achievable with that critical mass of individuals. The focus on support rather than issues and lobbying is arguably one area where women's networks have become too introspective.

Having the opportunity to practise and learn from experienced and successful individuals who are willing to teach younger members about the rules of the game was cited by a number of managers as advantageous to learning about competition. Teaching young women how to recognise competition was mentioned by only a couple of the managers, reflecting their own lack of knowledge and experience of the concept. In discussing competition it was made abundantly clear that men have more opportunity to practise being competitive through outside activities such as sport, and also by the dynamic itself. As one woman manager said to me, there are simply more men who want to play games and be competitive so it's easy to join in, have a go and have some fun before the competition gets serious.

Is engaging with competition and competitive relations at work mandatory and if it is, what effect does this have on the workplace and career choices and the wellbeing of the worker?

The ability of some women managers to overcome structural, behavioural and attitudinal obstacles to career progress has demonstrated their increasingly sophisticated approach to organisations even when they have not always been welcomed as managers. The group of pioneering women managers who have been instrumental in breaking down some of the stereotypes, which Schein (1975) and Schein and Mueller (1992) has studied over some time, have been rewarded with contributing to greater opportunities for women to reach senior management. However, progress is repeatedly being reported (Catalyst, 2005; EOC, 2007; Wittenberg-Cox and Maitland, 2009) as static, particularly in the upper echelons of management, and the relationship between confidence and progress has not seemingly transferred along the pipeline. That some women managers struggle with confidence over the course of a career continues to cited in research as a barrier to progress. For women managers, confidence comes from levels of acceptance from subordinates, peers and superiors and has strong links with receiving acknowledgement for delivering skills and expertise. Early in women's management careers the value of acknowledgement is underplayed in its role in developing confidence. The women I interviewed strongly viewed men as being acknowledged from the moment they enter the workplace in a way that women are not. The acknowledgement comes initially in terms of acceptance and gradually moves and shapes the confidence to succeed. However, what emerges from some women is that as time goes by they recognise confidence as being self-generating and a skill which requires practice and analysis to perfect. Of course, the support of peers and superiors can be valuable but equally, self-sufficiency can suffice, especially for those women who pick up the pioneering mantle which has been passed along from those who have gone before.

The relationship of confidence and competition is one which is limited by how active a person wants or is able to be. One of the issues associated with a lack of confidence is isolation, and for a significant number of women managers, isolation is a shared experience which is not the case for men. First, male managers within their gender group have a vast number of examples of success – a key resource to help assemble an identity which fits the individual and their desired environment. Second, male managers largely are not defined by their gender in the same way as women managers and consequently do not expend energy on assimilating and rationalising their gendered experiences. Third, male managers have more opportunities to get support in building confidence merely by being able to have one focus – work – compared with women, who too often remain bound by domestic and caring responsibilities.

For as long as this situation prevails competition cannot be mandatory except for the duty to compete externally as contractually required. Yet what is interesting is how men and women may answer this question differently in terms of their perceptions. If each dimension of competition is taken, personal and temporal competition is widespread, and symbolic and positional competition are difficult for managers to avoid at some level. This leaves internal and interpersonal competition which, while attracting the most anxiety are also the dimensions most actively avoided.

How do competitive relations at work impact on responsibilities and activities outside of work?

Personal competition is the most popular dimension which operates outside of work and is found in many activities people engage in through leisure, hobbies and self-development channels. For the managers I spoke to personal competition was often perceived as originating outside of the workplace. However, for senior managers who had reached points where peer comparison was no longer an option, personal competition did make an appearance in terms of benchmarking work performances. Asking managers if they were competitive off the back of activating personal competition was not rewarded in the affirmative.

At the centre of life, both inside and outside work, is temporal competition. In many ways this dimensions is where gender is distinctly visible, reinforcing social stereotypes and traditional roles such as men going to work and women staying at home. Beck (2000) explains that as the 'monogamous work society' has become more open, structures, attitudes and behaviours which support multiple activities for individuals require some transformation. This position is the insight which fuels competitive relations in the domestic environs as two adults vie with temporal competition to achieve their personal and professional responsibilities which can, as many people testify, clash and cause tensions. Sirriani and Negrey (2000), Simpson (1998) and Hochschild (1997) all support the argument that temporal competition is an important site to fuel change which can allow for production and reproduction to co-exist in a harmonious relationship which is fair and balanced. Gendered practices are not always intentional but, as Connell (2003) says, the collective practices of an organisation or workforce can create gender effects. For example, long hours as a prerequisite for management promotion can disadvantage women, particularly those who cannot commit to the double dose of work and care. Martin argues that gender has a social structure with practices which encompass multiple meanings, actions, behaviours, identities and discourses which are 'fluid and shifting, yet robust and persisting' (Martin, 2003, p. 345). In this social structure time touches all the elements.

The practices involved in temporal competition are highly visible as they focus on the two factors of time and presence, both of which are impossible to avoid, whether at work or at home. Women are certainly socialised to be more sensitive to the multiple facets of temporal competition than men, which illustrates a point where some transformation should focus. Men certainly experience temporal competition, but in ways such as presenteeism and long hours being enforced as tactics by organisational cultures to demonstrate commitment and ambition. It becomes clear how the clash between men's and women's experiences of temporal competition can overlay tensions which are construed as emanating in gender relations and not in the static structures of society which govern time for work and time for home as being distinct and in so doing maintain the viability of traditional caring roles for women whether they want/have to work or not. This is where part time work emerges with low paid options for women who seek to access the workplace in ways that fit with the dominant male version of work. I agree with Adam (2003) and Gerson and Jacobs (2004) who argue that until time is viewed as fluid and shifting then how managers work is likely to continue in the existing patterns constrained by static temporal structures which dominate organisations.

Communities of practice

The work of the eight dimensional competition model and the development of the competition cage offer frameworks for shedding light on the concept of competition to broaden our thinking and experiences in the workplace, on the sports field and more generally in society. In order to take this thinking one step further I have been drawn to the work of Etienne Wenger and how we learn and manage knowledge. He says that there are four premises for defining learning as social participation: first, we are social beings, second, knowledge is a matter of competencies, third, knowing relies on active engagement and fourth, meaning is about our ability to experience the world and decide what is important. To engage in learning, individuals and collectives need to find a way of talking which they practise to share their historical and social resources. The community then forms around the social configuration of what is being shared, which creates an identity to provide a structure for accumulating and analysing the experiences and information. So a 'community of practice is a practical way to frame the task of managing knowledge' (Wenger et al., 2002, p.4).

A good example of this was a group of women who lived in the same town and were looking for a business idea which would make them money and bring people to their town. The women shared an interest in bread making, although none were proficient in this skill. The town also had an empty mill with a broken water wheel. Someone close to the group found out that there was a fund available for restoration projects which were related to creating a business. The women expanded their team to include a building team and together they applied and were awarded the funds to restore the mill and the water wheel, and build a café which would serve food alongside a bakery. The mill would be open to the public who would be able to mill and buy flour. A television documentary which followed the project shone a light on how the core group of people grew as more people were required to deliver specific skills and knowledge. During this process the core group of organisers changed as the task of managing the knowledge grew exponentially as the project was actually redefined into a number of interdependent elements. The journey of learning was a rollercoaster of joy, fear, anticipation, frustration, conflict, determination and finally shared success. As the project was completed and began to operate as a business, what emerged was a community of people who were joined through a process of learning which arguably exceeded all their expectations. I have used this example because it centred on a geographically bound community who had, at the beginning, only one commonality – they lived in the same place. However, in a quest to save their society they extended their individual social participation to become quasi business partners, a structure they used to manage the vast array of knowledge and skills they acquired.

Communities of practice can equally be bound by working in the same place and for some groups this has been experienced in what are best described as networks based on gender, sexuality and disability, for example. Women's networks are an obvious example to draw on as the premise of social participation is key to offering a platform for sharing experiences and resources for women in the workplace. The networks can be defined by positional level, occupation, industry, geography or a combination of all four elements. Using tools such as mentoring programmes, skill development seminars, experiential content events and meeting other women, the networks could indeed be described as communities of practice. Where such networks are organisational, the knowledge transfer can be among the network and then more broadly filter into the organisation. For Wenger (1999), a community of practice shares a concern, a set of problems or a passion for a topic and by socially interacting members are able to deepen their own knowledge and expertise. In the 1970s and 1980s the topic of women in management was definable by a lack of numbers and the need to build a pipeline, which was addressed with more women graduates and more access to management jobs. However, as time has progressed the topic has become increasingly complex and the knowledge transfer has not delivered substantial progress.

The thread weaving through the practice of being a manager is the traditional career model which, as Edwards and Wajcman (2005) argue, remains intact in some organisations while it is becoming more flexible in others. Edwards states, 'The developmental trajectory of a career is still designed to fit men's life course. Women's careers, which are generally "broken" or "interrupted" to have and to care for children, are thereby rendered not just different but deficient' (Edwards and Wajcman, 2005, p.77). Flexible working has become a panacea for all the issues of working parents, and policies and practices for maternity and paternity leave are held up as the first step towards progressive societal changes. But combining work and family continues to reinforce stereotypes that working women are a problem – unable to fit into the rigid organisations and their equally static temporal structures. What is appearing out of the often stagnant and circular arguments of women in management and women's equality in the workplace is what Kelan (2009) describes as gender fatigue. As a community of practice the project of achieving access for women at work has reached a point where because women are visibly embedded in management further consideration in terms of policy, legislation and practice could be considered complete. Looking to the developing world and locating fundamental rights based issues can certainly appear to be more worthy of attention and energy. The presence of sport in development programmes appears to show that the work rate is increasing and that knowledge is growing, although arguably in somewhat erratic ways.

Outside of women in management, issues such as gender based violence, teenage pregnancy, illiteracy rates, HIV/AIDS, overpopulation and poverty strike a passion with many groups who seek to build projects which aim to educate, protect and build awareness of societal malfunctions. Gender fatigue does seem to be directed at women in management, who are perceived as privileged and yet can also be viewed as a catch all for an underlying attitude that says – enough about the women.

Media and sport: communities of practice in competition

The largest community of practice in my view comprises sports players, supporters and viewers who share a passion for watching and participating in a pure form of competition which delivers entertainment, health and fitness practices and employment. The structure for sharing knowledge is socially based and can be found in historical facts, commentary, playing and coaching skills. This aspect of knowledge transfer is active and engaged and enables passion and concerns to be discussed and shared in open forums, whether that is the team changing rooms, on the side-line, at the pub, in the home or the workplace.

Encouraging the sporting community to engage more girls and women in participating and watching sport is one way to start a project which focuses on sharing the knowledge of controlled competition in a structured game and accepting that competition is best understood from playing, from winning, from losing and from appreciating that sport is an introductory lesson.

Having read and spoken to key people who are involved in sport, from elite to local programmes, sport in development, researchers and players, what becomes apparent is the passionate belief these people have that sport in whatever form has purpose wider than the actual sport itself. Throughout my time writing this book I have been drawn to these people to find out what that wider purpose might be. My underlying hope was that it might be something to do with educating people about how to understand the basics of competition as means of connecting with society, economic empowerment and new ways of thinking about how we work in relation to time. It is highly likely that this was a big ask but sometimes connections seem so obvious it is hard to imagine others not recognising and joining the same dots. As sport has the scarcity and challenge models at its core it is not unreasonable to expect more awareness of competition than what I found. What at the end of this book I still find astonishing is how people remain locked in keeping competition invisible or limited to very defined structures. I have to wonder why.

Sometimes in order to answer a question one has to think about their own process of understanding, which in this instance meant looking at my own frame of reference and experience. This journey takes me back to my childhood and early adulthood (mid-twenties) when I was growing up in New Zealand. For me, life during this time was surrounded by sports. Seemingly everyone – boys, girls, mums, dads and grandparents did something. Even having lived in the UK for a long time now and looking at all the reports on sport, I simply don't see people playing in parks, and in sports fields every week in organised competitions. Fortunately as I was coming to the end of this book I spoke to an old friend who works for Sport New Zealand (Sport NZ) who told me about a report by Dalziel published in September 2011 which he thought might help build the picture I was looking for. The report examines the economic and social value of sport in New Zealand. So taking a look at numbers I was pleased to see that not too much had changed in terms of activity since my childhood.

The key points I want to share are that in 2008/09 young people spent on average 29 minutes per day in organised sport. In 2007/08, a staggering 96 per cent of adults had taken part in one or more sport/

recreation activities during the previous 12 months, though this figure includes gardening and walking. Volunteering time for sport/recreation activities was reported by 25 percent of adults, accounting for 51.3 million hours per year. In financial terms the contribution of sport and recreation to Gross Domestic Product (GDP) in New Zealand, including volunteered services, is estimated in 2008/09 to have been $5.2 billion, or 2.8 per cent (as much as the dairy industry in New Zealand). These facts and figures illustrate the cultural importance of sport to New Zealanders and while elite performance from the national teams and individuals is important, general access and participation rates is an important barometer.

With so much sport, how is competition viewed and perceived in New Zealand? While this is difficult to quantify, a case study from a typical sports club provides some insight. North's is a community based rugby club which has junior and senior teams and a strong sense of values which include being proud yet humble, dedicated and committed, supporting young people's development, passionate about being competitive and aiming for success (Research NZ, 2010).

While these facts and figures start to shape a picture where sport and competition are embedded into the cultural fabric, it is worth noting two other points. While on average adults spend five hours a week in all sport and recreation, men spend five hours and 24 minutes and women four hours and 45 minutes. The gender difference is not great but still reinforces the difference in leisure time and domestic/caring time. Dalziel makes an interesting analysis of how much time adults spend in such activities: on average they could have worked another 18 days in a year and earned accordingly. From an economist's perspective this reveals the preference for time in sport being prioritised over employment. This link is an indicator of preference and reinforces how culturally embedded sport and recreation are in adult life. The other key indicator of sport, competition and culture is media coverage. Rugby union is the most popular spectator sport in New Zealand and on television rugby, netball and tennis had an average reach of 200,000 (5% of the population) people daily. Public and private broadcasting devote a large section of programming to sport and the two national newspapers assign 11 per cent of each edition to sport. Horse racing accounts for about 3 per cent of this, and the other 8 per cent is for other sports, which is interesting as the national sport does not dominate any of the media in the way that football does in the UK. Again, this highlights how sport is not just about a single sport. The options are wide, varied and highly accessible.

The positioning of sport at WomenWin and Sport New Zealand (Sport NZ) have some interesting commonalities around language and intent. (Sport NZ is the new name for the government organisation responsible for sport and recreation formerly called SPARC.) Both organisations are less than ten years old and while one is government funded and the other an NGO, their approach to the value of sport in culture projects winning as an important measure of participation and support as grass roots levels. Does this focus on winning suggest that competition is gaining some traction as a concept which, through sport and education, can show that winning does not mean someone else has to lose? I would certainly like to think that if the language of competition can be reconstructed to deliver inclusive and active ideas through sport and/in development programmes, further ideas and notions can be introduced among the holistic messaging.

The key to participation in sport lies with opportunity and encouragement and from this position confidence, citizenship, team membership, friendship, rivalry, leadership, winning and losing can all be experienced. In whatever combination such experience is packaged there are many success stories which fill us with hope that the human spirit is strong. However, in the discussion of competition this is not enough. Gender in the media is at a critical crossroads in either changing or reinforcing the stereotypes of women in sport and women more broadly in society. The relationship between the media and society on local and international platforms is a powerful base for creating representations which make it too easy for people to subscribe to rather than challenge. Having shared the stories of so many managers for whom the value of young people is important for transforming the position of girls in society the media need to be charged by readers and viewers to deliver a more sophisticated offer which better represents both the men and women in our societies. Drawing on the words of C.S. Lewis, it is time to stop explaining the barriers and obstacles for why some people are rewarded with privilege and others are not. It is time to see something different, to say something different and to take responsibility for demanding new angles.

Leveraging competition for change is difficult if women are more reluctant to engage fully and consciously with it than men. In management the non-articulation around meanings of competition suggests that any distinct advantage of actively engaging with competition could be temporary and limited. Being open to competition operating in multiple ways and in multiple relationships is where those managers who do engage with the concept appear to have an additional strand to their management mind-set which can positively influence success factors and career progression.

Next steps

The scope for further research on competition is undoubtedly important. The relationship between sport and then understanding the basics of competition and how this can positively impact on career planning and career development requires further thinking. Whether promoting sport to girls over a longer period would encourage a greater understanding of competition once they enter the labour market would be worthy of attention. Perhaps the sport in development models which are making progress in capturing young women in the developing world might equally find a captive audience in the developed world which share common issues. Gender based violence, a right to play sport, health education and an objective of encouraging economic empowerment resonate with many of the social issues facing the Western world.

Being open to competition remains a challenge which will not be easily overcome while there is resistance from groups who will not see beyond the stereotype. Because competition is a dynamic, engagement needs to be accompanied by activity to heighten the sense of exposure of creating experiences and knowledge. Expanding the gender and management debate to include competition allows new ground to be broken in terms of attitudes and behaviours practised at work. Using the model and the cage provides a frameworks from which further examination can be conducted. For as long as gender equality challenges the thinking and practices of men and women managers and encourages them to engage actively with existing and ill-defined concepts – change is possible.

Temporal competition is fertile ground for additional research with sporting and business organisations to attempt to re-balance priorities and deliver a potentially fitter, healthier and more productive population. The combination of research, discussion and making connections with organisations who are progressive is key to bringing competition to life and to making it work for us.

Bibliography

Abramson, J. (1975) *The Invincible Woman: Discrimination in the Academic Profession* Jossey-Bass

Acker, J. (1990) 'Hierarchies, jobs, bodies: A theory of gendered organisations' *Gender and Society* Vol 4 (No 2)

Acker, J. (1998) 'The Future of Gender and Organizations: Connections and Boundaries' *Gender Work and Organization* Vol 5 (No 4)

Acker, J. (2000) 'Gendered Contradictions in Organizational Equity Projects.' *Organization* Vol 7(No 4)

Acker, J. (2001) 'Different Strategies are Necessary Now' *Monthly Review* Vol 1–4

Ackoff, R. (1979) 'The Future of Operational Research is Past' *The Journal of the Operational Research Society* Vol 30 (No 2)

Adam, B. (1995) *Timewatch: The Social Analysis of Time.* Cambridge, Polity Press

Adam, B. (2003) 'Reflexive Modernisation Temporalized' *Theory, Culture and Society* Vol 20

Adkins, L. (2005) 'The New Economy, Property and Personhood' *Theory, Culture & Society* Vol 22 (No 1)

Adler, M. and Izraeli, D. (1994) *Competitive Frontiers in a Global Economy*, Cambridge, Blackwell Publishers

Alcoff, L. and Potter, E. (1992) *Feminist Epistemologies*, New York Routledge

Aldridge, M. (2001) 'The Paradigm Contingent Career? Women in Regional Newspaper Journalism' *Sociological Research Online*

Alexander, S. (1994) 'Gender Bias in British Television Coverage of Major Athletic Championships' in *Women's Studies Int. Forum* Vol 17 (No 6)

Allen, T. Eby, L. and Lentz, E. (2006) 'The relationship between formal and mentoring program characteristics and perceived program effectiveness' *Personnel Psychology* Vol 59

Alvesson, M. and Hardy, C. et al. (2008) 'Reflecting on Reflexivity: Reflexive Textual Practices in Organization and Management Theory' *Journal of Management Studies* Vol 45(No 3)

Alvesson, M. and Karreman, D. (2000) 'Varieties of discourse: On the study of organizations through discourse analysis' *Human Relations* Vol 53 (No 9)

Amabile, T. (1982). 'Children's Artistic Creativity' *Personality and Social Psychology Bulletin* Vol 8 (No 3)

Anderson, D. Vlnnicombe, S. and Singh, V. (2010) 'Women partners leaving the firm: choice, what choice?' *Gender in Management* Vol 25(No 3)

Arabsheibani, G. (2005) 'Gay Pay Gap in the UK' *Economica* Vol 72

Arnsperger, C. and De Ville, P. (2004) 'Can Competition Ever be Fair? Challenging the Standard Prejudice' *Ethical Theory and Moral Practice* Vol 7

Atkinson, N. (2011) www.nzhistory.net.nz/page/new-zealand-s-rowing-eight-win-gold-munich, (Ministry for Culture and Heritage)

Atkinson, N. (2011) www.nzhistory.net.nz/culture/1981-springbok-tour/impact-of-the-tour, (Ministry for Culture and Heritage)

Auerbach, M. (1991) 'Women Managers Don't Aim for Queen Bee' *New York Times*. New York

Australian Institute of Management www.aim.com.au/about/management.html accessed 21/12/2011

Australian Sport www.ausport.gov.au/participating/women/resources/issues/sexploitation accessed 21/01/12

Baruch, Y. (2004) 'Transforming careers: from linear to multidirectional career paths' *Career Development International* Vol 9 (No 1)

Bateson, M.C. (1989) *Composing a Life* New York Grove Press

BBC http://news.bbc.co.uk/sport1/hi/football/9373280.stm accessed 12/12/11

Beck, U. (1992) *Risk Analysis* London, Sage Publications

Beck, U. (2000) *The Brave New World of Work* Cambridge, Polity Press

Beck, U. and Beck Gersheim, E. (2002) *Individualization* London, Sage Publications

Belbin, R. and Meredith, A. (2000) *Beyond the Team* Oxford, Butterworth Heinemann

Bittman, M. and Wajcman, J. (2000) 'The Rush Hour: The Character of Leisure Time and Gender Equity' *Social Forces* Vol 79 (No 1)

Black, D. Makar, H. Sanders, S. and Taylor, L. (2003) The Earnings Effects of Sexual Orientation' *Industrial and Labor Relations* Vol 56

Black, S. (1992) 'Improving Performance Effectiveness: Making Competition Work for You' *Management Quarterly* Vol 33(No 4)

Blackaby, D. Charles, N., Davies, C., Murphy, P. O'Leary, N. and Ransome, P. (1999) 'Women in Senior Management in Wales' Research Discussion Series, *Equal Opportunities Commission*. Swansea, University of Wales

Blair-Loy, M. and Jacobs, J. (2003) 'Globalization, Work Hours, and the Care Deficit Among Stockbrokers' *Gender and Society* Vol 17(No 2)

Booth, A. (2009). 'Gender and competition' *Labor Economics* Vol 16

Bowen, G. and Orthner, D. (1991) 'Effects of organizational culture on fatherhood', in Bozett, F. and Hanson, S. (eds) *Fatherhood and Families in Cultural Context* New York, Springer

Bowles, R. and Babcock, L. (2007) 'Social incentives for gender differences in the propensity to initiate negotiations: Sometimes it does hurt to ask' *Organizational Behaviour and Human Decision Processes* Vol 103

Bradley, H. (1996). *Fractured Identities* Cambridge, Polity Press

Bradley, H. (1999). *Gender and Power in the Workplace* Hampshire, Palgrave Macmillan

Braidotti, R. (2002) *Metamorphoses: Towards a Materialist Theory of Becoming.* Cambridge, Polity Press

Brannen, J. (2005) 'Time and the Negotiation of Work-Family Boundaries' *Time & Society* Vol 14(No 1)

Brannen, J. and Moss, P. (1996) *Dual Earner Households after Maternity Leave* Unwin and Hymer

Brenner, O. Tomkiewicz, J. and Schien, V. (1989) 'The Relationship Between Sex Role Stereotypes and Requisite Management Characteristics Revisited' *Academy of Management Journal* Vol 32(No 3)

Britton, D. (2000) 'The epistemology of the gendered organization' *Gender and Society* Vol 14(No 3)

Broadbridge, A. and Hearn, J. (2008) 'Gender and Management: New Directions in research and Continuing Patterns in Practice' *British Journal of Management* Vol 19

Brown, L. (2001) 'Adolescent girls, class and cultures of femininity' *Cultural and Critical Perspectives on Human Development: Implications for Research, Theory and Practice*. M. Packer and M. Tappan (eds), Albany

Brown, R. (1997) 'Flexibility and Security: Contradictions in the Contemporary Labour Market' in *The Changing Shape of Work*. R. Brown (ed.), Hampshire, Macmillan Press Ltd

Bruni, A., Gheradi, S. and Poggio, B. (2004) 'Doing gender, doing entrepreneurship: An ethnographic account of intertwined practices' *Gender Work and Organization* Vol 11(No 4)

Burke, R. (2006) *Research Companion to Working Time and Working Addiction* Massachusetts, Edward Elgar

Burke, R. and McKeen, C. (1997) 'Not every managerial woman who makes it has a mentor' *Women in Management Review* Vol12(No 4)

Butler, J. (1999) *Gender Trouble* London, Routledge

Butler, J. (2004) *Undoing Gender* London, Routledge

Callan, S. (2007) 'Implications of family-friendly policies for organizational culture' *Work Employment and Society* Vol 21(No 4)

Campbell, A. (2004) 'Female Competition: Causes, Constraints, Content and Contexts' *The Journal of Sex* Vol 41(No 1)

Carter, N. Silva, C. (2010) *Pipelines Broken Promise* New York, Catalyst

Catalyst (2005) *Women Take Care, Men Take Charge, Stereotyping of US Business Leaders* New York, Catalyst

Charles, N. and James, E. (2003) 'Gender and work orientations in conditions of job insecurity' *British Journal of Sociology* Vol 54(No 2): 239–257

Charmaz, K. (2000) 'Grounded Theory Objectivist and Constructivist Methods" *Handbook of Qualitative Research* N. Denzin and Y. Lincoln (eds), London, Sage Publications

Claes, M. (1999) 'Women, Men and Management Styles' *International Labour Review* Vol 138(No 4)

Clarke, A., E (2005) *Situational Analysis: Grounded Theory After the Postmodern Turn*. London, Sage

Coalter, F. and Taylor, J. (2010) *Sport-for-development Impact Study*, Stirling University

Cockburn, C. (1991) *In the Way of Women* Hampshire, Macmillan Press Ltd

Code, L. (1992) *Taking Subjectivity into Account* Cambridge, Routledge

Coe, T. (1992) *The Key to the Men's Club* Institute of Management

Collins, G. (2005) 'The Gendered Nature of Mergers' *Gender Work and Organization* Vol 12(No 3)

Collinson, D. and Hearn, J. (1996) *Men as Managers, Managers as Men* London, Sage

Connell, R. (1987) *Gender and Power Society, the Person and Sexual Politics*, Cambridge, Polity Press

Connell, R. (2002) *Gender*. Cambridge, Polity

Connell, R. (2003) 'Developing a Theory of Gender as Practice' *Gender and Society* Vol 17(No 3)

Connell, R. and Messerschmidt (2005) 'Hegemonic Masculinity: Rethinking the Concept' *Gender and Society* Vol 19(No 6)

Connell, R. and Wood, J. (2002) 'Globalization and business masculinities' in *Men and Masculinities*

Connelly, S. and M. Gregory (2008) 'Moving Down: Women's Part-time work and occupational change in Britain 1991–2001' *The Economic Journal* Vol 118 (February)

Corbin, J. and Strauss, A. (1990) 'Grounded Theory Research: Procedures, Cannons and Evaluative Criteria' *Qualitative Sociology* Vol 13(No 1)

Corrigall, E. and Konrad, A. (2006) 'The Relationship of Job Attribute Preferences to Employment, Hours of Paid Work and Family Responsibilities' *Sex Roles: A Journal of Research* Vol 54 (No 1–2)

Couprie, H (2007) 'Time Allocation within the Family' *Economic Journal* Vol 117, 516

Coward, R. (1992) *Our Treacherous Hearts* London, London, Faber and Faber

Coward, R. (2000) *Sacred Cows* London, HarperCollins

Crompton, R. (1999) *Restructuring Gender Relations and Employment* Oxford University Press

Crompton, R. and Harris, F. (1998a) 'Gender Relations and Employment: The Impact of Occupation' *Work Employment and Society* Vol 12(No 2)

Crompton, R. and Harris, F. (1998b) 'A reply to Hakim' *British Journal of Sociology* Vol 49(No 1)

Crompton, R. and Lyonette, C. (2005) 'The new gender essentialism -domestic and family choices and their relation to attitudes' *The British Journal of Sociology* Vol 56

Croteau, D. and Hoynes, W. (2001) *The Business of Media* London, Pine Forge Press

Dalziel, P. (2011) *The Economic and Social Impact of Sport and Recreation in New Zealand*, AERU Reports, Lincoln University

Daniels, K., Johnson, G. and de Chernatony, L. (1994) 'Differences in Managerial Cognitions of Competition' *British Journal of Management* Vol 5 (Special Issue S21–29)

Davidson, M. and Burke, R (2000) *Women in Management: Current Research Issues* Volume 2, London, Sage Publications

de Beauvoir, S. (1997) 'Introduction to The Second Sex' in *The Second Wave*. L. Nicholson (ed) Cambridge, Routledge

de Bruin, M. (2000) 'Gender, organizational and professional identities in journalism' *Journalism* Vol 1(No 2)

de Laine, M. (2000) *Fieldwork, Participation and Practice* London, Sage Publications

DeBoer, K. (2004) *Gender and Competition* Coaches Choice

Delphy, C. (1984) *Close to Home: A Materialist Analysis of Women's Oppression*. University of Massachusetts Press

Denzin, N. and Lincoln, Y. (2000) *Handbook of Qualitative Research* London, Sage

Deutsch, M. (1949) 'A Theory of co-operation and competition' *Human Relations* 2 Vol 2

DeVault, M. (1996) 'Talking Back to Sociology: Distinctive Contributions of Feminist Methodology' *Annual Review of Sociology* Vol 22: pp. 29–50

Dex, S. and Bond, S.(2005) 'Measuring work-life balance and its covariates' *Work Employment and Society* Vol 19(No 3)

Dopson, S. and Neumann, J. (1998) 'Uncertainty, contrariness and the double bind: middle managers' reactions to changing contracts' *British Journal of Management* Vol 9

Dowden, A. and Mitchelmore, K. (2010) Value of Sport and Recreation: Case Study of Northern United Rugby Football Club, Research NZ

Du Billing, Y. and Alvesson, M. (2000) 'Questioning the Notion of Feminine Leadership: A critical perspective on the gender labelling of leadership' *Gender Work and Organization* 7(3)

Duncan, M and Hasbrook, C (1988) 'Denial of power in televised women's sports' Sociology of Sport Vol 5(No 1)

Dunning, E. and Sheard, K. (1979) *Barbarians, Gentlemen and Players: A Sociological Study of the Development of Rugby Football,* London, Routledge

Edwards, C., Woodall, J. and Welchman, R. (1996). 'Organizational Change and women managers' careers: the restructuring of disadvantage.' *Employee Relations* Vol 18(No 5)

Edwards, P. and Wajcman, J. (2005) *The Politics of Working Life* Oxford University Press

Eisenhardt, K., and Kahwajy, J. et al. (1997) 'Managing Conflict' *Harvard Business Review* July-August

Ekinsmyth, C. (1999) 'Professional Workers in a Risk Society' *Transactions of the Institute of British Geographers* Vol 24(No 3)

Ely, R. (1994) 'The Social Construction of Relationships Among Professional Women at Work' *Women in Management: Current Research Issues.* M. Davidson and R. Burke (eds) Paul Chapman Publishing

Ely, R. and Meyerson, D. (2000) 'Advancing Gender Equity in Organizations: The Challenge and Importance of Maintaining a Gender Narrative' *Organization* Vol 7(No 4)

England, K. (1994) 'Getting Personal: Reflexivity, Positionality and Feminist Research' *Professional Geographer* Vol 46(No 1)

English, J (1978) 'Sex Equality in Sports' *Philosophy and Public Affairs* Vol 7(No 3)

Engwall, L. (1978) *Newspapers as Organizations* Gower Publishing Co

EOC (2005) *Britain's Hidden Brain Drain – Final Report* Equal Opportunities Commission

Eveline, J. (2005) 'Woman in the Ivory Tower' *Journal of Organizational Change* Vol 18(No 6)

Evetts, J. (2000) 'Analysing Change in Women's Careers: Culture, Structure and Action Dimensions' *Gender Work and Organization* Vol 7(No 1)

Fels, A. (2004) 'Do Women Lack Ambition?' *Harvard Business Review* April

Fenton, N. (1995) 'Women, communication and theory: a glimpse of feminist approaches to media and communications studies' *Feminism and Psychology* Vol 5(No 3)

Ferree, M. (2003) 'Practice Makes Perfect? A Comment on Yancey Martin's Gendering Practices, Practicing Gender' *Gender and Society* Vol 17(No 3)

Fine, B. (1992) *Women's Employment and the Capitalist Family.* Routledge

Finlay. L. (2002) 'Negotiating the swamp: the opportunity and challenge of reflexivity in research practice' *Qualitative Research* Vol 2 (No 2)

FIFA www.fifa.com/mm/document/fifafacts/bcoffsurv/emaga_9384_10704.pdf accessed 11/12/11

Flanagan, J.C. (1954) The Critical Incident Technique, *Psychological Bulletin*, 54 pp. 327–358

Fleming, P. (2007) 'Sexuality, Power and Resistance in the Workplace' *Organization Studies* Vol 28

Fonow, M. and Cook, J. (1991) *Beyond Methodology: Feminist Scholarship as Lived Research* Indiana University Press

Foucault, M. (1979) *The Will of Knowledge The History of Sexuality Vol 1* Penguin

Franks, S. (2000). *Having None of It.* Granta Books

George, C. Hartley, A. and Paris, J. (2001) 'Focus on Communication in Sport' *Corporate Communications* Vol 6 (No 2)

Gerson, K. and Jacobs, J. (2004) *The Time Divide: Work, Family and Gender Inequality* Harvard University Press

Gibson, D. (2004) 'Role models in career development: new directions for theory and research' *Journal of Vocational Behaviour* Vol 65

Gilligan, C. (1993) *In a Different Voice* Harvard University Press

Gneezy, U. and Niederle, M. et al. (2003) 'Performance in Competitive Environments Gender Differences' *The Quarterly Journal of Economics* August

Goldberg, S. (1993) *Why Men Rule: A Theory of Male Dominance* Open Court Publishing Company

Gordon,S.(1991) `Prisoners of Men's Dreams Striking Out for a New Feminist Future' in Davidson,M.J. and Burke,J. (eds) *Women in Management Current Research Issues* Volume II. London Sage

Gosling, J. and Mintzberg, H. (2003) 'The Five Minds of a Manager' *Harvard Business* Review November

Greater Expectations, 2005, Equal Opportunities Commission (EOC)

Grimshaw, J. (1993) 'Practices of Freedom' *Up Against Foucault*. C. Ramazanoglu (ed). Routledge

Guillaume, C. and Pochic, S. (2007) 'What Would You Sacrifice? Access to Top Management and the Work-Life Balance' *Gender Work and Organization* Vol 14

Hakim, C. (2000) *Work-Lifestyle Choices in the 21st Century* Oxford University Press

Halford, S. and Leonard, P. (2001) *Gender, Power and Organisations* Palgrave

Halford, S., Savage, M. and Witz, A. (1997) *Gender, Careers and Organisations* Macmillan Press Ltd

Hall, D.V. (1963) 'Making Things Happen: A history of the National Federation of Business and Professional Women's Clubs of Great Britain and Northern Ireland'

Hancock, P. and Tyler, M. (2001) *Work, Postmodernism and Organization* London, Sage Publications

Hancock, P. and Tyler, M. (2007) 'Un/doing Gender and the Aesthetics of Organizational Performance' *Gender Work and Organization* Vol 14(No 6)

Handy, C. (1993) *Understanding Organisations* London, Penguin Group

Haraway, D. (1988) 'Situated knowledges: the science question in feminism and the privilege of partial perspective' *Feminist Studies* Vol 14

Harding, S. (1987) *Feminism and Methodology* Indiana University Press

Harding, S. (2004) *Rethinking Standpoint Epistemology* Oxford University Press

Harding, S. and K. Norberg (2005) 'New Feminist Approaches to Social Science Methodologies: An Introduction' *Signs: Journal of Women in Culture and Society* Vol 30(No 4)

Hargreaves, J (1986) *Sport, Power and Culture: Social and Historical Analysis of Popular Sports in Britain* Oxford University Press

Harstock, N. (1983) *The Feminist Standpoint: Developing the Ground for a Specifically Feminist Historical Materialism* D Reidel Publishing

Harstock, N. (1997) 'The Feminist Standpoint' in *The Second Wave*. L. Nicholson (ed). London, Routledge

Hartman, H. (1997) *The Unhappy Marriage of Marxism and Feminism* London, Routledge

Headlan-Wells, J. (2004) 'E-mentoring for aspiring women managers' *Women in Management Review* Vol 19 (No 4)

Hearn, J. and Broadbridge, A. (2008) 'Gender and Management new directions in research and continuing patterns in practice' *British Journal of Management* Vol 19

Hearn, J. and Parkin, W. (2003) *Gender Sexuality and Violence in Organizations* London, Sage

Heslin, P. (2005) 'Conceptualizing and evaluating career success' *Journal of Organizational Behaviour* Vol 26

Hesse-Biber, S. and Leavy, P. (2004) *Feminist Approaches to Research as a Process* Oxford University Press

Hewlett, S. (2002) 'Executive Women and the Myth of Having it All' *Harvard Business Review* April

Hill-Collins, P. (1991) *Black Feminist Thought* New York Routledge

Hill-Collins, P. (1997) 'Defining Black Feminist Thought' in *The Second Wave*. L. Nicholson (ed). Cambridge, Routledge

Himmelweit, S. and Sigala, M. (2001) 'Choice and the Relationship between Identities and behaviour for Mothers with Pre-school Children: Some Implications for Policy from a UK Study' *Soc. Pol* Vol 33(No 3)

Hochschild, A. (1990) *The Second Shift* New York, Piatkus

Hochschild, A. (1997) *The Time Bind* New York, Henry Holt and Company

Hodgson, D. (2005) 'Putting on a Professional Performance: Performativity, Subversion and Project Management' *Organization* Vol 12(No 51)

Holt, H. and Thaulow, I. (1996) *Formal and Informal Flexibility in the Workplace: The Work-Family Challenge* London, Sage Publications

Horin, A. (2004) 'Women Bosses take sting out of queen bee' *Sydney Morning Herald*

Horlick, N. (1997) *Can You Have It All? (How to Succeed in a Man's World)* Hampshire, Macmillan

Horne, J., Tomlinson, A., Whannel, G (1999) *Understanding Sport* London, Routledge

Houston, J., Mcintire, S., Kinnie, J. and Terry, C. (2002) 'A Factorial Analysis of Scales Measuring Competitiveness' *Educational and Psychological Measurement* Vol 62

Hughes, C. (2004) 'Class and Other Identifications in the Managerial Careers: The Case of the Lemon Dress' *Gender Work and Organization* Vol 11(No 5)

Hughes, C. and Kerfoot, D. (2002) 'Rethinking Gender Work and Organization' *Gender Work and Organization* Vol 9(No 5)

Hyde, M. (2012) www.guardian.co.uk/sport/blog/2012/jan/18/london-2012-olympics-security?INTCMP=SRCH access 21/01/12

Ibarra, H. (1999) Provisional Selves: Experimenting with image and identity in professional adaptation, *Administrative Science Quarterly,* 44 pp. 764–791

Ibarra, H. (1993) 'Personal networks of women and minorities in management: a conceptual framework' *Academy of Management Review* Vol 18(No 1)

Ibarra, H. and Hunter, M. (2007) 'How Leaders Create and Use Networks' *Harvard Business Review* January

Indiana Gazette, August 6, 1921 'British Peer and Publisher Starts Lively Discussion Among American Thinkers'

Inglis, F. (1990) *Media Theory, An Introduction* Cambridge, Blackwell

Itzin, C. (1995) 'The Gender Culture in Organizations' in *Gender Culture and Organizational Change*. C. Itzin and J. Newman (eds) Cambridge, Routledge

Itzin, C. and J. Newman (1995). *Gender, Culture and Organizational Change* Cambridge, Routledge

Jackson, J. C. (2001) 'Women middle managers' perception of the glass ceiling' *Women in Management Review* Vol 16(No 1)

Jacobs, J. and Gerson, K. (2004) *The Time Divide Work, Family and Gender Inequality* Boston, Harvard University Press

Johnson, P. and Duberley, J. (2003) 'Reflexivity in Management Research' *Journal of Management Studies* Vol 40(No 5)

Jones, D. (2002) *Boss Talk* Sydney, Allen & Unwin

Kakabadse, A., J. Bank, et al. (2004) *Working in Organisations* Farnham, Gower Publishing

Kanter, R. (1977) *Men and Women of the Corporation* New York, Basic Books

Kanter, R. (1989) *When Giants Learn to Dance* London, Simon & Schuster

Karsten, M. (1994) *Management and Gender Issues and Attitudes* Santa Barabara, Praeger

Kearney, AT *www.atkearney.com/index.php/Publications/the-sports-market.html* accessed 11/12/11

Kay, T. (2009) 'Developing through sport: evidencing sport impacts on young People' *Sport in Society*, Vol 12 (No 9)

Kelan, E. (2009) 'Gender Fatigue: The Ideological Dilemma of Gender Neutrality and Discrimination in Organizations' *Canadian Journal of Administrative Sciences* Vol 26 (No 3)

Kelan, E. (2009) *Performing Gender at Work* Hampshire, Palgrave Macmillan

Kelinske, B., Mayer, B. and Chen, K. (2001) 'Perceived benefits from participation in sports: a gender study' *Women in Management Review* Vol 16(No 2)

Killinger, B. (2006) 'The workaholic breakdown syndrome' In *Research companion to working time and work addiction* R. Burke (ed). Massachusetts, Edward Elgar

Kitzinger, J. (2000) 'Media templates: patterns of association and the (re)construction of meaning over time' *Media, Culture and Society* 22: 61–84

Kleinjans, K. (2009) 'Do gender differences in preferences for competition matter for occupational expectations?' *Journal of Economic Psychology* Vol 30

Knights, D. and Kerfoot, D. (2004) 'Between Representations and Subjectivity: Gender Binaries and the Politics of Organizational Transformation' *Gender Work and Organization* Vol 11

Kohn, A. (1992) *No Contest: The Case Against Competition* Boston, Houghton Mifflin

Kuhn, T. (2006) 'A Demented Work Ethic and a Lifestyle Firm: Discourse, Identity and Workplace Time Commitments' *Organization Studies* Vol 27(No 9)

Kunz, V. (2008) 'Sport as a Post-Disaster Psychosocial Intervention in Bam, Iran' *Sport and Society*, Vol 12 (No 9)

Kvale, S. (1996) *Interviews: An Introduction to Qualitative Research Interviewing.* London, Sage

Le Feurve, N. (1999) 'Gender, Occupational Feminization and Reflexivity: A cross-national perspective' in *Restructuring Gender Relations and Employment.* R. Crompton (ed). Oxford University Press

Leathwood, C. (2005) 'Treat me as a human being –don't look at me as a woman: femininities and professional identities in further education' *Gender and Education* Vol 17 (No 4)

Leavitt, H. (2005) 'The Necessary Evil of Hierarchies' *Stanford Business Magazine*

Leonard, P. (2002) 'Organizing Gender? Looking at Metaphors as Frames of Meaning in Gender/Organizational Texts' *Gender Work and Organization* Vol 9(No 1)

Levermore, R. (2008) 'Sport: A New Engine of Development' *Progress in Development Studies* Vol 8(No 2)

Lewis, C. S. (1978) *The Abolition of Man*, 1943, 1946, 1978. CS Lewis Pte Ltd

Lewis, S. (1996) 'Rethinking Employment: An Organizational Culture Change Framework' in *The Work-Family Challenge*. S. Lewis and J. Lewis (eds) London, Sage Publications

Lewis, S. (2001) 'Restructuring workplace cultures: the ultimate work-family challenge?' *Women in Management Review* Vol 16

Liff S and Ward, K. (2001) 'Distorted Views Through the Glass Ceiling: The Construction of Women's Understanding of Promotions and Senior Management Positions' *Gender Work and Organization* Vol 8(No 1)

Linstead, A. and Thomas, R. (2002) 'What do you want from me?' A poststructuralist feminist reading of middle managers' identities' *Culture and Organisation* Vol 8 (No 1)

Lucas, G. (2010) http://www.thisislondon.co.uk/standard-sport/article-23974482-five-great-acts-of-sportsmanship.do accessed 21/02/2012

Luthehaus, N. (2002) *The Making of an American Icon* Oxford, Princeton University Press

McCarthy, H. (2004) *Girlfriends In High Places* London, Demos

McIntosh, P. (1979) *Fair Play* Portsmouth, Heinemann

Magretta, J. (2002) *What Management Is* London, HarperCollins

Maguire, J. (2011) 'Towards a sociology of sport' *Sport in Society* 14:7–8

Mallon, M. and Cohen, L. (2001) 'Time for a Change? Women's Accounts of the Move from Organizational Careers to Self-Employment' *British Journal of Management* Vol 12

Major, J http://www.johnmajor.co.uk/page1389.html accessed 05/09/2011

Mamman, A. and Rees, C (2005) 'Australian managerial attitudes towards employee relations: a comparison with the British National Survey' *Asia Pacific Journal of Human Resources* Vol 43(No 3)

Markiewicz, D., Devine, I. and Kausilas, D. (1999) 'Friendships of women and men at work' *Journal of Managerial Psychology* Vol 15(No 2)

Marshall, J. (1984) *Women Managers: Travellers in a Male World* Oxford, John Wiley & Sons

Marshall, J. (1995) *Women Managers Moving On* London, Routledge

Martin, B. (2005) 'Mangers after the era of organizational restructuring: towards a second managerial revolution?' *Work Employment and Society* Vol 19(No 4)

Martin, B. and J. Wajcman (2004) 'Markets, contingency and preferences: contemporary manager' narrative identities' The Editorial Board of the *Sociological Review*

Martin, Y. (2003) 'Said and Done versus Saying and Doing: Gendering Practices, Practicing Gender at Work' *Gender and Society* Vol 17(No 3)

Martin, Y. (2006) 'Practising Gender at Work: Further Thoughts on Reflexivity' *Gender Work and Organization* Vol 13 (No 3)

Massey, D. (1995) 'Masculinity, dualism and high technology' *Trans Inst British Geographers* Vol 20

Matsumoto, D. (1987) 'One Young Woman In Publishing' in *Competition A Feminist Taboo* H. Miner and V. Longino (eds) New York, The Feminist Press

Mattingly, D. and Al-Hindi, K. (1995) 'Should Women Count? A Context for the Debate' *Professional Geographer* Vol 47(No 4)

Mavin, S. (2006) 'Venus envy: problematizing solidarity behaviour and queen bees' *Women in Management Review* Vol 21(No 4)

Mavin, S. (2008) 'Queen Bees, Wannabees and Afraid to Bees: No More 'Best Enemies' for Women in Management?' *British Journal of Management* Vol 19: S75-S84

Maynard, M. (1994) 'Methods, Practice and Epistemology: The Debate about Feminism and Research' in *Researching Women's Lives from a Feminist Perspective* Maynard and Purvis (eds) London, Taylor and Francis

Maynard, M. and Purvis, J. (1994). *Researching Women's Lives from a Feminist Perspective London*, London, Taylor and Francis

McDowell, L. (1997) *Capital Culture Gender at Work in the City* Cambridge, Blackwell

McKenna, E. (1997) *When Work Doesn't Work Anymore* London, Simon and Schuster

McNair, B. (2003) 'From control to chaos: towards a new sociology of journalism' *Media, Culture and Society* Vol 25

McQuail, D. (1985) 'Sociology of Mass Communication' *Annual Review of Sociology* Vol 11

McKenzie Davey, K. (2008) 'Women's accounts of organizational politics as a gendering process' *Gender, Work and Organization* Vol 6

McRae, S. (2003) 'Constraints and choices in mothers' employment careers: a consideration of Hakim's Preference Theory' *British Journal of Sociology* Vol 54(No 3): pp. 317–338

Mead, M. (2002) *Cooperation and Competition Among Primitive Peoples.* New Jersey, Transaction Publishers

Meara, N. and Day, J. (1993) 'The Perspectives on Achieving Via Interpersonal Competition' *Sex Roles: A Journal of Research* Vol 28(Issue 1–2)

Messner, M. (2007) *Out of Play* New York, State University of New York

Meyerson, D. and Fletcher, J (2000) 'A Modest Manifesto for Shattering the Glass Ceiling' *Harvard Business Review* (January-February)

Meyerson, D. and Kolb, D. (2000) 'Moving out of the 'Armchair': Developing a Framework to Bridge the Gap between Feminist Theory and Practice' *Organization* Vol 7 (No 4)

Mies, M. (1993) 'Towards a Methodology for Feminist Research' in *Social Research Philosophy, Politics and Practice.* M. Hammersley (ed). London, Sage

Miller, J. (2005) 'Get A Life' *Fortune Magazine*

Miller, N. (2006) 'IT Women in the Industry' *Sydney Morning Herald*

Mills, A. and Tancred, P. (1992) *Gendering Organisational Analysis* London, Sage

Mills, A. J. (2002) 'Studying the Gendering of Organizational Culture Over Time: Concerns, Issues and Strategies' *Gender Work and Organization* Vol 9(No 3)

Miner, H. and Longino, V. (1987) *Competition A Feminist Issue* New York The Feminist Press

Mintzberg, H. (1973). *The Nature of Managerial Work.* London, HarperCollins

Mintzberg, H. (1998). 'On Managing Professionals; *Harvard Business Review* November-December

Mintzberg, H. (2004). *Managers Not MBAs* San Francisco Berret-Koehler Publishers Inc

Mohanty, C. (1988). 'Under Western Eyes: Feminist Scholarship and Discourse' *Feminist Review* Vol 30

Muse, D. (1987). 'High Stakes, Meagre Yields: Competition Among Black Girls.' in *Competition A Feminist Taboo.* Miner and Longino (eds). New York, The Feminist Press

Newton, J. (1984) 'Making and Remaking History: Another Look at Patriarchy' *Tulsa Studies in Women's Literature* Vol 3(No 1/2)

Ng, T., Eby, L., Sorensen, K. and Feldman, D. (2005). 'Predictors of objective and subjective career success' *Personnel Psychology* Vol 58

Nickell, S. (1996) 'Competition and Corporate Performance' *The Journal of Political Economy* Vol 104(No 4)

Niederle, M. and Vesterlund, L. (2007) 'Do Women Shy Away From Competition? Do Men Compete Too Much' *The Quarterly Journal of Economics* August

Noon, M. and Blyton, P. (1997) *The Realities of Work* London Macmillan Press

Oakley, A. (2000) *Experiments in Knowing* Cambridge, Polity Press

Oakley, J. (2000) 'Gender-based barriers to senior management positions: understanding the scarcity of female CEO's' *Journal of Business Ethics* Vol 27

O'Leary, J. (1997) 'Developing a new mindset: the 'career ambitious individual' *Women in Management Review* Vol 12(No 3): pp 91–99

Olesen, V. (2000) *Feminisms and Qualitative Research at and into the Millennium.* Sage

Olsson, S. (2000) 'Acknowledging the female archetype: women managers' narratives of gender' *Women in Management Review* Vol 15(No 5/6): pp 296–302

Parry, K. (1998) 'Grounded Theory and Social Process: A New Direction for Leadership Research' *Leadership Quarterly* Vol 9(No 1)

Perrons, D., Fagan, C. McDowell, L., Ray, K. and Ward, K. (2005). 'Work, Life and Time in the New Economy: An Introduction' *Time & Society* Vol 14(No 1)

Personnel Today (2006) 'Venus Envy: Sisters are ruining it for themselves' Personnel Today

Peters, T. (1997) *The Circle of Innovation* London, Hodder and Stoughton

Pfister, G. (2010) 'Women in sport – gender relations and future perspective' *Sport in Society* Vol 13(No 2)

Potter, E. and Wetherell, M. (1987). *Discourse and Social Psychology: Beyond Attitudes and Behaviour* London, Sage

Powell, G. (1988) *Women and Men in Management* London, Sage

Powell, C. (1996) *My American Journey,* Ballantine Books, New York p. 55

Powell, G., Butterfield, A. and Parent, J. (2002) Gender and Managerial Stereotypes: Have the Times Changed?' *Journal of Management* Vol 28(No 2)

Powell, G. and Graves, L (2003) *Women and Men in Management* London, Sage

Pratt, M. and Foreman, P. (2000) 'Classifying Managerial Responses to Multiple Organizational Identities' *Academy of Management Review* Vol 25

Pringle, R (1989) *Secretaries Talk* London, Verso Publishing

Procter, I. and Padfield, M. (1999) 'Work Orientations and Women's Work: A critique of Hakim's Theory of the Heterogeneity of Women' *Gender Work and Organization* Vol 6(No 3)

Price Waterhouse Cooper (PWC) (2010) 'Back on track? The outlook for the global sports market to 2013 Report'

Ragins, B. and Cotton, J. (1991) 'Easier Said than Done: Gender Differences in Perceived Barriers of Gaining a Mentor' *The Academy of Management Journal* Vol 34

Ramazanoglu, C. (1993) *Up Against Foucault* London, Routledge

Ramazanoglu, C. (2002) *Feminist Methodology Challenges and Choices.* Sage

Ransom, J. (1993) 'Feminism, Difference and Discourse' in *Up Against Foucault.* C. Ramazanoglu (ed). London, Routledge

Ranson, G. (2003) 'Beyond 'Gender Differences': A Canadian Study of Women's and Men's Career in Engineering' *Gender Work and Organization* Vol 10(No 1)

Rasmussen, B. (2004) 'Between endless needs and Limited Resources: The Gendered Construction of a Greedy Organization' *Gender Work and Organization* Vol 11(No 5)

Rees, B. (2003) *The Construction of Management* Cheltenham, Edward Elgar

Reich, R. (2000) *The Future of Success* New York, Alfred A Knopf

Richardson, D. (2007) 'Patterned Fluidities: (Re)Imagining the Relationship between Gender and Sexuality' Sociology Vol 41 (3) pp. 457–474

Richman, E. and Shaffer, D. (2000) 'If You Let Me Play Sports' *Psychology of Women Quarterly* Vol 24: 189–199

Rindfleish, J. (2000) 'Senior management women in Australia, diverse perspectives' *Women in Management Review* Vol 15(No 4)

Rindfleish, J. (2002) 'Senior Management Women and Gender Equity: A comparison of public and private sector women in Australia' *Equal Opportunities International* Vol 21(No 7)

Roe, R., Waller, M. and Clegg, S. (2009) *Time in Organizational Research.* London, Routledge

Romaine, S. (1989) *Bilingualism* Oxford, Blackwell Ltd

Romaine, S. (1999) *Communicating Gender* London, Lawrence Erlbaum Associates

Rosener, J. (1990). 'Ways Women Lead.' *Harvard Business Review* Vol Nov-Dec

Ross, A. (1995) 'The Great White Dude' *Constructing Masculinity.* M. Berger (ed). London, Routledge

Ross, S. and Rausch, K. (2003) 'Competition and Cooperation in the Five Factor Model: Individual Difference in Achievement Orientation' *The Journal of Psychology* Vol 137(No 4)

Rubery, J. and Grimshaw, D. (2003) *The Organisation of Employment* Hampshire, Palgrave Macmillan

Rutherford, S. (2001) 'Are you going home already?' *Time and Society* Vol 10(No 2)

Ryan, M. and Haslam, S. (2005) 'The Glass Cliff: Evidence that Women are Over-represented in Precarious Leadership Positions' *British Journal of Management* Vol 16

Ryckman, R. and Borne, B. (1997) 'Values of Hypercompetitive and Personal Development Competitive Individuals' *Journal of Personality Assessment* Vol 69 (No 2)

Ryska, T. (2003) 'Sportsmanship in Young Athletes: The Role of Competitiveness, Motivational Orientation and Perceived Purposes of Sport' *The Journal of Psychology* Vol 137(No 3)

Schaafsma, H. (1997) 'A networking model of change for middle managers' *Leadership & Organization* Vol 18(No 1)

Schatzki, T. (2006) 'On Organizations as they Happen '*Organizational Studies* Vol 27

Schein, V. (1975) 'Relationships between sex role stereotypes and requisite management characteristics' *Journal of Applied Psychology* Vol 60

Schein, V. (1994) Power, Sex and Systems' *Women in Management Review* Vol 9(No 1)

Schein, V. (2001) 'A Global Look at Psychological Barriers to Women's Progress in Management' *Journal of Social Issues* Vol 57(No 4)

Schein, V. (2007) 'Women in Management: reflections and projections' *Women in Management Review* Vol 22(No 1)

Schein, V. and Mueller, R. (1992) 'Sex role stereotyping and requisite management characteristics: a cross cultural look' *Journal of Organizational Behaviour* Vol 13

Schein, V., Mueller, R., Lituchi, T. and Liu, J. (1996) 'Think manager -think male: a global phenomenon?' *Journal of Organizational Behaviour* Vol 17

Schlesinger, P. (2006) 'Is there a crisis in British journalism?' *Media, Culture and Society* Vol 28(No 2)

Schwartz, F. (1989) 'Management Women and the New Facts of Life' *Harvard Business Review* January/February

Schwartz, F. (1992) 'Women as a Business Imperative' *Harvard Business Review* March/April

Scott, J. (1986) 'Gender: A Useful Category of Analysis' *The American Historical Review* March/April

Scully, D. (1990) *Understanding Sexual Violence* London, HarperCollins

Sealy, R. (2010) 'Changing perceptions of meritocracy in senior women's careers' *Gender in Management* Vol 25(No 3)

Segal, L. (1990). *Slow Motion* London, Virago Press

Segal, L. (1999). *Why Feminism?* Cambridge, Polity Press

Sheppard, D. (1992) 'Women Managers Perceptions of Gender and Organizational Life' *Gendering Organizational Analysis*. Mills and Tancred (eds). London, Sage

Skillset Report (2009) *Strategic Skills Assessment for the Creative Media Industry*

Simpson, R. (1998) 'Presenteeism, Power and Organizational Change: long Hours as a Career Barrier and the Impact on the Working Lives of Women Managers' *British Journal of Management* Vol 9 (Special Issue)

Simpson, R. (2000) 'Gender Mix and organisational fit: how gender imbalance at different levels of the organisation impacts on women managers' *Women in Management Review* Vol 15(No 1)

Sinclair, A. (1998) *Doing Leadership Differently* Melbourne University Press

Sinclair, A. (2000) 'Teaching managers about masculinities: are you kidding?' *Management Learning* Vol 31(No 1)

Singh, V. Vinnicombe, S. and James, K. (2005) 'Constructing A professional Identity: How Young Female Managers use Role Models' *Women in Management Review* Vol. 21(No 1)

Siranni, C. and Negrey, C. (2000) 'Working Time as Gendered Time' *Feminist Economics* Vol 6(No 1)

Sommer, S. (1992) 'Improving Performance Effectiveness: Making Competition Work for You' *Management Quarterly* Vol 33(No 4)

Sport England www.sportengland.org/research/active_people_survey accessed 19/02/2012

Spaaij, R. (2009) 'The social impact of sport: diversities, complexities and Contexts' *Sport in Society* Vol 12(No 9)

Spaaij, R. (2009) 'Personal and social change in and through sport: crosscutting Themes' *Sport in Society* Vol 12(No 9)

Sprague, J. and Kobrynowicz, D. (2004) *A Feminist Epistemology* Oxford University Press

Staines, G., Travis, C. and Jayerante, T. (1973) 'The Queen Bee Syndrome' *Psychology Today* Vol 7

Stanley, L. and Wise, S. (1993) *Breaking Out Again* London, Routledge

Stanne, M., Johnson, D. and Johnson, R. (1999) 'Does Competition Enhance or Inhibit Motor Performance A Meta-Analysis' *Psychological Bulletin* Vol 125(No 1)

Stapel, D. and Koonmen, W. (2005) 'Competition, Cooperation and the Effects of Others on Me' *Journal of Personality and Social Psychology* Vol 88(No 6)

Steiner, S (2012) www.guardian.co.uk/lifeandstyle/2012/feb/01/top-five-regrets-of-the-dying?

Still, L. (1997) *Glass ceilings and sticky floors* Human Rights and Equal Opportunity Commission

Still, L. and Timms, W. (2000) 'Women's business: the flexible alternative workstyle for women' *Women in Management Review* Vol 15(No 5/6)

Strauss, A. and Corbin, J. (1998) *Basics of Qualitative Research: Techniques and Procedures for Developing Grounded Theory* London, Sage

Street-Porter, J. (2008). *Life's Too F***ing Short* London, Quadrille Publishing

Sturges, J. (1999) 'What it means to succeed: Personal conception of career success held by male and female managers at different ages' *British Journal of Management* Vol 10

Sullivan, O. (2000) 'The Division of Domestic Labour: Twenty Years of Change?' *Sociology* Vol 34(No 3)

Tauer, J. and Harackiewiez, J. (2001) 'The Effects of Cooperation and Competition on Intrinsic Motivation and Performance' *Journal of Personality and Social Psychology* Vol 86 (No 6)

Taylor, S. (ed.) (1998) *Emotional Labour and the New Workplace. Workplaces of the Future* Hampshire, Macmillan Press Ltd

Thomas, R. and Davies, A. (2005) 'What Have the Feminists Done for Us? Feminist Theory and Organizational Resistance' *Organization* Vol 12

Thompson, J. and Bunderson, J. (2001) 'Work-Nonwork Conflict and the Phenomenology of Time: Beyond the Balance Metaphor' *Work and Occupations* Vol 28(No 17)

Tietze, S. and Musson, G. (2005) 'Recasting the Home-Work Relationship: A Case of Mutual Adjustment?' *Organization Studies* Vol 26(No 9)

Tjovold, D., Johnson, D. and Johnson, R. (2003) 'Can Interpersonal Competition Be Constructive Within Organizations?' *The Journal of Psychology* Vol 137 (No 1)

Tomlinson, J. (2006) 'Routes to Part time management in UK service sector organizations: implications for women's skills, flexibility and progression' *Gender Work and Organization* Vol 13

Tomlinson, J. Olsen, W. and Purdam, K. (2009) 'Women Returners and Potential Returners: Employment Profiles and Labour Market Opportunities – A Case Study of the UK' *European Sociological Review* Vol 24(No 2)

Uhl-Bien, M. and Maslyn, J. (2003) 'Reciprocity in managers subordinates relationships: components, configurations and outcomes' *Journal of Management* Vol 29

UNESCO (1978) *The International Charter of Physical Education and Sport.* 21 November 1978. Paris, France

United Nations (1989) *Convention on the Rights of the Child* 20 November 1989. New York

UN (2001a) www.un.org/esa/socdev/ageing/waa/isaale accessed 1 February 2012

UN Division for the Advancement of Women Department of Economic and Social Affairs *Women 2000 and Beyond* December 2007

Wajcman, J. (1998) *Managing Like A Man* Cambridge, Polity Press

Wajcman, J. and Bittman, M. (2000) 'The Rush Hour: The Character of Leisure Time and Gender Equity' *Social Forces* Vol 79 (No 1)

Wajcman, J. and Martin, B. (2002) 'Narratives of Identity in Modern Management: The Corrosion of Gender Difference' *Sociology* Vol 36(No 4)

Walby, S. (1990) *Theorizing Patriarchy* Cambridge, Blackwell

Walby, S. (1997). *Gender Transformations* London, Routledge

Walby, S. (2004) 'The European Union and Gender Equality: Emergent Varieties of Gender Regime' *Social Politics* Vol 11

Walby, S. and Olsen, W. (2002) '*The impact of women's position in the labour market on pay and implications for UK productivity*' Women and Equality Unit

Waldstorm, C. and Madsen, H. (2007) 'Social relations among managers: old boys and young women's networks' *Women in Management Review* Vol 2

Walters, S. (2005) 'Making the best of a bad job? Female part-timers orientations and attitudes to work' *Gender Work and Organization* Vol 12

Wanneberg, P.L. (2011) 'The Sexualisation of Sport: A gender analysis of Swedish elite sport from 1967 to the present day' *European Journal of Women's Studies* Vol 18 (No 3)

Warhurst, C. and Thompson, P. (eds) (1998) *Hands, Hearts and Minds: Changing Work and Workers at the End of the Century. Workplaces of the Future* Hampshire, Macmillan Press

Wenger, E (1999) *Communities of Practice: Learning, Meaning and Identity* Cambridge University Press

Wenger, E. McDermott, R. Snyder, W. (2002) *Cultivating Communities of Practice: A Guide to Managing Knowledge* Harvard Business School Press

Weyer, B. (2007) 'Twenty years later: explaining the persistence of the glass ceiling for women leaders' *Women in Management Review* Vol 22(No 6)

Wheeler, M. (2006) 'Is Teaching Negotiation Too Easy, Too Hard or Both?' *Negotiation Journal* Vol 22

Whelehan, I. (2004) 'Having it all (again?)' ESRC seminar on new femininities LSE London, LSE

Whipp, R., Adam, B. and Sabelis, I. (2002) *Making Time: Time and Management in Modern Organizations* Oxford University Press

White, B. (2000) 'Lessons from the careers of successful women' In *Women in Management: Current Research Issues Volume 2.* Davidson and Burke (eds) London Sage

White, B. and Cox, C. (1997) 'A portrait of successful woman' *Women in Management Review* Vol 12(No 1)

Whitehead, S. (2001) 'Woman as Manager: A seductive ontology' *Gender Work and Organization* Vol 8(No 1)

Whitely, W. and Dougherty, T. (1992) 'Correlates of career-oriented mentoring for early career managers and professionals' *Journal of Organizational Behaviour* Vol 13

Wilson, F. (1996) 'Research Note: Organizational Theory: Blind and Deaf to Gender?' *Organization Studies* Vol 15(No 5)

Wittenberg-Cox, A. and Maitland, A. (2009) *'Why Women Mean Business'* Oxford, Wiley

Witz, A. and Savage, M. (1992) 'The gender of organisations' in *Gender Bureaucracy.* Witz and Savage (eds). London, Blackwell

Wood, G. and Newton, J. (2006) 'Childlessness and Women Managers: Choice, Context and Discourses' *Gender Work and Organization* Vol 13(No 4)

Worchel, S. and Shebilske, W. et al. (1997) 'Competition and Performance on a Computer Based Complex Perceptual Motor Task' *Human Factors* Vol 39(No 3)

Working Outside the Box, 2007, Equal Opportunities Commission (EOC)

WSFF (2010) *Prime Time The case for commercial investment in women's sport – The Commission on the Future of Women's Sport*

WSFF wsff.org.uk/publications/fact-sheets/teenage-girls-and-dropout accessed 10/01/12

Zinn, C. (2005) www.guardian.co.uk/news/2005/dec/28/guardianobituaries. cricket accessed 14/12/11

http://www.britannica.com/blogs/2009/02/alfie-kohn-is-bad-for-you-and-dangerous-for-your-children/ - accessed 28/05/2012

http://www.healthboard.com/websites%20accessed%2028/05/2012

Index

0 1341 1502412 4

RECEIVED

DEC 2 0 2012

GUELPH HUMBER LIBRARY
205 Humber College Blvd
Toronto, ON   M9W 5L7